FARM CONVENIENCES

AND HOW TO BUILD THEM

Classic American Labor-Saving Devices

LYONS PRESS
Essex, Connecticut

LYONS PRESS

An imprint of The Globe Pequot Publishing Group, Inc.
64 South Main Street
Essex, CT 06426
www.globepequot.com

2026 edition by The Globe Pequot Publishing Group, Inc.

British Library Cataloguing in Publication Information available

Library of Congress Control Number: 2026943329

ISBN 978-1-4930-9630-5 (paper)
ISBN 978-1-4930-9631-2 (e-book)

FOREWORD.

Not too long ago, this planet was a very rural, and exceedingly improvisational, place. The bumpkins of Earth, whether they were in the mountains of Turkey or on the coast of Australia, when confronted with the complexities of the physical universe were often forced to simply take a good look at the problem in front of them and then wing it with whatever was handy. Hence, a board and a stick became a stool; a handful of hardware and a creek became a mill; a stick, a round rock, and a hole in the ground became an obsession; and a bottle, a plank, two sheets, and some wind became a drunk in a sailboat.

We don't live like that any more, and that's probably a pity. Divorced from nature, most of us live in cities, where problems are more complex but have fewer and fewer moving parts—and chances are that one of them is a bureaucrat. So while the spirit of make-it-up inventiveness survives, it has become overwhelmingly technical. And this, in turn, is a source of anguish, often involving a call to a customer-support number and a lifetime spent on hold.

What would the men and women who designed these handy devices think of our manufactured universe? I think they'd like it a lot. After all, a century ago, nobody wanted to spend a whole day making a thingamabob to pick apples. They just wanted the apples. Making the apple picker was in fact so inconvenient that they made sure it was designed and built to last a long, long time.

The inconvenient items in *Farm Conveniences* represent the best of the golden age of ad hoc engineering, the make-do inspiration of our great-grandparents. They represent a willingness and an enthusiasm to create some pretty good stuff out of very little. And if we've nearly lost that kind of goofy inventiveness, it's because the opportunities to invent often no longer involve the mundane artifacts of daily life—clothes-wringers, cow-milkers, spud-diggers—

where the novelty of invention can be seen in high contrast to the ordinariness of the tasks for which these things were made. Now inventiveness is almost invisible. The design of "conveniences" has now moved into the thin air of cyberspace, where nothing lives for very long, and where any specific innovation is kind of hard to notice, as virtually everything there is innovative, one way or another.

For those of us who are hopelessly analog in this age of digital excess, that isn't very comforting. The items in *Farm Conveniences*, however, have the power to reassure—because of their ability to demonstrate that the world really can make a kind of sense if you can just see how it all fits together, how it works. Making conveniences such as a gate or building a trellis aren't the kinds of activities that seem likely to contribute much to a man's life, unless you happen to want a gate or a trellis. But convenience is not the point of this collection of farm conveniences—a modest part of an even more grand collection, *Homemade Contrivances*. The point of this collection is to remind us that given enough common sense and enough free time and a big enough pile of junk, there's a solution for almost every problem.

I found this book, long forgotten by those whose grandfathers once relied on it for sound advice, on a dusty shelf in a junk shop in the Allegheny Mountains of Pennsylvania. In fact, the shopkeeper had forgotten the book was even there. That seems right, for if nothing else, *Farm Conveniences* will demonstrate that there is a lot of useful knowledge out there, if we could only remember where we put it. Admittedly, some of that knowledge is technical and some is theoretical. But some of it—like the items in this book—is hugely practical and just the kind of stuff that can make a man's life ever so slightly more convenient.

—Denis Boyles

PREFACE.

SKILL in the construction and use of simple labor-saving devices is of vast importance to the farmer, and any aid to the development of this manual dexterity is always very welcome.

The volume, herewith presented, abounds in valuable hints and suggestions for the easy and rapid construction of a large number of home-made contrivances within the reach of all. It is an every-day hand-book of farm work, and contains the best ideas gathered from the experience of a score of practical men in all departments of farm labor. Every one of the two hundred and forty pages, and two hundred and twelve engravings, teaches a valuable lesson in rural economy. "FARM CONVENIENCES" is a manual of what to do, and how to do it quickly and readily.

CONTENTS.

FARM CONVENIENCES.

A CONVENIENT BIN FOR OATS.

THE usual receptacle for oats, corn, or mill feed, or other grain for domestic animals, is a common bin or box about four feet in hight. It is difficult to get the grain out of such a place when the quantity is half or more exhausted. To obviate this inconvenience, there may be affixed, about one foot from the bottom on one side of the bin, a board, (*B*) figure 1. This is nailed so as to project into the bin at an angle sufficient to allow the filling of a measure between the lower edge of board *B* and top edge of the opening at *M*. The opposite lower side of the bin is covered with boards, as indicated

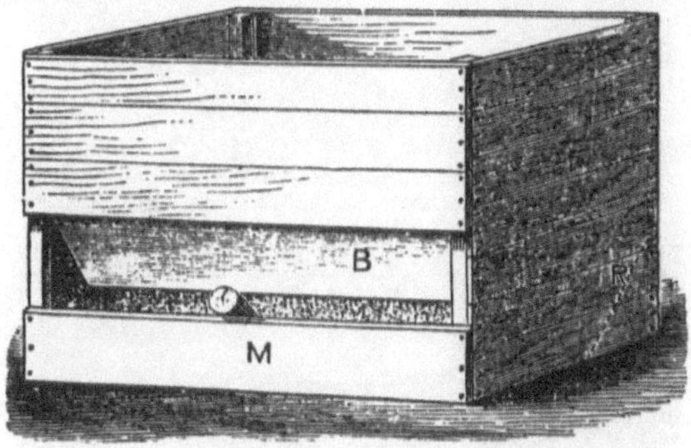

Fig. 1.—A BIN FOR OATS OR OTHER FEED.

by the dotted line at *R*, for the purpose of placing the contents within easy reach. The top can be completed with hinged cover as well as the delivery space By using a bin of this form, the last bushel is as easily removed as the first one.

FASTENINGS FOR COWS.

Although stanchions are really the safest fastening for cows, yet some persons object to them because the animals are held in a too confined position, and one which is supposed to be painful, or otherwise objectionable to the cows. Most owners of valuable cows consider safety to be the first requisite in their management, and the question as to what the cow would like as of minor importance. Stanchions have the valuable recommendation that one always finds his cows in the morning just where they were left at night, if they have been properly secured. Nevertheless, for those who dislike stanchions, there are other safe ways of fastening cows. For some years we used the method shown in figures 2 and 3. In

Fig. 2.—FASTENING BY SLIDING RING ON A POLE

the first a strong smooth pole was inserted through the floor and "stepped" into the beam beneath and into the floor above. It was also fastened by an iron strap bolted through the front of the trough. A steel ring to which a steel chain was attached was made to slide up and down upon the post, and a leather neck strap, or, in some cases, a leather head stall, was attached to the chain by a suitable ring or loop. The ring could not fall so low as the floor, being held by the edge of the feed-trough, and the cow's feet could not, therefore, be entangled in the chain by getting over it. This is the chief danger in the use of neck straps and chains, but it may be avoided in this way. Another plan is to have an iron rod bolted to the feed-trough, upon which the ring may slide. This is equally secure, and gives more room for movement to the cow. With these ring-ties it is best to have

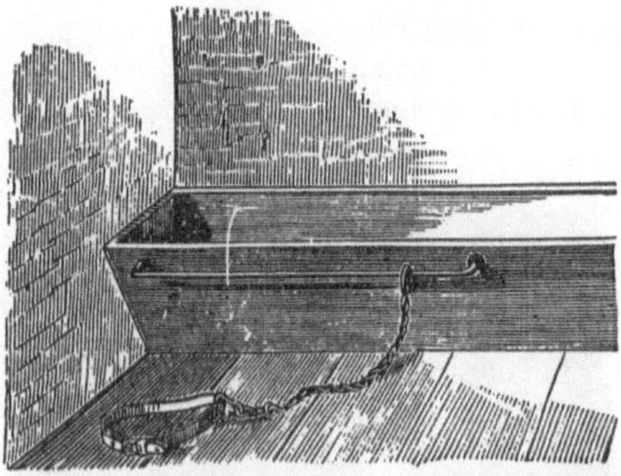

Fig. 3.—FASTENING ATTACHED TO FEED-TROUGH.

short stalls to prevent the cows interfering with each other, else one of them may step on to another as it is lying down. The teats are sometimes injured even when stanchions are used, but the danger of this is greater with chain ties.

MOVABLE NESTS FOR HENS.

Hens, as a general thing, are remarkably self-willed and obstinate. Perhaps an exception may be made as regards the Brahmas, which are very docile and easily managed. On account of this general peculiarity of fowls, many people who possess a somewhat similar disposition, find no success in keeping them. Their hens will not lay in the nests provided for them, or after sitting a few days upon a nest of eggs, leave them and never return. The consequences are, either no eggs at all, or nests hidden where they cannot be reached; no chickens, and time and labor lost. This may all be avoided if the owners will only study the habits and instincts of their poultry reasonably. One of the most inveterate habits of hens is that of hiding their nests, or seeking them in retired, shaded places. Those who would have plenty of eggs must make their arrangements accordingly. A very cheap and convenient nest is shown in figure 4. It is made of pieces of board eighteen

Fig. 4.—A MOVABLE HEN'S NEST.

inches long, nailed endwise to three-sided cleats at the top and bottom. The box need not be more than eighteen or twenty inches in length. Some corner pieces are nailed at the front to make it firm, and the back should be closed. These nests may be placed in secluded corners, behind sheds, or beneath bushes in the back yard, or behind a barrel or a bundle of straw. The nest egg should be of glass or porcelain, and every evening the eggs that have been laid during the day should be removed. A little cut straw mixed with clean earth or sand, will make the best material for the nest. This should be renewed occasionally, for the sake of cleanliness. When a hen has taken possession of one of these nests, it may be removed at night to the hatching-house, without disturbing her. Before the nests are used, they should be thoroughly well lime-washed around the joints, to keep away lice.

HOW TO GET RID OF STRAW.

Many farmers in "the West," and some in what we call "the East," are troubled as to what they shall do with the piles of straw which lie about their fields. Upon the same farms with these nearly useless straw piles, many head of stock are kept, and many more might be kept, which could be made useful in reducing the straw to a condition in which it would serve as manure. If the already urgent necessity for manure upon the western and southern fields were realized, there would be little hesitation in taking measures to remove the difficulty. The chief obstacle is, that these involve either personal or hired labor; the first is objectionable to many, and the second cannot be had for want of the money necessary to pay for it. The least laborious method of using this straw and making it serve the double purpose of a shelter for stock and a fertilizer for the field upon which it has been grown, is as follows: Some poles are set in the ground, and rails or other poles are laid upon them so as to form a sloping roof. This is made near or around the place chosen for thrashing the grain. The straw from the thrashing-machine is heaped upon the rails, making a long stack, which forms three sides of a square, with the open side towards the south, and leaving a space beneath it in which cattle may be sheltered from storms. In this enclosure some rough troughs or racks may be placed, from which to feed corn. Here the cattle will feed and lie, or will lie at nights under shelter, while feeding during the day upon corn in the field. As the straw that is given them becomes trampled and mixed with the droppings, a further supply is thrown down from the stack. The accumulation may be removed and spread upon the field to be plowed in when it is so required, and the stakes pulled up and carried to another place, where they may be needed for the same purpose. Such a shelter as this would be very serviceable for the purpose of making manure, even where straw is scarce, as in parts of the Southern States. There pine boughs may be made to serve as a covering, and leaves, pine straw, dry pond muck, swamp muck, "trash" from cotton fields, corn stalks, or pea vines, and any other such materials may be gathered and thrown from time to time beneath the cattle. Cotton-seed meal, straw, and coarse hay would keep stock in excellent order, and although there may be little snow or ice during the winter months in those States, yet the animals will be very much better for even this rude but comfortable shelter. In many other places such a temporary arrangement will be found useful in saving the hauling of straw, stalks, or hay from distant fields, and the carting of manure back again to them. It will be found vastly easier to keep a few young cattle in such a field, and go thither daily to attend to them during the winter when work is not pressing, than to haul many loads of hay or straw to the barn at harvest time, or many loads of manure in the busy weeks of spring.

THE MANAGEMENT OF YOUNG BULLS.

Many farmers want a method of disciplining bulls so that they may be made more docile and manageable. To do this it would be advisable to work them occasionally in a one-horse tread power. They should be used to this when young, and thus being made amenable to restraint, there will be no "breaking" needed afterwards and consequently no trouble. We have used a Jersey bull in a tread-power in which he worked with more steadiness than a horse, and twice a week he served a very useful purpose in cutting the fodder for the stock. Nothing more was needed than to lead him by a rope from the nose-ring into the tread-power, and tie him short so that he could not get too far forward. He was very quiet, not at all mischievous, and was a very sure stock bull; and besides this, the value of his work was at least equal to the cost of his keep. Where there is no tread-power, a substitute may be found in the arrangement shown in figure 5. Set a post in the barn-yard, bore a hole in the top, and drive a two-inch iron pin into the hole. Take the wheel of a wagon that has an iron axle, and set it upon the top of the post so that it will turn on the pin as on an axle. Fasten a strong pole (such as a binding pole for a hay wagon) by one end to the wheel, and bore two holes in the other end, large enough to take the arms of an ox-bow in them. Fix a light-elastic rod to the wheel, so that the end will be in advance of the end of the larger pole. Yoke the bull to the pole, and tie the nose-ring to the end of the elastic rod, in such a way that a slight pull is exerted upon the ring. Then

Fig. 5.—MANNER OF EXERCISING A BULL.

lead the bull around a few times until he gets used to it; he will then travel in the ring alone until he is tired, when he will stop. Two hours of this exercise a day will keep a bull in good temper, good condition and excellent health.

A CONVENIENT ICE-HOOK.

A very handy ice-hook may be made as shown in figure 6. The handle is firmly fastened and keyed into a socket; at the end are two sharply-pointed spikes, one of which serves to push pieces of ice, and the other to draw them to the shore, or out of the water, to be loaded and removed. It may be made of light iron, horse-shoe bar will be heavy enough, and there is no need to have the points steeled; it will be sufficient if they are chilled, after they are sharpened, in salt and ice pounded together.

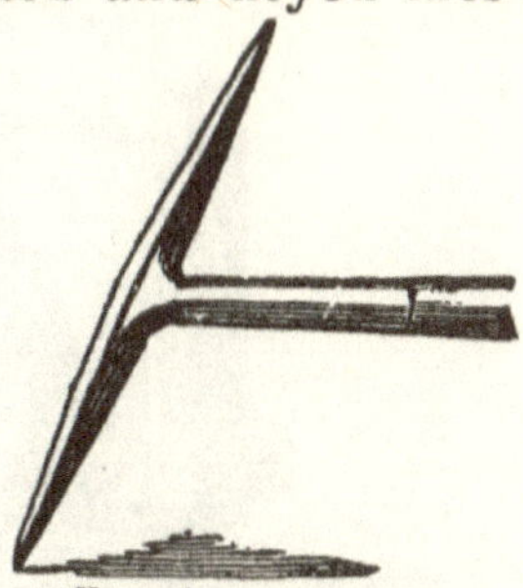

Fig. 6.—ICE-HOOK.

HINTS FOR THE WORKSHOP.

A grindstone is very seldom kept in good working order; generally it is "out of true," as it is called, or worn out of a perfectly circular shape. A new stone is frequently hung so that it does not run "true," and the longer it is used, the worse it becomes. When this is the case, it may be brought into a circular shape by turning it down with a worn-out mill-file. It is very difficult to do this perfectly by hand, but it is easily done by the use of the contrivance shown in figure 7. A post, slotted in the upper part, is bolted to the frame. A piece of hard wood, long enough to reach over the frame, is pivoted in the slot. This should be made two inches wider than the stone, and be pivoted, so that an opening can be made in the middle of it, of the same width as the stone. This opening is made with sloping ends, so that a broad mill-file may be wedged into it in the same manner as a plane-iron is set in a plane. At the opposite end of the frame a second post is bolted to

Fig. 7.—TRUEING A GRINDSTONE.

it. A long slot, or a series of holes, is made in the lower part of this post, so that it may be raised or lowered at pleasure by sliding it up or down upon the bolt. If a slot is made, a washer is used with the bolt; this will make it easy to set the post at any desired height. It should be placed so that the upper piece of wood may rest upon it, exactly in the same position in which the file will be brought into contact with the stone. A weight is laid upon the upper piece to keep it down, and hold the cutter upon the stone. When the stone is turned around slowly, the uneven parts are cut away, while those which do not project beyond the proper line of the circumference are not touched.

A Grinding Frame to hold tools is shown in figure 8.

Fig. 8.—HOLDER FOR TOOLS.

It is made of light pieces of pine, or hard wood. The tool to be ground is fastened to the cross-piece. A sharp point, a nail, or a screw, is fastened to the narrow end of the frame, and, when in use, the point is stuck into the wall of the shed, which forms a rest.

A NON-PATENTED BARREL-HEADER.

Not long since we saw in operation a useful contrivance for pressing the heads of apple or egg barrels into place. Both apples and eggs require to be packed very firmly to enable them to be transported in barrels with safety. Apples loosely packed in a barrel will come to market in a very badly bruised condition, and if the packing around eggs is not very firmly compressed, the eggs and packing change places or get mixed up, and it is the eggs, and not the packing, which then suffers. A barrel of eggs properly packed, with layers of chaff or oats an inch thick between the layers of eggs, and three inches at each end of the barrel, will bear to be compressed as much as three inches with safety; without this compression, eggs are almost sure to be greatly damaged. A barrel of apples may fill the barrel to about two inches above the chime, and will bear to have the head brought down to its place. When barrels containing these perishable articles are thus packed they may receive very rough usage without injury to the contents. The header referred to consists of a bar of half-inch square iron rod, with a large eye or loop at one end, and at the other end two diverging hooks which grasp the bottom of the barrel. The bar is bent to fit the curve of the barrel. When in use, the hooks are placed beneath the lower chime of the barrel, one end of a short lever is placed in the eye, and the lever rests upon a block, which is set upon the head of a barrel properly placed in position. A strap or cord, with a loop or stirrup at one end, is fastened to the other end of the lever. The foot is placed in the loop or stirrup, and the weight of the body thrown upon it brings the head of the barrel into its place; the hands being free, the hoops can be driven down tightly without the help of an assistant. Without the

Fig. 9.—BARREL-HEADER.

use of the cord and stirrup, two persons are required to head barrels, but with the aid of these the services of one can be dispensed with.

BUILDING RIBLESS BOATS.

A method of building boats, by which ribs are dispensed with, has recently been brought into use for coast, lake, and river crafts. These boats are light, swift, strong, and cheap. They have been found to be remarkably good sea boats, and to stand rough weather without shipping water. By this method of building, fishermen and others who use boats can construct their own at their leisure, and in many cases become independent of the skill of the professional boat builder. The materials needed are clear pine boards, one inch thick, a keel of oak or elm, a stem and stern-post of the same timber, and some galvanized iron nails. For small boats the boards and keel should be the whole length of the boat intended to be built; for boats over sixteen feet in length, splices may be made without injuring the strength, if they are properly put together. The materials having been procured, a frame or a set of tressels are made, and the keel is fitted to them in the usual manner, by means of cleats on each side, and wedges. The stem and stern-post are then fitted to the keel in the usual manner, the joints being made water-tight by means of layers of freshly-tarred brown paper laid between the pieces, or by the use of a coating of thick white lead and oil. Previously to being fitted together, the sides of the keel, stem, and stern-post are deeply grooved to receive the first strip of planking. The boards are then ripped into strips one inch, or an inch and a half wide, according to the desired strength of the boat. For rough work,

Fig. 10.—BUILDING A RIBLESS BOAT.

such as fishing with nets, or dredging, an inch and a half would be a proper width for the strips. The ripping may be done with one of the hand circular sawing machines, or at a saw-mill, with great rapidity. The first strip is then nailed to the keel, a coating of tar or white lead having first been given to the groove in the keel already prepared for it. The broad side of the strip is laid next to the keel. A set of molds, corresponding to the lines or form of the boat, are cut out of inch boards, and tacked to the keel in the manner shown in figure 10, with the help of cleats upon each side. Then one strip after another is nailed to each preceding one, and the shell of the boat is built up of these strips. Each strip is trimmed down at the ends in a proper manner, with a drawn knife, or a plane, and as each one is nailed to the preceding one, some of the tar or white lead is brushed over it, to make the joint tight and close. A sufficient number of nails is used to hold the strips firmly together, and the heads are driven down level with the surface of each strip. The work proceeds in this manner, forming the strips as each is fitted, bending them to the shape of the molds, and nailing one alternately upon each side, so that the molds are not displaced by the spring of the timber. When the sides of the boat are completed, the fender and gunwales are fitted, and bolted to them to strengthen them, and cleats are bolted inside for the seats to rest upon. The molds are now removed, and the boat consists of a solid shell an inch and a half thick, with not a nail visible excepting on the top strip, and conforming exactly in shape to the model. To give extra strength, short pieces of the strips are nailed diagonally across the inside, from side to side, and across the keel. In this manner a great deal of additional stiffness and strength is given to the boat. A boat of this kind is easily repaired when injured, by cutting out the broken part and inserting pieces of the strips. For a larger boat, which requires a deck, the strips are wider and thicker, or a diagonal lining may be put into it ; knees are bolted to the sides, and the beams to the knees, the deck being laid upon the beams. The method is applicable to boats of all sizes and for all purposes, and its cheapness and convenience are rapidly bringing it into favor. If the material is ready for use, two men can finish a large boat in two weeks, and a small one in one week. These boats being very light and buoyant, considerable ballast will be necessary to make them steady enough in case sails are used.

TO MEND A BROKEN TUG.

No one should go from home with a buggy or a wagon without a small coil of copper wire and a "*multum in parvo*" pocket-knife. This knife, as its name implies, has many parts in a little space, and, among other useful things, has a contrivance for boring holes in leather straps. In case a strap or a leather trace breaks, while one is on a journey, and at a distance from any house, one would be in an awkward "fix" if without any means of repairing damages. With the copper wire and an implement for boring some holes, repairs can be made in a very few minutes. The ends of the broken strap or tug may be laid over each other or spliced ; a few holes bored in the manner shown in figure 11, and some stitches of wire passed through in the way known among the ladies as "back stitching." The ends of the wire are twisted together, and the job will be finished almost as quickly as this may be read. If it is a chain that breaks, the next links may be brought together and wire wound around them in place of the broken link, which will make the chain serviceable until home is reached. In fact, the uses of a piece of wire are almost endless. Nothing holds a button upon one's working clothes so securely as a piece of wire, and once put on in this manner, there is never any call upon the women of the house at inconvenient times for thread

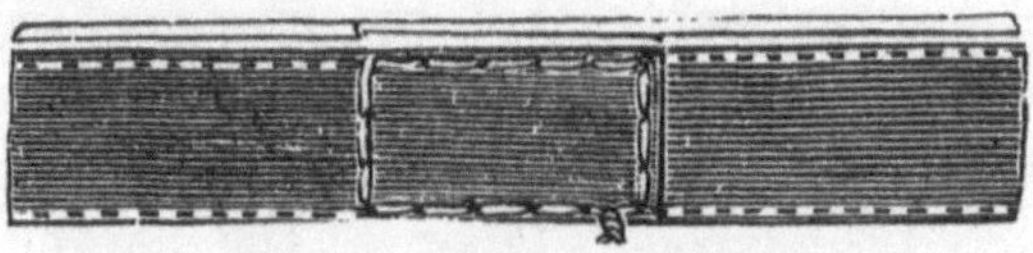

Fig. 11.—REPAIRING TUG.

and needle to replace it. The wire will pierce the cloth without any help, and nothing more is needed than to pass it through each hole of the button and twist the ends to secure them, cutting them off close with a knife. There is scarcely any little thing that will be found of so great use about a farm, or a workshop, or in a mill, or even in a house, as a small stock of soft copper wire.

BUSINESS HABITS.

There is probably not one farmer in ten thousand who keeps a set of accounts from which he can at any moment learn the cost of anything he may have produced, or even the cost of his real property. A very few farmers who have been brought up to business habits keep such accounts, and are able to tell how their affairs progress, what each crop, each kind of stock, or each animal has cost, and what each produces. Knowing these points, a farmer can, to a very great extent, properly decide what crops he will grow, and what kind of stock he will keep. He will thus be able to apply his labor and money where it will do the most good. He can weed out his stock and retain only such animals as may be kept with profit. For the want of such knowledge, farmers continue, year after year, to feed cows that are unprofitable, and frequently sell for less than her value one that is the best of the herd, because she is not known to be any better than the rest. Feed is also wasted upon ill-bred stock, the keep of which costs three or four times that of well-bred animals, which, as has been proved by figures that cannot be mistaken, pay a large profit on their keeping. For want of knowing what they cost, poor crops are raised year by year at an actual loss, provided the farmer's labor, at the rates current for common labor, were charged against them. To learn that he has been working for fifty cents a day, during a number of years, while he has been paying his help twice as much, would open the eyes of many a farmer who has actually been doing this, and it would convince him that there is some value in figures and book accounts. It is not generally understood that a man who raises twenty bushels of corn per acre, pays twice as much for his plowing and harrowing, twice as much for labor, and twice as great interest upon the cost of his farm, as a neighbor who raises forty bushels per acre. Nor is it understood that when he raises a pig that makes one hundred and fifty pounds of pork in a year, that his pork costs him twice as much, or the corn he feeds brings him but half as much as that of his neighbor, whose pig weighs three hundred pounds at a year old. If all these things were clearly set down in figures upon a page in an account book, and were studied, there would be not only a sudden awakening to the unprofitableness of such farming, but an immediate remedy would be sought. For no person could resist evidence of this kind if it were once brought plainly home to him. If storekeepers, merchants, or manufacturers kept no accounts, they could not possibly carry on their business, and it is only because the farmer's business is one of the most safe that he can still go on working in the dark, and throwing away opportunities of bettering his condition and increasing his profits.

HAY-RACKS.

We here illustrate two kinds of hay-racks, which have

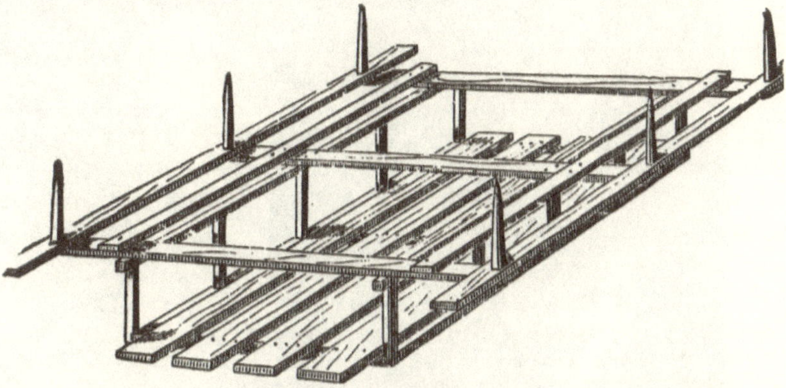

Fig. 12.—HAY-RACK.

been found more convenient in use than some of the old

Fig. 13.—RACK FOR GRAIN.

kinds. That shown in figure 12 consists of a frame made

Fig. 15.—EXTRICATING A MIRED COW

of scantlings, mortised together, and fitting upon the wagon after the box has been removed. Cross-pieces, which project over the wheels, are bolted to the frame, and to these one or two side-boards are bolted. A few short, sharpened stakes are fixed into the sides of the frame, which help to hold the load, and prevent it from slipping off from the rack during the loading. A strong rack of this kind may be made to carry a very large load of hay. We have seen over thirty hundred-weight loaded upon one of them, and more might have been easily added to the load. The plan of building this rack is readily seen by studying the engraving. At figure 13 is shown a rack made to fit upon a wagon body. When grain is hauled, much is sometimes lost through the rack, by shelling. This is almost always the case in hauling ripe oats, and always in drawing buckwheat. To avoid this loss, we have used a strong wagon-box of rough planks, fitted with iron sockets, bolted securely to the sides. Into these sockets were fitted head and tail racks, as shown in the engraving. For the sides we procured natural crooks, shown in figure 14.

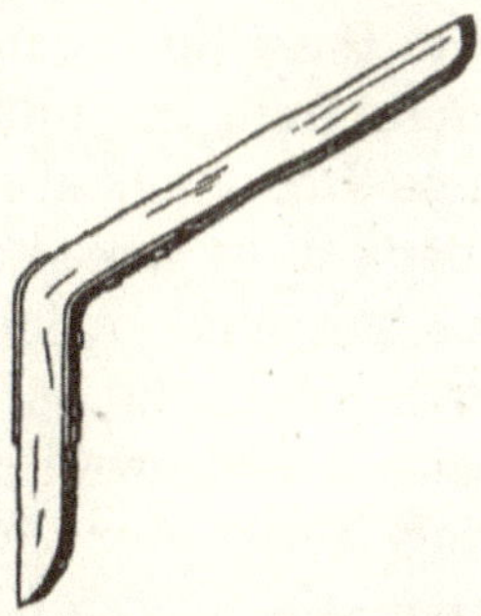

Fig. 14.—SUPPORT FOR RACK.

HOW TO EXTRICATE A MIRED ANIMAL.]

An animal mired in a swamp gets into a worse predicament the longer it struggles. The effort to extricate it should be made in an effective manner, so that the animal may not be encouraged to exhaust itself in repeated exertions, which are useless, and only sink it deeper in the mire. The usual method is to fasten a rope around the animal's horns or neck, and while this is pulled by some of the assistants, others place rails beneath the body of the animal for the purpose of lifting it out of the hole. This plan is sometimes effective, but it often is not, and at best it is a slow, clumsy, and laborious method. The materials needed for the method here referred to are all that are required for a much better one, which is illustrated in Figure 15. This is very simple, and two men can operate it, and, at a pinch, even one man alone may succeed with it. A strong stake or an iron bar is driven into the solid ground at a distance of twenty-five feet or more from the mired animal. Two short rails, about nine feet long, are tied together near the ends, so that they can be spread apart in the form of a pair of shears, for hoisting. A long rope is fastened around the horns or neck of the animal, with such a knot that the loop cannot be drawn tight enough to do any injury. The rope is cast over the ends of the rails as they are set up upon the edge of the solid ground, and carried to the stake or crow-bar beyond. The end of the rope is fastened to a stout hand-spike, leaving about a foot of the end of it free. This end is laid against the bar or stake, and the other end is moved around it so that the rope is wound upon it, drawing it up and with it drawing the animal out of the mire. The rope being held up by the tied rails, tends to lift the animal and make its extrication very easy.

HOW TO SAVE AND KEEP MANURE.

There is no question more frequently or seriously considered by the farmer, than how he shall get, keep, and spend an adequate supply of manure; nor is there anything about the farm which is of greater importance to its successful management than the manure heap

There are few farmers now left who pretend to ignore this feed for the land; and few localities, even in the newer Western States, where manure now is thought to be a nuisance. We have gradually come to the inevitable final end of our "virgin farms," and have now either to save what is left of their wonderful natural fertility, or to restore them slowly and laboriously to a profitable condition. We have reached the end of our tether, and are obliged to confess that we have trespassed over the line which bounds the territory of the locust, or have improved the face of the country so much that, the protecting timber being removed, the water supply is becoming precarious, and springs, brooks, and rivers no longer flow as they did heretofore. To some extent the tide of emigration, which has flowed westward so many years, is now eddying or even ebbing, and the cheap, worn lands of the East are finding purchasers, who undertake to bring them back to their former condition. At the same time Eastern farmers are discovering more and more certainly that they must increase their crops, and make one acre produce as much as two have heretofore done. The only way in which either of these classes can succeed, is by keeping sufficient stock to manure their farms liberally; to feed these animals so skillfully and well that they shall pay for their feed with a profit, and in addition leave a supply of rich manure, with which the soil can be kept in a productive state, and to save and use the manure with such care that no particle of it be lost. It is not every farmer who can procure all the manure he needs; but very many can save what they have, with far greater economy than they now do; and this, although it may seem a question secondary to that of getting manure, is really of primary importance; for by using what one has to better purpose, he opens a way to increase his supply. We have found this to be the case in our own experience, and by strict attention to saving and preserving every particle of manure in its best condition, we have succeeded in so enlarging our supply of fodder that the number of stock that could be fed was largely increased each year, and very soon it was necessary to go out and buy animals to consume the surplus. To bring a farm into improved condition, there is no cheaper or more effective method than this.

The ordinary management of manure, in open barnyards, where it is washed by rains, dried by the sun's scorching heat, and wasted by every wind that blows, is the worst that is possible. In this way half or more of the value of the manure is lost. By figuring up what it would cost to purchase a quantity of manure equal to what is thus lost, the costliness of this common method would be discovered, and the question how much could be afforded to take care of the manure would be settled. When properly littered, one cow or ox will make a ton of manure every month, if the liquid as well as the solid portion is saved. Ten head would thus make one hundred and twenty tons, or sixty two-horse wagon loads in a year. A pair of horses will make as much manure as one cow, or twelve tons in the year. A hundred sheep, if yarded every night and well littered, will make one hundred tons of manure in the year, and ten pigs will work up a wagon load in a month, if supplied with sufficient coarse material. The stock of a one hundred acre farm, which should consist of at least ten cows, ten head of steers, heifers, and calves, a pair of horses, one hundred sheep, and ten pigs, would then make, in the aggregate, three hundred and sixteen tons of manure every year, or sufficient to give twelve tons per acre every fourth year. If this were well cared for, it would be, in effect, equal to double the quantity of ordinary yard manure; and if a plenty of swamp muck could be procured, at least six hundred tons of the best manure could be made upon a one hundred acre farm. If this were the rule instead of a rare exception, or only a possibility, what a change would appear upon the face of the country, and what an addition would be made to the wealth of the nation!

GRINDING TOOLS.

The useful effect of many tools depends greatly upon the exact grinding of their edges to a proper bevel. A cold chisel, for instance, requires an edge of a certain

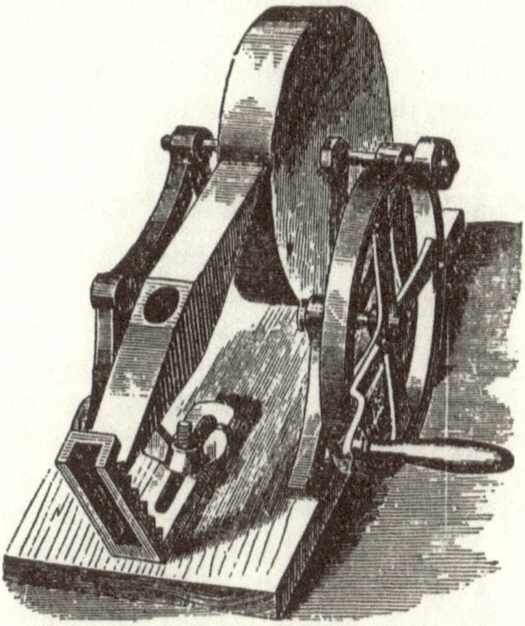

Fig. 16.—DEVICE FOR GRINDING MILL-PICKS.

bevel to cut hard metal, and one of a different angle for softer metal; the harder the work to be cut, the greater should be the angle formed by the edge, and the softer the material, the more acute the edge. The same rule is to be observed in wood-cutting tools. But there are no tools which require more exact and careful grinding than mill-picks, and the first business of a miller is to know how to grind his picks. Upon this depends the dress of the stones, and the quality of work turned out by them. Figure 16 represents a small grindstone for sharpening picks, which is run by means of friction wheels covered with leather, and provided with a gauge for setting the pick at a variable angle to the stone. This gauge, shown in the engraving, is so serviceable as to be well worth a place in any farm workshop. It consists of a series of steps raised upon a slotted plank, which is screwed upon the frame of the grindstone. By means of the slot and a set screw, seen below the pick, the gauge can be set for tools of different lengths, and each step causes the tool set in it to be ground at a different angle.

A METHOD OF HANGING HOGS.

An easy method of hanging a hog or a beef, is by the use of the tripod shown in figure 17. It is made of three by three oak scantling, six feet long, connected at one end, in the manner shown, by means of an iron bar one inch thick, passed through a hole bored in each piece. The two outside pieces are fastened together by two cross-pieces, bolted to them, so that they are spread at the bottom sufficiently, which would be about three feet. A hook is fastened to the lower cross-piece, upon which the hog is suspended. To hang the hog the frame is laid upon the ground with the hog between the outside

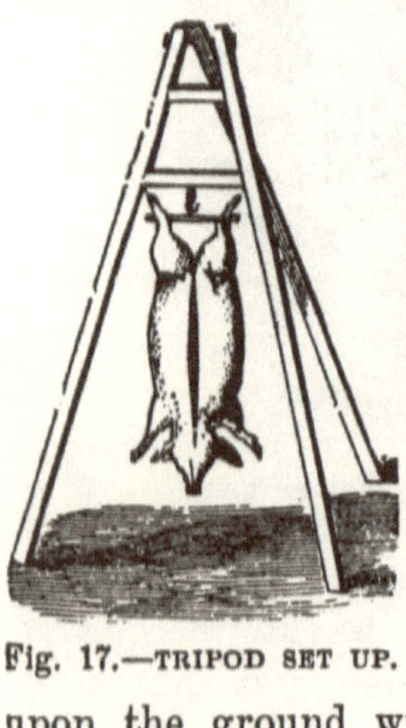

Fig. 17.—TRIPOD SET UP.

legs, the third leg being drawn backwards. The hog is hooked by the gambrel stick to the cross-piece, the frame is lifted up, and the hinder leg is spread out so as to support it, as shown in figure 17. The frame may be lowered easily when the hog has to be taken down, and as the frames are cheaply made, and occupy little room, it will be well to have several of them. They may be made to serve other useful purposes.

RELIEF FOR BOG-SPAVIN AND THOROUGH-PIN.

Bog-spavin, and thorough-pin, which are in reality the same disease, differing in position only, and that very slightly, may be considered as incurable. But like many chronic disorders, they may be very much relieved by proper methods. They are caused by an inflammatory condition of the synovial membrane of the hock joint, and are chiefly located in the vicinity of the junction of the bones of the leg, or the capsule between the tibia and the astragalus. This inflammation may be primarily caused by sudden shocks, or by continued strains from hard work, and the troubles are common among those horses which are of a lymphatic constitution, soft boned, or hereditarily subject to scrofulous or inflammatory conditions. They are also found lower down the leg, in which case they are the result of inflammation of the sheath of the tendons. They do not always cause lameness, except when the horse is first brought from the stable, and after a short time the stiffness may pass away. At other times there is great heat and tenderness in the parts, and the animal is decidedly lame. The best treatment is by cold applications and pressure upon the part. Blistering, which is sometimes resorted to, generally increases the trouble, and may cause a permanent thickening of the tissues, and a stiff joint. Pressure is best applied by a sort of truss, or strap, provided with a single pad in case of spavin or wind-gall, or double pads in case of thorough-pin, which is simply a spavin or wind-gall, so placed that the liquid which is gathered in the sac or puff may be pressed between the tendons or joint, and made to appear on the opposite side of the leg. In this case it is obviously necessary to apply the pressure upon both sides of the leg, and a double pad strap will be needed, of the form shown in figure 18. A common broad leather strap, lined with flannel, or chamois leather, to prevent chafing, is used; pads of soft leather, stuffed with wool, are sewn to the strap, and the exact spots where the pressure is to bear, disks of several thicknesses of soft leather or rubber are affixed. The pads must necessarily be made to fit each individual case, as success will depend upon their properly fitting the limb. The pads should be worn continually until the swelling disappears, and meanwhile, at least twice daily, the parts should be bathed for some time with cold water, and cloths wetted with cold water, with which a small quantity of ether has been mixed, should be bound around the parts, and the pads buckled over them so tightly as to exert a considerable pressure. Absolute rest is necessary while the animal is under this treatment.

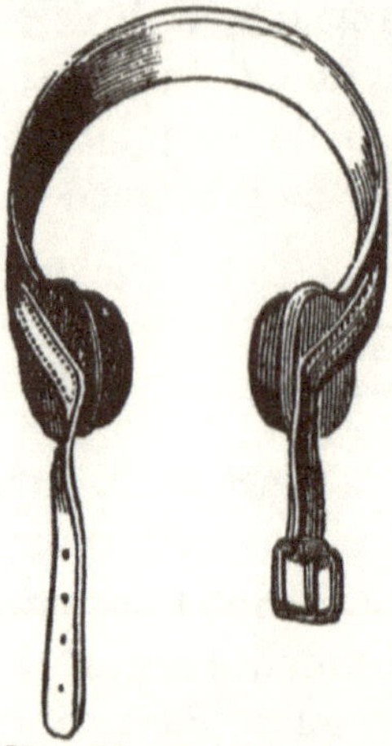

Fig. 18.—SPAVIN PAD.

TOOL-BOXES FOR WAGONS, ETC.

To go from home with a wagon without taking a few tools, is to risk a break-down from some unforeseen accident, without the means of repairing it, and perhaps a consequent serious or costly delay. Those who do business regularly upon the roads, as those who haul lumber, wood, coal, or ores of different kinds, should especially be provided with a set of tools, as a regular appurtenance to the wagon, and the careful farmer in going to market or the mill, or even to and fro upon the farm, should be equally well provided. We have found by experience that a break-down generally happens in the worst possible place, and where it is most difficult to help one's self. The loss of so simple a thing as a nut or a bolt may wreck a loaded wagon, or render it impossible to continue the journey, or some breakage by a sudden jerk upon a rough road may do the same. It is safe to be provided for any event, and the comfort of knowing that he is thus provided greatly lightens a man's labor. At one time, when we had several wagons and teams at work upon the road, we provided the foreman's wagon with a box such as is here described, and it was in frequent use, saving a considerable outlay that would otherwise have been necessary for repairs, besides much loss of valuable time. It was a box about eighteen inches long, sixteen inches wide, and six inches deep, divided into several compartments. It was supplied with a spare king-bolt, a hammer-strap, wrench, some staples, bolts, nuts, screws, a screw-driver, a hammer, cold-chisel, wood-chisel, punch, pincers, a hoof-pick, copper rivets, a roll of copper wire, a knife heavy and strong enough to cut down a small sapling, a roll of narrow hoop-iron, some cut and wrought nails, and such other things as experience proved to be convenient to have. The shape of the box is shown in figure 19. The middle of the top is fixed, and on each side of it is a lid

Fig. 19.—WAGON BOX.

hinged to it, and which is fastened by a hasp and staple, and a padlock or a spring key. The box is suspended to the wagon reach, beneath the box or load, by two strong leather straps with common buckles. Being only six inches deep, it is not in the way of anything, and is readily accessible when wanted.

MAKING A HINGE.

A gate with a broken hinge is a very forlorn object, and one that declares to every passer-by, "here lives a poor farmer." If there is one thing more than another worthy of note and a cause of congratulation in this one hundredth year of the existence of the United States, it is the infinite number of small conveniences with which we are supplied, every one of which adds to the sum of our daily comfort. More than this, the majority of these little things, which are in use all over the world, are the inventions and productions of Americans. So plentifully are we supplied with these small conveniences, that we cannot turn our eyes in any direction without coming across some of them. It is these small matters which enable us to have so many neat and pleasant things about our homes, at so little cost of money, time, or labor. One of the greatest of the small conveniences around the farm, or the mechanic's rural home, is the small forge. To make a gate-hinge with the help of this portable forge is a very easy thing. We take a piece of half-inch square bar-iron, as long as may be needed, and heating one end, round it for an inch or two ; then, heating the other end, flatten it out gradually to a point for the same length, and bend it over a mandrel, or the nose of an anvil, into the shape shown in figure 20. We then cut off a piece of round half-inch bar, about two inches long, and drive it into the loop, tightening the loop around it as much as possible.

Fig. 20.

The loop-end is then brought to a welding heat, and the joint closed around the pin, and neatly worked smooth with the hammer. Another piece of square iron is then taken, and worked at each end the same as the first one, the loop, however, is worked open upon a piece of cold $\frac{5}{8}$-inch round bar, so that it will be large enough to work easily upon the pin of the first piece. A thread may now be cut upon the round ends, or they may be riveted over a piece of iron plate, or a large washer, when they are driven through the gate-post and the heel-post of the gate. It is best, however, to have a screw-thread and a nut, using a washer under each nut, to prevent the wood from being crushed. The whole then appears as at figure 21, and is a hinge that cannot easily be broken or worn out.

Fig. 21.

In boring the holes for a hinge of this kind, a bit or an auger of only half-an-inch diameter should be used, so that the edges of the iron should cut their own way into the wood, and when the hinges are driven, a piece of hard wood should be laid upon the ends that are struck, so that they will not be battered by the hammer. Care must be exercised to have them driven in squarely, so that the gate may swing without binding on the hinges. For lighter hinges, the same sized iron may be used, but the ends should be hammered out to a point, and the edges should be notched or bearded with a cold-chisel, as shown at figure 22. These may be driven into a post

Fig. 22.

very readily, if a hole smaller than the iron be bored to

lead the way, and when driven in, will not be easily drawn out. When it is necessary to draw a hinge out of a post or gate, that has become rusted in, or that has been very tightly driven, it may easily be done by boring a hole above it, or on one side of it, or beneath it, a little larger than the iron, and then forcing it into the hole by means of a wooden wedge driven close to it. It will then be loose, and may easily be taken out without difficulty.

SHELTER FOR THE HEAD.

Many a severe headache, and a restless night after an exhausting day's work in the harvest field, might be prevented by the use of some simple precautions. The sun beats down upon the head and neck with great force, when the thermometer marks ninety degrees and over in the shade, and the scorching effect of a heat of one hundred and twenty degrees in the direct sunshine is both uncomfortable and dangerous to the health. The head should be protected in such cases by wearing a straw hat, or one of some open material, with a broad brim, and by placing a leaf of cabbage or lettuce, or a wetted cambric handkerchief in the crown of it. The very sensitive back of the head and neck is best protected by means of a white handkerchief fastened by one border to the hat-band, figure 23, and the rest made to hang down loosely over the neck and shoulders. The neck is thus shaded from the sun's rays, and the loosely flapping handkerchief causes a constant current of air to

Fig. 23.—NECK-PROTECTOR.

pass around and cool the neck and head. We have found this to be a most comfortable thing to wear, and its value as a protector to the base of the brain and the spinal marrow is so well known in hot countries, that the use of a similar protection is made imperative in armies when on the march.

HOW TO LEVEL WITH SQUARE AND PLUMB-LINE.

The common carpenter's square and a plumb-line may be made to serve as a substitute for the spirit level for many purposes on the farm or elsewhere, when a level is not at hand. The manner of getting the square in position to level a wall, for instance, is shown in figure

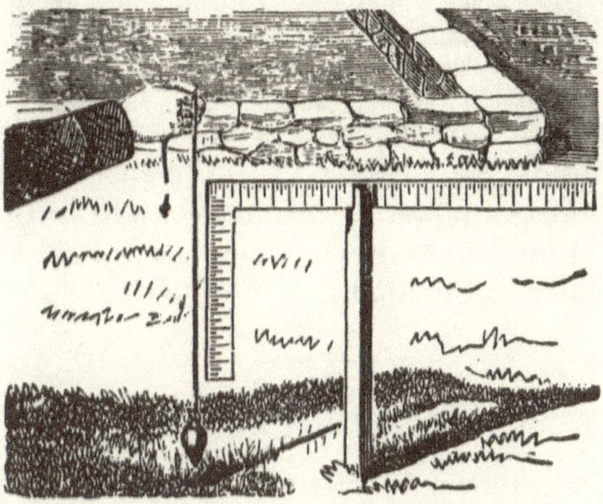

Fig. 24.—MANNER OF LEVELLING A WALL.

24. A piece of board, three feet in length, having one end sharpened, is driven into the ground for a rest; a notch is made in the top of the stick large enough to hold the square firmly in position, as shown in the engraving. A line and weight, held near the short arm, and parallel to it, will leave the long arm of the square level. By sighting over the top of the square, any irreg-

ularities in the object to be levelled are readily discovered. A method to find the number of feet in a descent in the ground is illustrated by figure 25. The square is placed as before directed; then a sight is taken over and along the upper edge of the square to a pole or rod placed at a

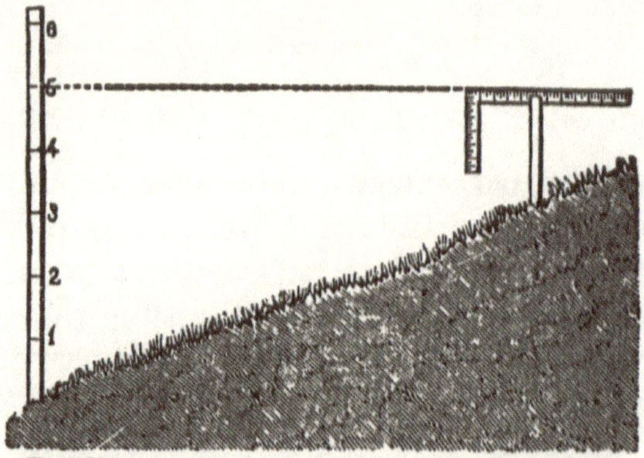

Fig. 25.—MEASURING A SLOPE WITH A SQUARE.

desired point. The point on the pole which is struck by the line of sight shows the difference between the levels of the two places. This method will be found applicable in laying out drains, where a certain desired fall is to be given to the ditch.

KEEP THE CATTLE UNDER COVER.

Even now, in some of the newer regions of the West, the easiest way to get rid of the manure is considered the best. The English farmers have long been obliged to feed farm animals largely for the fertilizers they yield, and this has proved that covered yards are the most economical. These covers are not so expensive as might be supposed at first thought. Substantial sheds, large enough to accommodate a hundred head of cattle, may be built at a cost all the way from $1,000 to $1,500, according to the locality and price of labor and lumber. The roof may be made with three ridge poles resting upon outside walls, and two rows of pillars. There should be ample provision for ventilation and the escape of the water falling upon the roof. The original cost will not be many dollars per head, and the interest on this will represent the yearly cost. If this should be placed at two dollars for each animal, it will be seen that this outlay is more than repaid by the increased value of the housed manure over that made in the open yard, and exposed to the sun and drenching rains. The saving in food consequent upon the warm protection of the animals has been carefully estimated to be at least one-tenth the whole amount consumed. In the saving alone, the covered yard gives a handsome return upon the investment.

WATERING PLACES FOR STOCK ON LEVEL LAND.

It is frequently the case that there are underdrains of living water passing through level fields, in which there is no water available for stock. In such a case, a simple

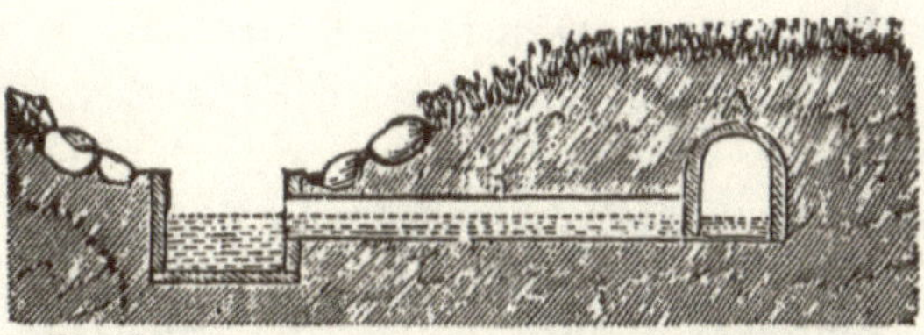

Fig. 26.—TAKING WATER FROM UNDERDRAIN.

plan for bringing the water to the surface is shown in figures 26 and 27, in which is indicated an underdrain of stone or tile; a pipe of two-inch bore of wood or tile, and about 15 feet in length, is laid level with the bottom of the drain, and connecting with a box one foot or more square sunk into the ground. If the soil be soft, the box is surrounded with stones as shown. A low place or small hollow at some point along the drain is selected for the watering box, or, should the land be

Fig. 27.—THE WATERING PLACE.

nearly level, then with plow and scraper an artificial hollow is soon made at any point desired. Two fields may be thus easily watered by making the box two feet in length, and placing it so that the fence will divide it.

A SHAVING-HORSE.

The shingle-horse, shown in figure 28, is made of a plank ten feet long, six inches wide, and an inch and

Fig. 28.—SHAVING-HORSE FOR SHINGLES.

a half thick. A slot is cut through this plank, and a lever, made of a natural crook, is hinged into it. A wooden spring is fixed behind the lever, and is fastened to it by a cord. This pulls back the lever when the foot is removed from the step beneath. The horse may have four legs, but two will be sufficient, if the rear end is made to rest upon the ground. Figure 29 is made of a plank, six feet long, ten inches wide, and two inches thick. Four legs, two feet long, are fixed in inch and a half holes, as shown below. A bench, eighteen inches

Fig. 29.—HORSE FOR GENERAL USE.

long, eight and a half inches wide, and an inch and a half thick, is fixed upon the horse. A slot, eight by one and a half inches, is cut through the bench and the plank, and the lever, two feet eight inches long, is fixed in this by means of a pin passing through the bench. Some extra holes are made in the lever, by which the height of the head above the bench may be changed to suit different sizes of work. A head is put upon the lever, six inches square each way, but bevelled off at the front. The foot-board, five by ten inches, is fastened to the bottom of the lever by a strong pin.

A MILKING-STOOL.

The front of the stool (figure 30) is hollowed to receive the pail, which is kept in its place by a wire, fixed as shown in the engraving. The front leg has a projecting rest upon which the bottom of the pail is placed to keep it from the ground, and also from breaking

Fig. 30.—A MILKING-STOOL.

away the wire by its weight. The milker may either sit astride of this stool, or sideways upon it.

HOW TO TREAT THRUSH.

Thrush is a disease of the horse's hoof, quite common in this country. It results oftener from neglect in the stables than from any other cause. The symptoms are fetid odor and morbid exudation from the frog, accompanied with softening of the same. A case recently came under our observation. A young carriage horse, used mostly on the road, and kept in the stable through the year, showed lameness in the left fore foot one morning after standing idle in the stable all the previous day. On removing the shoe, and examining the hoof, a fetid odor was observed. The stable was examined, when the sawdust used for bedding was found to be saturated with urine. The stable was cleaned immediately. Dry sawdust was placed in the stall, and a few sods packed in the space where the horse usually rested his fore feet. The lameness diminished without medical treatment.

and in ten days disappeared altogether. A bedding of sawdust or earth, covered with straw or leaves, promotes the comfort of the horse, but it needs watching and systematic renewing. The limit of the absorbing power of the driest soil, or sawdust, is soon reached. If a horse is kept most of the time in the stable, his bedding soon becomes wet, and unfit for his use. It is all the better for the compost heap, and for the horse, to have frequent renewals of absorbments of some kind, that fermentation may not be in progress under his hoofs. The proper place for this fermentation is in the compost heap. Too often the care of the horse is left to a servant without experience in the stable, and the result is permanent disease in the hoofs and legs of the horse. This is most certainly one of the cases in which "an ounce of prevention is worth a pound of cure."

A WESTERN LOCUST TRAP.

A great many devices have been used for the destruction of the locusts in those Western States where they have done so much mischief for a few years past. Whether the locusts are to remain as a permanent pest to the Western farmers, or not, remains to be proved. It is certain, however, that through some effects of the climate, the attacks of parasitic enemies, their consumption by birds and other animals, and by the efforts of the farmers themselves, the locusts have of late been greatly reduced in numbers, and their depredations have become almost inconsiderable. Many methods have been adopted for their destruction. Rolling the ground; plowing furrows, and making pits in them in which the insects are caught; burning them in long piles of dry grass; catching them in large sacks, and upon frames smeared with gas tar, and upon large sheet-iron pans containing burning fuel; all these have been tried with more or less success, as well as the negative means of diverting them from their course by means of thick smoke from smothered fires of prairie hay. A most effective method is one invented by a woman in Minnesota. This consists of a large strip of sheet-iron, figure 31, from ten to thirty feet long, turned up a few inches at the ends and one side; a wire is fixed to each end, or at proper places in the front, by which it can be drawn over the ground by a pair of horses or oxen. A light chain or rope is fixed so as to drag upon the ground a foot in advance of

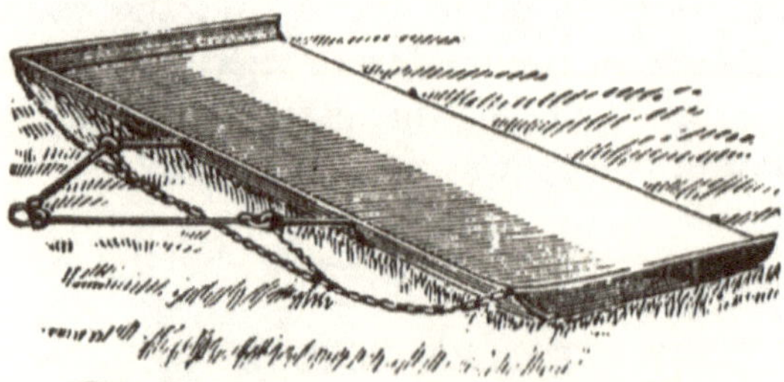

Fig. 31.—TRAP FOR CATCHING LOCUSTS.

the front of the sheet-iron, by which the locusts are disturbed and made to jump, and as the machine is moving on at the same time, they drop upon it. A thick coat of gas-tar is smeared over the surface of the iron, in which the locusts are imbedded and stick fast. The vigorous kicking of the trapped insects helps to keep the mass stirred up, and present a sticky surface. When the trap is full, the locusts are raked off into a pile, and set on fire and consumed. This machine can be drawn over young wheat without injury, as it is not heavy enough to break it down, and being flexible, conforms to the surface of the ground it is passing over. The engraving shows the manner of preparing the sheet-iron for this purpose. The season when the locusts have formerly damaged the newly sprouted wheat is in the spring, and it will be useful for many Western farmers to know of this cheap and effective method, which is not patented, and for which they may thank a farmer's wife of more than usual ingenuity and habits of observation.

SPREADING MANURE.

The winter is a good season for spreading manure. It is immaterial whether the ground is covered with snow or not, or whether it is frozen or soft, provided it is not too soft to draw loads over, and that the ground is not upon a steep hill-side, from which the manure may be washed by heavy rains or by sudden thaws. We have spread manure upon our fields several winters, and always with advantage, not only in saving labor and time, but also to the crops grown after it, more especially to oats and potatoes. In spreading the manure, it

Fig. 32.—WAGON WITH RAISED BOX.

is the best to drop it in heaps, leaving it to be spread by a man as soon as possible afterwards. This may be done most readily by using a manure hook, with which the manure is drawn out of the sled or wagon-box. Sloping wagon-beds are used for hauling various heavy materials, and why should they not be used for this, the heaviest and most bulky load a farmer has to handle? A wagon, having the box raised (figure 32), so that the forward wheels could pass beneath it, would be very convenient on a farm. It could be turned in its own length, and handled with vastly greater facility than the ordinary farm wagon, which needs a large yard to be turned in. Such a wagon could be unloaded with great ease and

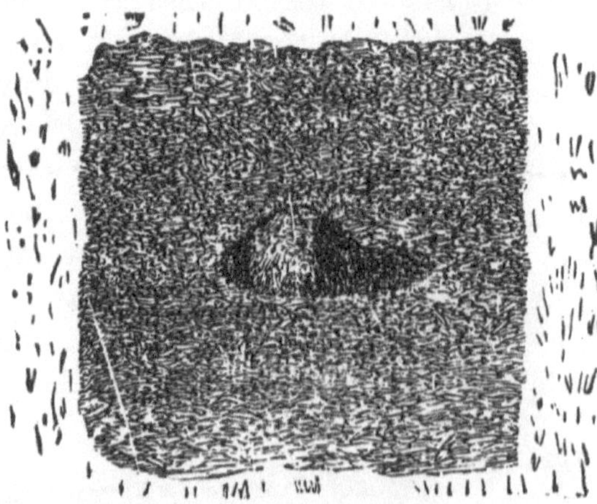

Fig. 33.—MANNER OF SPREADING.

very rapidly by the use of the hook, and in case it was desired to spread the load broadcast from the wagon, that could be done perfectly well. But to do this keeps the horses idle the greater part of the time, and is an unprofitable practice. Two teams hauling will keep one man busy in the yard helping to load, and another in the field spreading; the work will then go on without loss of time. In dropping the heaps, they may be left in rows, one rod apart, and one rod apart in the row· each load being divided into eight heaps. This will give twenty loads per acre. If ten loads only are to be spread. the rows should be one rod apart, and the heaps two rods apart in the rows. In spreading the manure, it should be done evenly, and the heaps should not be made to overlap. If there is one heap to the square rod, it should be thrown eight feet each way from the centre, covering a square of sixteen and one half feet, as shown in figure 33. One heap then is made to join up to another, and the whole ground is equally manured. There is more in this point than is generally supposed by farmers, many of whom are careless and wasteful in this respect, giving too much in some places, and too little in others. The consequence is uneven growth over the field, rusted grain, or perhaps laid straw in some places, and in others a half-starved crop. Another important point in spreading is, to break up the lumps, and scatter the fine manure. Unless this is done, the field cannot be evenly fertilized. There is work about this, which would tempt some hired men to neglect it, but it should not only be insisted upon, but looked to, and its performance insured.

PUTTING AWAY TOOLS.

The wearing out of farm implements is, as a rule, due more to neglect than to use. If tools can be well taken care of, it will pay to buy those made of the best steel, and finished in the best manner; but in common hands, and with common care, such are of little advantage. Iron and steel parts should be cleaned with dry sand and a cob, or scraped with a piece of soft iron, washed and oiled if necessary, and in a day or two cleaned off with the corn-cob and dry sand. Finally, paint the iron part with rosin and beeswax, in the proportion of four of rosin to one of wax, melted together and applied hot. This is good for the iron or steel parts of every sort of tool.

Wood-work should be painted with good, boiled, linseed oil, white lead and turpentine, colored of any desired tint; red is probably the best color. Keep the cattle away until the paint is dry and hard, or they will lick, with death as the result. If it is not desired to use paint on hand tools, the boiled oil, with turpentine and "liquid drier," does just as well. Many prefer to saturate the wood-work of farm implements with crude petroleum. This cannot be used with color, but is applied by itself, so long as any is absorbed by the pores of the wood.

SELF-CLOSING DOORS.

A self-opening, rolling door is shown in figure 34. A half-inch rope, attached to a staple driven into the upper edge of the door, passes parallel with the track, and beyond the boundary of the door when open, over a small

Fig. 34.—SELF-CLOSING SLIDING DOOR.

grooved pulley and thence downward; a weight is attached to its end. The door is shown closed, and the weight drawn up. As the door is a self-fastening one, when the fastening is disengaged the weight will draw the door open. By a string or wire connected to the fastening, the door may be opened while standing at any part of the building, or if one end be attached to a post outside, near the carriage way, the door may be opened without leaving the vehicle, a desirable plan, especially during inclement weather. The weight and pulleys should be located inside the building, but are shown outside to make the plan more readily understood. By attaching the rope to the opposite side of the door, it may be made self-closing instead of self-opening, as thought most convenient. The manner of closing a swing-door, as in figure 35, is so clearly shown as to need no description.

Fig. 35.—SWING-DOOR.

VENTILATORS FOR FODDER STACKS.

The perfect curing of fodder corn is difficult, even with the best appliances ; as usually done, the curing i very imperfect. The fodder corn crop is one that merits not only the best preparation of the ground and the best culture, but it is worthy of special care in harvesting and curing. The French farmers are giving much attention to this crop, and by good culture are raising most extraordinary and very profitable yields. Seventy tons per acre is not unfrequently grown by the best farmers. We do not average more than eight tons per acre, yet with

Fig. 36.—FRAME.

us the corn crop may be grown under the most favorable circumstances. In a few instances, a yield of thirty tons per acre has been reached by one farmer, but this is the highest within our knowledge. One of the most prominent defects in ordinary American agriculture is, the neglect with which this easily grown and very valuable crop is treated ; and one of the most promising improvements in our advancing system of culture is, the attention now being given to fodder corn. A drawback under which we labor is the difficulty of curing such heavy and succulent herbage ; this, however, will by and by be removed, both by the adoption of the French system of ensilage, and by better methods of drying the fodder. On the whole, the system of ensilage offers by far the greatest advantages ; the fodder being preserved in a fresh and succulent condition, and the labor of preparing the silos, cutting the stalks, and properly protecting them from the atmosphere, being actually no more than that of drying the crop in the usual manner, storing it in stacks, and cutting it afterwards for use when it is needed. It is impossible, however, that even the best improvements can be introduced otherwise than slowly and with caution ; the old system, although it may be less effective and profitable than the new, will be long retained by many ; and even in the old methods improvements are being made from season to season by the ingenuity of farmers. We recently saw a very simple but useful arrangement for the ventilation of stacks, and mows in

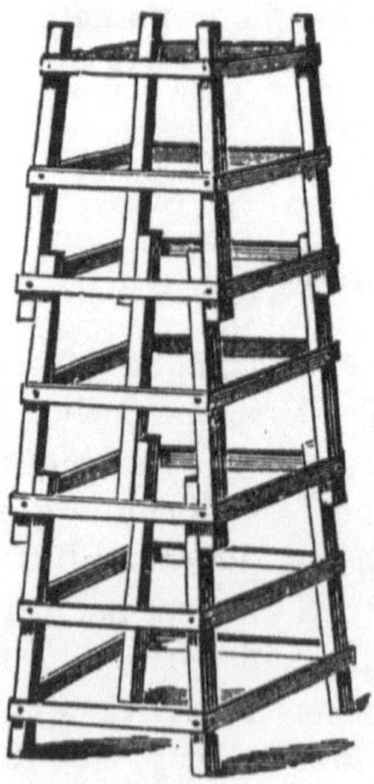

Fig. 37.—VENTILATOR.

barns, which is applicable to the curing of corn fodder. It consists of a frame, figure 36, made of strips of wood, put together with small carriage bolts. The strips may be made of chestnut, pine, or hemlock, the first being the most durable and best, two inches wide and one inch thick. The illustration shows how these strips are put together. The length of the section shown may be three or four feet. In figure 37 is seen the manner in which the sections are put together. A small stack may have a column of these ventilators in the centre ; a large one may have three or four of them ; in a mow in the barn, there may be as many as are needful, two or three, or more, as the case may be. When made in this shape, they are so portable, and easy to use, that the greatest objections against ventilators are removed. In stacking fodder corn, it is safest to make the stacks small. Three of these sections, placed together in one column, are sufficient for a stack containing three tons, and which would be about fourteen feet high. The sheaves should be small, and the stack somewhat open at the bottom, so as to freely admit currents of air. The top of the stack should be well protected to keep out the rain ; a hay cap fastened over the top would be very effective for this. If a quantity of dry straw could be thrown in between the bundles, and on the top of each layer of them, the perfect curing of the fodder would be then secured.

CORN-MARKER FOR UNEVEN GROUND.

The corn-marker, shown in figure 38, is so constructed that it will readily accommodate itself to uneven ground. It consists of two pieces of plank, these form the middle set of runners. Upon these pin two straight pieces of two by four scantling, with each end projecting over the runner six inches; through these ends are bored holes for a four-inch rod. Two other pieces of plank, like the former, are procured, and one end of two other pieces of scantling are pinned to each runner; then these beams are connected to the middle pair by the

Fig. 38.—FLEXIBLE CORN-MARKER.

bolts, as seen in the engraving, so that, while one runner is on high ground, the other may be in the land furrow. In turning around, the two outside runners may be turned up against the seat.

A HOME-MADE HARROW.

The harrow, figure 39, is a square one. The teeth are set twelve inches from centre to centre, each way. There are four beams in each half, and five teeth in each beam. These beams are four feet eight inches long, mortised into the front piece, which is three feet seven inches in length. The rear ends of the beam are secured by a piece of timber, two by one and a half inches, halved on to the beams and then bolted. The harrow is made of two and a half by two and a half-inch scantling, using locust wood, because of its great durability and firmness. There is nothing particularly new about this harrow, except that it is larger than common, and the novel way of hitching to it by which it is kept steady.

The teeth can be made to cut six inches or one inch apart. The manner of hitching is shown in the engraving. The draw-bar is made of three-eighths by one and three-quarter iron, three feet four inches in length.

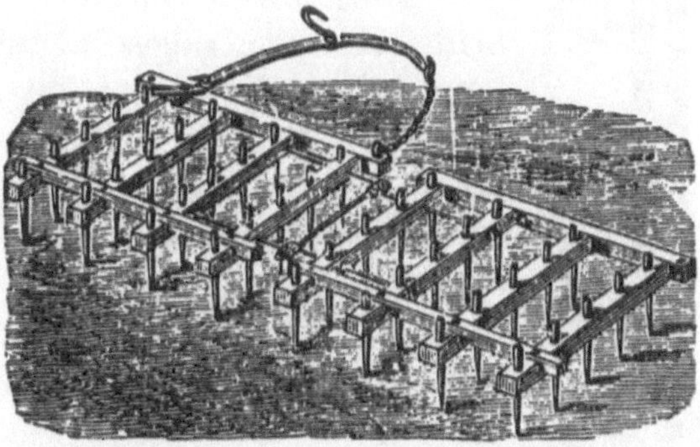

Fig. 39.—AN EXCELLENT HARROW.

The chain is attached to this by a hook at one end, the other being fastened to the harrow by a staple. The chain is about two feet long. The entire cost is about twelve dollars.

CLEARING LAND BY BLASTING.

The explosive used is dynamite or giant powder. It is a mixture of nitro-glycerine with some absorbents, by which this dangerously explosive liquid is made into a perfectly safe solid substance, of a consistence and appearance not unlike light-brown sugar. It is not possible to explode dynamite by ordinary accident, nor even by the application of a lighted match. A quantity of it placed upon a stump and fired with a lighted match, burns away very much as a piece of camphor or resin would do, with little flame but much smoke, and boils and bubbles until only a crust is left. There is not the least danger, therefore of igniting the powder dangerously, until properly placed for the blast. In this respect it has a very great advantage over ordinary blasting powder, which may be exploded by a spark. The powder, as it is manufactured, is made into cartridges about eight inches in length, and of any required diameter. The cartridges are wrapped in strong parchment paper, covered with paraffine, and the true form is shown at figure 40. They are fired by a cap (also in figure 40), which is inserted into the end of the cartridge. The fuse, which is of the common kind, is inserted into the open end of the cap, which is pinched close upon it with a small pair of pliers, so as to hold it firmly. The cartridge

Fig. 40. Fig. 41.

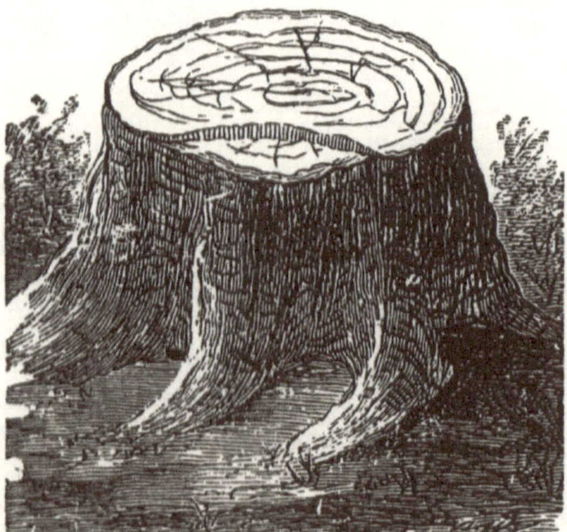

Fig. 42.—THE STUMP BEFORE THE EXPLOSION.

is then opened at one end, the cap with the fuse attached inserted, and the paper tied tightly around the fuse, with a piece of twine. The cartridge ready for firing is shown at figure 41.

Our first operation was upon a green white-oak stump, thirty inches in diameter, with roots deeply bedded in the ground. To have cut and dug out this stump with axe and spades would have been a hard day's work for two or more good men. The shape of the stump is shown at figure 42. A hole was punched beneath the stump, as shown in the figure, with an iron bar (figure 43), so as to reach the centre of it. Two of the cartridges were placed beneath the stump, and were tamped with some earth ; a pail of water was then poured into the hole, which had the effect of consolidating the earth around the charge. The fuse was then fired. The result was to split the stump into numerous fragments, and to throw it entirely out of the ground, leaving only a few shreds of roots loose in the soil. The result is shown in figure 44, on the next page ; the fragments of the stump in the engraving were thrown to a distance of thirty to fifty feet, and many smaller ones were carried over one hundred feet. The quantity of powder used was less than two pounds. A portion of the useful effect produced by the explosion, consisted in the tearing of the stump into such pieces as could easily be sawed up into fire-wood ; by which much after-labor in breaking it up, when taking it out in the usual manner, was saved. This test was perfectly successful, and proved not only the thorough effectiveness of this method, but its economy in cost and in time.

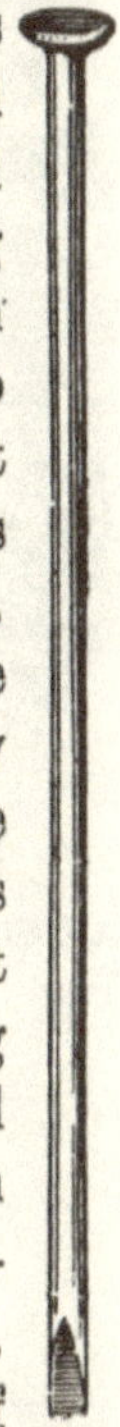

Fig. 43.

Several other stumps were taken out in the same manner ; the time occupied with each being from five to ten minutes. Smaller stumps were thrown out with single cartridges, and in not one case was anything left in the ground that might not be turned out with the plow, or that would interfere with the plowing of the ground. The explosive was then tried upon a fast rock, of about

Fig. 44.—THE EFFECT OF BLASTING THE STUMP.

one hundred and fifty cubic feet, weighing about ten tons. The shape of the rock before the explosion is

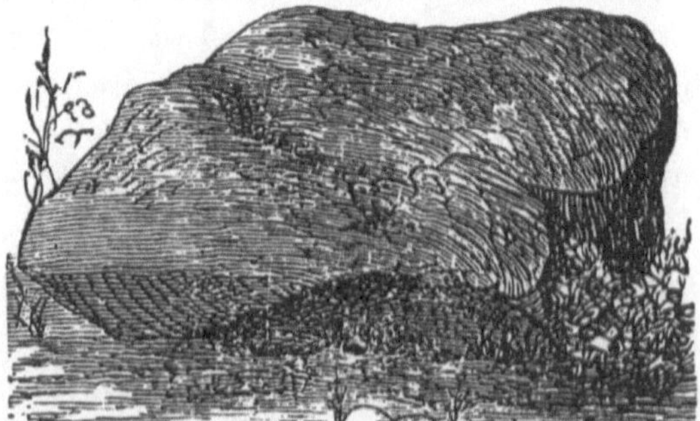

Fig. 45.—THE ROCK AS IT WAS.

shown in figure 45. A hole was made, with the bar, in the ground beneath the rock, and three cartridges were inserted and exploded. To have produced this result (shown in figure 46), by the ordinary method, that was here done in a few minutes by one man, would have occupied, at least, two men, with drills, sledge, etc., two or three days. The application of this method is seen to be of great value where the saving of time is an object. An acre of stumps or rocks may be cleared in one day by one or two men, and the material left ready

Fig. 46.—THE ROCK AFTER BLASTING.

for use as fire-wood, or as stones for fences or buildings. The cost in money is also reduced in some cases very considerably, and almost absolute safety to the careful operator is insured. It would be generally advisable to secure the services of an expert, and that the parties who have work of this character to be performed, should jointly engage such a man, who could either do the whole work, or do it in part, and instruct a foreman or skilful workman sufficiently in a day to perform the remainder. The most favorable seasons for operating upon stumps and rocks are fall and spring, when the ground is saturated with water. It should be explained that this explosive is not injured by water, although a long-continued exposure to it would affect some qualities of it.

PREVENTABLE LOSSES ON THE FARM.

It is a "penny wise and pound foolish" system, to breed from scrub stock. There is not a farmer in this region who has not access to a pedigreed Shorthorn bull, by a payment of a small fee of two to five dollars, and yet we find only one animal in ten with Shorthorn blood. It is a common practice to breed to a yearling, and as he is almost sure to become breechy, to sell him for what he will bring the second summer. Many farmers neglect castrating their calves until they are a year old. We think ten per cent. are thus permanently injured, must be classed as stags, and sold at a reduced price. Fully half the calves so stunted never recover.

With many, the starving process continues through the entire year. They are first fed an insufficient quantity of skim milk; then in July or August, just at the season when flies are at their worst, and pastures driest, they are weaned, and turned out to shift for themselves, and left on the pastures until snows fall, long after the fields yield them a good support. They are wintered without grain, spring finds them poor and hide-bound, and the best grazing season is over before they are fairly thrifty.

The keeping of old cows long past their prime is another thing which largely reduces the profits of the farmer. We have found quite a large per cent. of cows, whose wrinkled horns and generally run-down condition show that they have long since passed the point of profit. A few years ago, these cows would have sold at full prices for beef, now they will sell only for Bologna at two cents per pound. Thus cows have, in a majority of cases, been kept, not because they were favorites, or even because they were profitable, but from sheer carelessness and want of forethought. Another fruitful cause of loss to the farmer is, attempting to winter more stock than he has feed for. Instead of estimating his resources in the fall, and knowing that he has enough feed even for a hard winter, he gives the matter no thought, and March finds him with the choice of two evils, either to sell stock, or buy feed. If he chooses the former, he will often sell for much less than the animals would have brought four months earlier, and if the latter, will usually pay a much higher price for feed than if it had been bought in autumn. Too often he scrimps the feed, hoping for an early spring, and so soon as he can see the grass showing a shade of green around the fence rows, or in some sheltered ravine, turns his stock out to make their own living. This brings one of the most potent causes of unprofitable cattle raising; namely, short pastures. The farmer who is overstocked in winter, is almost sure to turn his cattle on his pastures too early in the spring, and this generally results in short pasture all summer, and consequently the stock do not thrive as they ought, and in addition, the land which should be greatly benefited and enriched, is injured, for the development of the roots in the soil must correspond to that of the tops, and if the latter are constantly cropped short, the roots must be small. The benefit of shade is lost, and the land is trampled by the cattle in their wanderings to fill themselves, so that it is in a worse condition than if a crop of grain had been grown on it. From all these causes combined, there is a large aggregate of loss, and it is the exception to find a farm on which one or more of them does not exist, and yet without exception they may be classed as "preventable," if thought and practical common sense are brought to bear in the management.

A CRADLE FOR DRAWING A BOAT.

When it is necessary to draw a boat out of the water, a cradle should be used. This is very easily made out of some short boards and a piece of plank. The boards are cut so that when three thicknesses are bolted together, the joints shall be broken and not come opposite

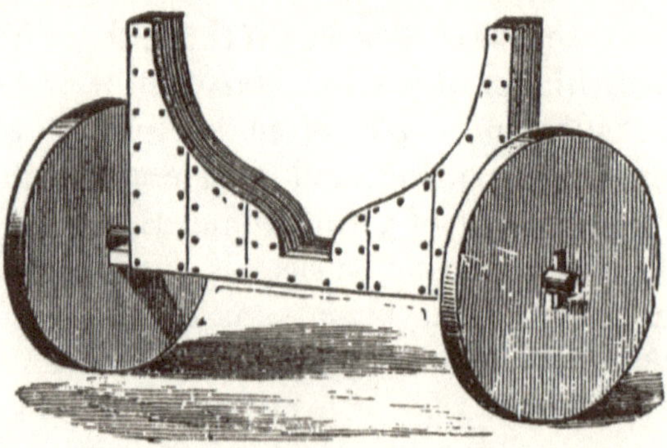

Fig. 47.—CRADLE FOR A BOAT.

each other, as shown in figure 47. The cradle should be made to fit the boat tightly, midway between stem and stern, so that when it rests upon it, the boat will be evenly balanced and firmly held. The cradle is mounted upon two wheels, which may be made of hard wood plank. A piece of two-inch plank may be sawn out for the axle, and the upper part of the cradle firmly bolted to it. Such a cradle as this may be made light or heavy, and if desired may be furnished with iron wheels, so that it will sink in the water. It can then be run down under the boat, and that be drawn upon it. By hauling upon the ring-bolt in its stern, the boat can be drawn up out of the water, and easily moved on land.

When it is desired to lift a boat out of the water, and suspend it in a boat-house, all that is necessary to be done is to fix two strong hooks, or rings, in the top of the house, and a ring-bolt at each end of the boat. A pair of double-sheaved blocks is provided for each end of the boat. The blocks are hooked to the rings in the house and to those in the boat, which is then drawn up, one end at a time, alternately, until high enough. If two persons are in the boat, both ends may be hauled up at once. The loose end of the rope is fastened to the ring of the boat, or to a ring or a cleat at the side of the boat-house. Then the boat remains suspended in the boat-house.

FEED-RACK FOR SHEEP.

The rack, figure 48, is made of poles for the bottom

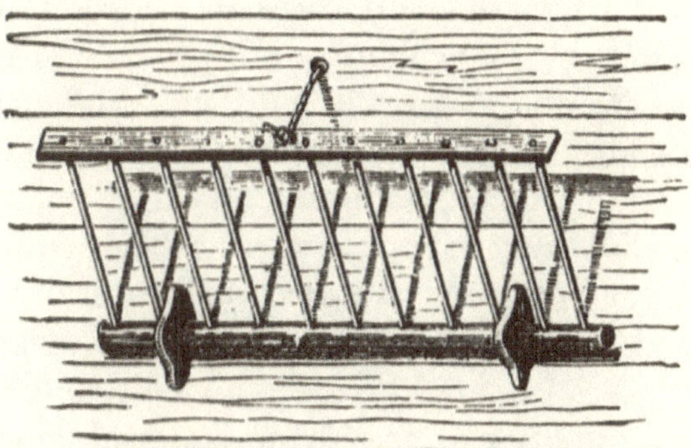

Fig. 48.—FEED-RACK FOR SHEEP.

and top, and cross-bars fitted into them. The bottom bar slides loosely in brackets, which are fixed to the wall of the shed, and the upper bar is secured by a cord, which passes over a small pulley in a hole in the wall above the rack; a weight being attached to the outside end of the rope, serves to keep the rack always against the wall. When the hay is put in the rack is drawn down, and, when filled, is pushed back against the wall, holding the hay closely, and being kept in place by the weight. This prevents the hay from being pulled out too freely by the sheep or cattle. It is recommended that the grain-trough be placed beneath a rack of this kind, so that the chaff which falls from it may be caught in the trough and saved for use, instead of being trampled under foot.

HOW TO MANAGE NIGHT-SOIL.

The fertilizing properties of night-soil are well known. The principal reason why this valuable material is neglected and permitted to go to waste, is the difficulty of handling it. If improperly handled, it is disagreeable and difficult to apply to the uses to which it is best adapted. There are many cases in which it could be made use of very conveniently, if rightly managed. In country towns and villages it is difficult to dispose of it, and it becomes a serious nuisance to householders, and a detriment to the public health, when it ought to be turned to profitable uses. In some other countries this refuse matter is eagerly collected and carefully used by the farmers. The methods employed in England, Germany, and France might very well be adopted by us, and a large quantity of fertilizing material be gathered. By the methods there in use, the night-soil is easily handled and prepared for distribution upon the land, or for mixing in composts. Arrangements are made with persons in towns and villages who wish to have the soil removed, and the time being fixed (this is always in the night, from which circumstance the name given to the material is derived), wagons with tight boxes, or carts, are sent to the place. Carts are mostly used, as indeed they are in Europe for most of the farm work. The carts, or wagons, carry out a quantity of earth, chopped straw, ashes, or such other absorbent as may be conveniently procured, and some sheaves of long straw, or else the ashes or other absorbent used, which is frequently the sweepings and scrapings of streets, is prepared upon the ground or near by. This material is then disposed

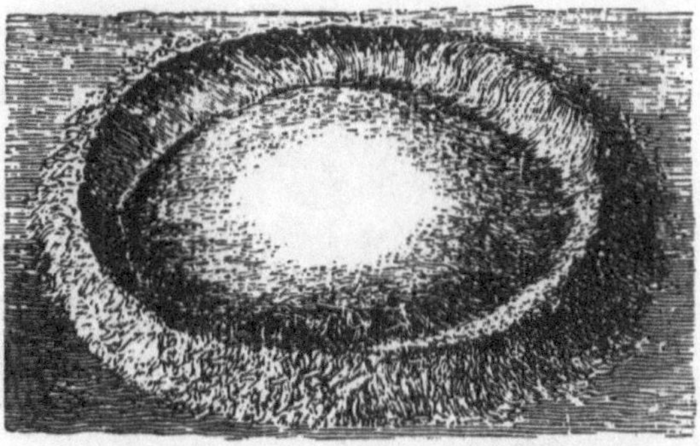

Fig. 49.—PREPARING NIGHT-SOIL.

in the form of a bank enclosing a space of sufficient size to hold the night-soil, as shown in figure 49. A reserve heap is kept to be mixed with the night-soil as it is emptied into the place prepared for it. Wheelbarrows with tight boxes are generally used to convey the soil from the cesspool. When the whole has been removed from the cesspool, the cut straw is mixed in and the banks of earth are turned over upon the pile, which can then be handled with shovels or forks, and is ready to be loaded into the wagon. Some of the long straw is laid in the bottom of the wagon-box, and the mixed mass is thrown upon it, layer after layer alternately with straw, until the top of the wagon-box is reached. It is most convenient to have a rack, or flaring side-boards, to confine the upper part of the load, but this is not necessary if the loading is properly done. The manner of loading the top is as follows: a bundle of straw is spread so that half of it projects over the side or end of the load. A quantity of the mixed stuff is forked on to the straw, the loose projecting ends of which are turned back on to the load when more is laid upon it. The doubled straw holds the loose stuff together, which might else be shaken off the load as it is carried home. In this manner the load is built up until it is completed, when it appears as

Fig. 50.—MANNER OF LOADING NIGHT-SOIL.

shown in figure 50. Loads thus made are carried many miles without losing anything on the journey, and the mass, which would seem to have no coherence, is kept solidly together. Carts are sometimes loaded to a hight of two or three feet above the side-boards, and are made to carry a load for three horses. By this management, this material is no more disagreeable than ordinary manure, and the work of moving it is rendered quite easy.

THE USE OF LIME IN BLASTING.

There are some forces, apparently insignificant, which act with irresistible power through short distances. The expansion of water in freezing is a force of this kind. The increase in bulk in changing from the liquid to the solid state of ice is only about one-tenth, yet it exercises a power sufficient to break iron vessels and rend the hardest rocks. Every one who has slaked a lump of quicklime by gradually pouring water upon it, has observed that the first effect of the contact between the water and lime is to cause a swelling of the lump. It generally expands and takes up considerable more room than before. This expansive force has recently been successfully applied to coal mining in England. Powdered quicklime is strongly compressed into cartridges about three inches in diameter, and each has running through it a perforated iron tube, through which water can be forced. These cartridges were used in a coal mine in place of the usual blasting charge, water was forced into them, and the expansion of the lime threw down a mass of coal weighing about ten tons, with little of the small coal made with the usual blast. The exemption from danger and the avoidance of smoke, have caused coal mine owners to regard this new method with favor. Some of our ingenious reapers may find a useful hint in this.

A WATER AND FEED TROUGH.

A supply of water in the cow-stable is a great convenience; a simple arrangement for furnishing it to the cows in their stalls may be made as follows: Sheets of galvanized iron are bent to form a trough, and fitted into the floor joists under the feed-box, as indicated in figure 51, making a trough three inches deep and sixteen inches wide. The flanges on each side are nailed to the joists, and the sheets of iron riveted together at the ends, and made water-tight by cement. The trough runs the entire length of the feed floor, and is supplied with water from a pipe, pump, or hose; a pipe at the other end carries away the surplus water and prevents overflow, and another pipe with a faucet is provided for emptying the trough. The feed-box is built over the

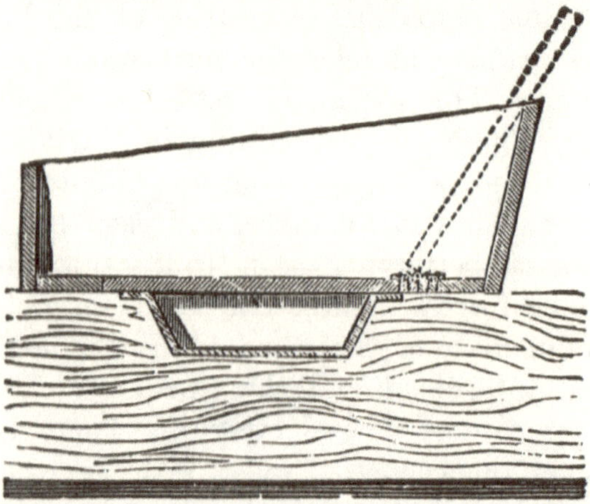

Fig. 51.—WATER AND FEED TROUGH COMBINED.

water trough, a part of its floor being a trap—indicated by dotted lines in the engraving—by which admission to the water is gained. Before opening this trap, the manger is swept clean; and if there were no other advantage than this compulsory cleansing of the mangers after each feeding, it would be sufficient to pay for the cost of constructing such a watering arrangement.

THE CONSTRUCTION OF STALLS.

It is rare, even in these days of progress, to see a well-arranged stall in a farmer's barn. No horse stall should be less than six feet in width, nor of a length less than nine feet. This affords room for the animal to lie down and rise comfortably without bruising hips and limbs, and also for the attendant to pass in and out. The partition between stalls should be of sufficient hight to prevent playing, biting, and kicking. Racks of iron are neat and serviceable. The horse eats its food from the ground, and because many first pull out a greater portion of the hay from the rack, we shall dispense with the rack as commonly used, and substitute a single manger which serves for both hay and grain.

Whatever may be the foundation of the stall, whether of brick, stone, cement, clay, or wood, it should have inclination enough to carry off all fluid. Over this place a flooring composed of strips of plank, four inches in width by two inches in thickness, with an inch intervening between each strip. This need not extend more than half the length of the stall, the upper portion being compact. The essential point is that the horse shall stand with an equal weight upon all the extremities. This custom of confining a horse to a sloping stall, in one position sometimes for days, is a cruel one, and very detrimental to the limbs and feet, as it brings about, sooner or later, serious affections in these parts. A loose box is far preferable to the stall, wherever practicable. Every stable or barn should be provided with one at least, in case of sickness or accident. By the arrangement of a floor as just described, the bedding is kept dry and the animal clean and comfortable. Litter should be always kept beneath the animal; it gives an air of comfort to the place and invites to repose of body and limbs by day and night. Stalls for both horses and cattle should be of sufficient hight. as also all door and passage ways about a barn. Formerly, it was the custom to build in such a way that no horse, and not even a man of respectable hight could enter a door-way without danger of knocking his skull, and inflicting serious injury. There are stalls in country barns so low that a horse cannot throw up his head without receiving a blow against the beams above. Animals undoubtedly acquire the trick of pulling back, or of making a sudden spring when passing a door-way, from having been obliged to run the gauntlet of some narrow, low, ill-contrived passage-way. The man who should now be guilty of building in this way would deserve to have his own brains knocked, every time he passes in and out, as a gentle reminder of his folly. All barn-doors should be high, wide, and, when practicable, always slide.

The common mode of securing cattle in the barn, especially milch cows, by placing their necks between stanchions, is not to be advocated, especially when they are confined in this way for many hours at a time without relief, as is often necessary in the winter season. A simple chain about the neck with a ring upon an upright post affords perfect security, while it gives the animal freedom of movement to head and limbs—and conduces to its comfort in various other ways. Animals should not be overcrowded, as is too often the case in large dairy establishments—a fact which will make itself evident sooner or later in the sanitary qualities of the milk, if in no other manner. We cannot deny the fact, if we would, that everything, however trifling, that contributes to the welfare of our domestic animals is a gain to the owner of them pecuniarily, and what touches a man's pocket is generally considered to be worth looking after, at all times and in all places.

HOG-KILLING IMPLEMENTS—RINGING.

The stout table on which the dead porkers are lain to be scraped and dressed after being scalded, is made with its top curving about four inches in a width of four feet, and consisting of strips of oak plank, as represented in figure 52. This curved top conforms to the form of the

Fig. 52.—A DRESSING TABLE.

carcass, and holds it in any desired position better than a flat surface. For scrapers, old-fashioned iron candlesticks are used; the curved and sufficiently sharp edges

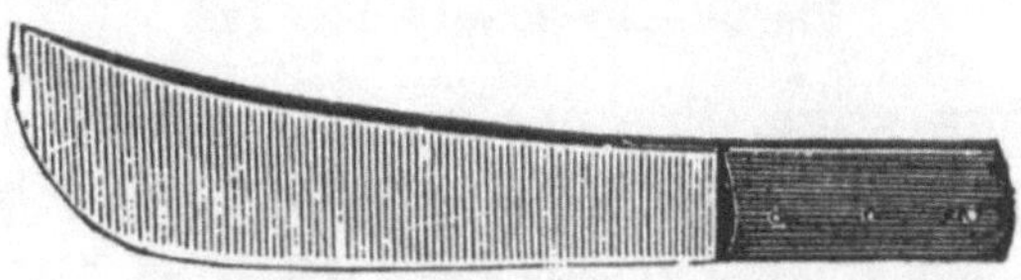

Fig. 53.—HANDY MEAT CLEAVER.

at either end serving as well as a scraper made for the purpose, and its small end has an advantage over the latter for working about the eyes and other sharp depressions. A cleaver for use in cutting up the pork is shown in figure 53; it has a thirteen-inch blade, three inches wide at the widest part, and one-quarter inch thick at the back. This is a convenient implement, easily and cheaply made by a good blacksmith, if it cannot be had at the stores ; any mechanic can put on the wooden handle. In figure 54 is represented a home-made hog-ringing apparatus. The blacksmith makes an instrument resembling a horse-shoe nail, of good iron, about three inches long, three-sixteenths of an inch wide, and one-thirty-second of an inch thick, tapering to a point; the "head" is merely the broad flat end curled up.

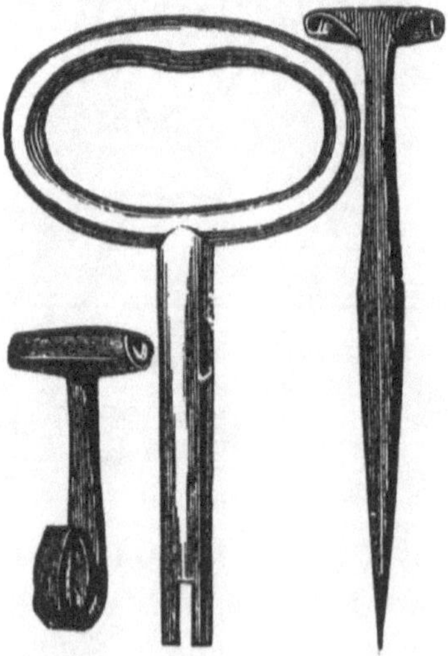

Fig. 54.—HOG-RINGER AND KEY.

Just before using, this needle-like instrument has its corners rubbed off on a file ; it then is easily pushed through the septum of the pig's nose. A key with its tongue broken off and a slot filed in the end, is used to curl up the projecting end, and the ringing is done. The "rings" cost about seventy-five cents a hundred, and are effective and easily applied.

HOW TO MIX CEMENT.

The article to be used is the Rosendale cement. This is nearly as good as the imported Portland cement, and much cheaper. The cement is made from what is known as hydraulic lime-stone—that is a rock which contains, besides ordinary lime-stone, some clay, silica, and magnesia. Pure lime-stone contains only lime and carbonic acid, in the proportions of fifty-six parts of the former to forty-four of the latter in one hundred. When this stone is burned, the carbonic acid is driven off by the heat, and pure or quick-lime is left. When this is brought in contact with water, the two combine, forming hydrate of lime; during the combination, heat is given out; the operation is called slaking. When the water is just sufficient to form the combination, a fine, dry powder is produced, which we call dry slaked-lime. When the water is in excess, the surplus is mixed mechanically with the lime, and forms what is called the milk of lime, or cream of lime, according to its consistence; it is this pasty substance which we mix with sand, to form building mortar. But when we have clay mixed in a certain proportion, either naturally or artificially, with the lime-stone, and this stone or mixture is burned in the same manner as ordinary lime-stone, we get what is known as hydraulic lime, because it combines with a much larger proportion of water than pure lime, and in combining with it, instead of falling to powder, like ordinary lime, it hardens into stone again. This hardening takes place even under water; the hydraulic lime combines with just so much water as is required to "set" or harden, and leaves the remainder. It possesses this property, also, when mixed, with sand in proper proportions, and when so mixed, the cement will adhere very firmly to the surface of any stone to which it may be applied. This property is made available in constructing works of concrete, which consists of broken stone mixed with such a quantity of cement, that, when it is packed closely, the surfaces of all the pieces of stone are brought into contact with the cement, and the spaces between the fragments of stone are filled with it. That there may be no more cement used than is actually needed, the mixture is rammed down solidly, until the fragments of stone are brought into close contact with

Fig. 55.—BOX FOR MIXING CEMENT.

each other. The composition of the impure or hydraulic lime-stone, which behaves in this useful manner, is, in the case of some of the Kingston stone, as follows: Carbonic acid, 34.20 per cent.; lime, 25.50; magnesia, 12.35; silica, 15.37; alumina (clay), 9.13; and peroxide of iron (which is useless or worse), 2.25. On account of this difference in character between lime and cement, a different treatment is necessary for each, and each is put to different uses. The cement makes a much harder and more solid combination with sand, and is therefore chosen

Fig. 56.—SIDE OF CEMENT BOX.

when great strength is required. Its rapid setting, when mixed with water, also requires that it be used as soon as it is mixed, and renders a rapid mixture necessary. The cement and sand should, therefore, be mixed together dry, and very thoroughly. Four parts of sand to one part of cement are the proportions generally used. These may be mingled in a box of suitable character, and the mass is so spread as to have a hollow in the centre, into which water is poured. The sides of the heap are gradually worked into the water, with a common hoe, in such a way as to prevent the water from spreading about, and as it is absorbed more water is poured in, until the whole is brought to a thin semi-liquid condition. A box very suitable for this operation is shown in figure 55. This is made of pieces of plank, prepared as follows: The side pieces are shown at figure 56. The end pieces are made with tenons, which fit in mortises in the side pieces, and the frame thus made is held to-

Fig. 57.—MACHINE FOR MIXING CEMENT.

gether by keys driven into the holes seen in the tenons. The bottom planks are fastened together with cleats, so placed as to receive the frame and fit snugly. Iron bolts are put through holes in the cleats, and through the holes in figure 56, and by means of nuts with washers under them, the whole box is brought firmly together. Such a box, after having been used for this purpose, will be found very useful for mixing feed in the barn, or for many other purposes, and may, therefore, be well made at the first. When the mortar is mixed, the broken stone may be thrown into it, beginning at one side, and the whole is worked up thoroughly with the hoe, so that every piece of stone is coated with the cement. A machine, that is easily made, may be used for this mixing, and is also very useful for mixing ordinary mortar for building or plastering. It is shown in figure 57. It consists of a box set upon feet, with a smaller box attached at the rear end, having an opening at the bottom where the mortar is seen escaping, and a shaft, having broad, flat arms on it, placed at a somewhat acute angle with the line of the shaft, so that they will operate as a screw to force the mass along the spout and out of it at the opening. A crank handle is fitted to this shaft, and if a fly-wheel can be borrowed from a feed-cutter, or a corn-sheller, and attached to the shaft as shown, so much the better. The materials to be mixed are thrown into the box, and by turning the handle, the whole will be thoroughly incorporated with great rapidity and ease.

RINGING AND HANDLING BULLS

Now that more attention is given to improving farm stock, a bull is kept upon nearly every large farm. The high-bred bulls are spirited animals, and are exceedingly dangerous if the utmost caution is not exercised in managing them. Experienced breeders are not unfrequently caught unawares, and unceremoniously lifted over the fence, or forced to escape ingloriously from one of their playful animals, or even seriously injured by the vicious ones. It should be made a rule, wherever a bull is kept, to have him ringed, before he is a year old, and brought under subjection and discipline at an early age, while he can be safely and easily handled. Some time ago we assisted at the ringing of a yearling bull, which severely taxed the utmost exertions of six persons with ropes and stanchions to hold him. A slip of the foot might have caused the loss of a life, or some serious injuries. To avoid such dangerous struggles, a strong frame, similar to that in figure 58, in which to confine the bull, may

Fig. 58.—STALL FOR BULL.

be used. The frame consists of four or six stout posts set deeply in the ground, with side-bars bolted to it, forming a stall in which the bull can be confined so that he cannot turn around. The frame may be placed in the barn-yard or a stable, and may be made to serve as a stall. At the front, a breast-bar should be bolted, and the upper side-bars should project beyond this for eighteen or twenty inches. The forward posts project above the side-bars some inches. The ends of these posts, and the side-bars, are bored with one-inch holes, and at the rear of the frame there should be tenons or iron straps to receive a strong cross-bar, to prevent the animal from escaping should the fastenings become broken or loosened.

Fig. 59.—STRAP.

The bull, led into the frame, is placed with his head

over the breast-bar, and the horns are tied with ropes an inch in diameter to the holes in the bars and posts. He is then secured, and his head is elevated so that the trochar and cannula can be readily used to pierce the cartilage of the nose, and the ring inserted and screwed together. Before the ring is used, it should be tested to ascertain that it is sound and safe.

When the ring is inserted, the straps shown in figure 59 should be used, for the purpose of holding it up and out of the way, so as not to interfere with the feeding of the animal until the nose has healed and become calloused. The straps may be left upon the head permanently, if desired, when the front strap will offer a convenient means of catching him by the staff, when necessary to do so in the field. The staff is a matter of the greatest importance. This should be made of the toughest ash or hickory, and not less than five feet long. With a staff of this length, the herdsman can check the wildest bull, and by resting the butt-end of it upon the ground, can throw the animal's head up, and prevent him from approaching too near. The hook of the staff is shown of two kinds in figures 60 and 61. One is furnished with a spring, by which it is closed. A metal bar attached to the spring and passing through a hole in the staff, prevents the ring from slipping along the spring. The other is provided with a screw by which it is closed.

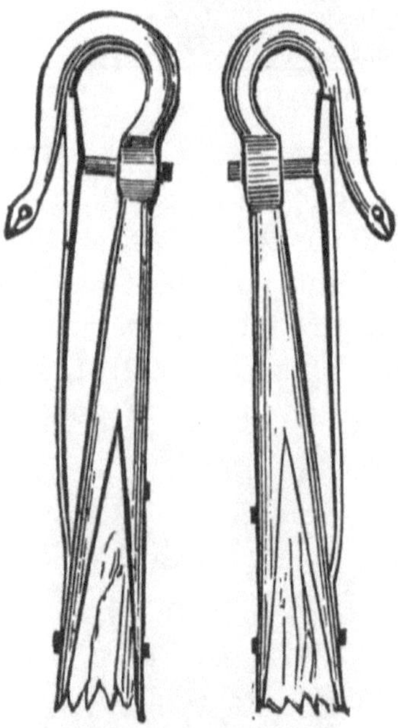

Fig. 60. STAVES. Fig. 61.

SLED FOR REMOVING CORN-SHOCKS.

A sled used for moving corn-shocks from a field which is to be sown with winter grain is shown in figure 62. It is simply a sled of the most ordinary construction, and which any farmer can build. It is made of two joists or planks of hemlock, though oak might be better; say three inches thick, a foot wide, and fourteen to sixteen feet long, rounded at one end and connected by three strong cross-pieces, being in form just

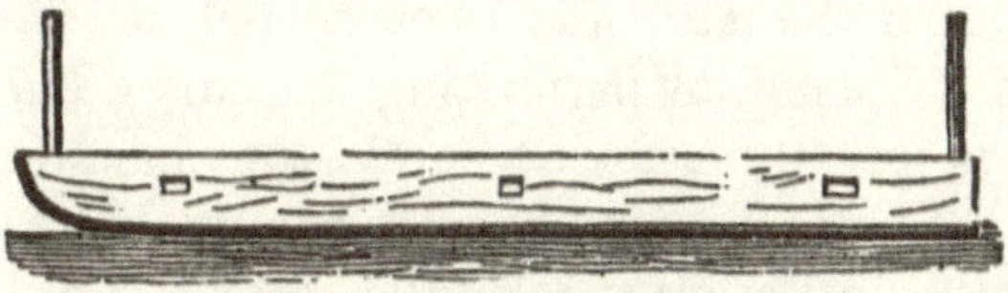

Fig. 62.—SIDE OF SLED.

such a sled as a farmer boy would make to use in the snow, with the addition of cross braces before and behind. The under edge of the runners should be rounded off to the extent of one and a half to two inches, to turn more easily. There should be also short standards before and behind. The runners may be four to five feet apart, according to the length of the corn. A side view of the runner with the standards is given in figure 62.

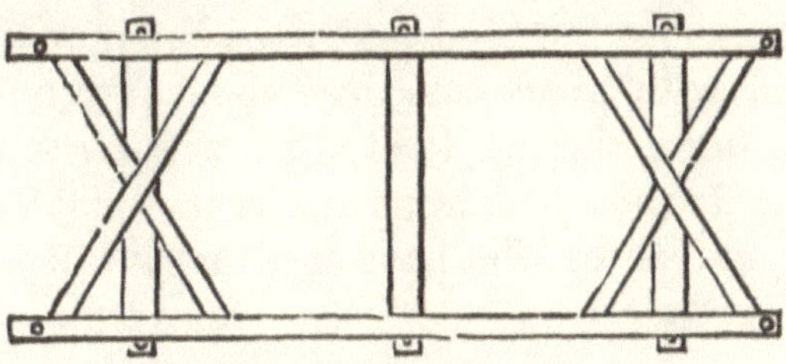

Fig. 63.—TOP OF SLED.

and a top view of the complete sled in figure 63. First, cut off the corn and put it in shocks in the usual way, making the shock smaller than usual. Let it stand thus a few days to dry, then a pair of horses are hitched to the sled, which is driven alongside the shock. The shock is pushed over on to the sled, and so one shock after another until the sled is full. The load is then driven to an adjoining field, where the shocks are set up on end again, and about four of them made into one and tied at the top, or reared against a fence.

The particular advantages of this plan are: First, that by use of the sled and method of loading and unloading the shocks, all actual lifting of the corn is avoided, and the labor and expense reduced more than one-half. Second, by permitting it to dry a few days, its weight is greatly reduced, and the handling much lighter. Third, the corn being partially dried, it can be put together in larger shocks the second time, and will keep better. By this method one man can clear two acres or more in a day, according to the weight of the crop.

A TAGGING TROUGH.

Sheep should be tagged in early spring, and a table for this purpose is shown in figure 64. The sheep is placed on this table feet upwards, in which position it is perfectly helpless, and will not struggle. Then the soiled wool about the hind parts, the belly, or the legs is clipped off with great ease, less than a minute being needed to tag a sheep. Half time will serve for some shearers to do this. In large flocks these tables will be necessary, and those who have small ones will find them very useful.

LIME AND LIME KILNS.

The periodical use of lime as a fertilizer is necessary to good culture. In the best cultivated parts of the country, lime is used once in every rotation of five crops, the usual rotation being two years, grass, corn, oats, wheat, or rye, seeded to grass or clover again. The lime is applied to the land when it is plowed for the fall grain, and is harrowed in before the seed is drilled, or it is harrowed in with the seed, sown broadcast. The quantity used is from forty to fifty bushels per acre. The effect of lime is both mechanical and chemical; it opens and

Fig. 64.—TROUGH FOR TAGGING SHEEP.

loosens heavy clays, and consolidates light, loose, sandy, or peaty vegetable soils; it has the effect of liberating potash from the soil, and of decomposing inert organic matter, and reducing it to an available condition. But while it is beneficial, it cannot be used alone without exhausting the soil of its fertile properties. This is evident from what has been said of its character; at least this is true, so far as regards its effects beyond affording directly to the crops any lime that they may appropriate from the supply thus given. All the benefits received beyond this is a direct draft on the natural stores of the soil. It is therefore necessary, to good agriculture, that either a thrifty clover sod should be plowed under, at least once in the rotation, or that a liberal dressing of manure be given, or both of these. In those localities where the benefits to be derived from the skilful use of lime are best known and appreciated, this method is practised; a heavy sod being plowed under, after having been pastured one year, for the corn, and a good coating of manure being given when the land is plowed for fall grain. Under such treatment, the soil is able to maintain itself and return profitable crops. It is not where

Fig. 65.—IMPROVED LIME KILN WITH ELEVATED TRACK.

this course is pursued that complaints are prevalent of the unprofitableness of farming. The use of lime is spreading gradually into the Western States, where the competition of the still farther and fresher western fields is being severely felt. The experience of Eastern farmers is now being repeated in what were once the Western States, and every appliance of scientific and thorough agriculture is found to be needed to maintain those Western farmers in the close contest for a living. This kiln, figure 65, is intended to stand upon level ground, and is furnished with a sloping track, upon which self-dumping cars containing fuel or lime may be drawn up by horse-power with a rope and pulleys. The body of the kiln may be twenty feet square at the bottom, and thirty feet high, with a flue above the stack of ten to twenty feet. The stack may be built of stone or brick, but should be lined with fire-brick or refractory sandstone. The arch is protected by the shed under the track. At *B*, *B*, are two bearing bars of cast-iron, three by two inches thick, which support the draw-bars, *C*. These are made of one and a half inch round wrought iron, having rings at the outer end, and of which there are four to the foot across the throat of the kiln, which is four or five feet in diameter. The rings serve to admit a crow-bar, by which the bars, or some of them, are drawn out to let down the charge of lime. The open space, *D*, is intended for the insertion of the bar to loosen or break the lime, should the throat become gorged. A cast-iron frame, with an aperture of three by twenty-four inches, is built into this opening. It also serves to kindle the kiln, and is closed by an iron door. The car should be made of wood, and lined with sheet-iron ; it is hinged to the front axle, and hooked to the draft-rope, so that when the fore-wheels strike the block, *E*, at the mouth of the kiln, the car tips and dumps its load. The iron door, *F*, which closes the kiln, is raised or lowered by means of the rope and ring, *G*, which passes over a pulley fixed upon the side of the flue. A covered shed will be needed to protect the top of the stack, and a gallery should be made around it, for a passage-way for the workmen. This kind of kiln is suited only for the use of coal as fuel ; when wood is used for burning the lime, common pits or temporary kilns are to be constructed.

FALL FALLOWING.

The old practice of summer fallowing, or working the soil for one year without a crop, for the purpose of gaining a double crop the second season, is now, very properly, obsolete. While some may question the propriety of this opinion, there can be no doubt as to the value of fall fallowing. The constant turning and working of the ground during the fall months cost nothing but time and labor, at a season when these cannot be otherwise employed, and so, in reality, cost nothing. But the benefits to the soil are very considerable. Especially is this the case with heavy clay soils, and less, in a descending ratio, through the gradations from heavy clay down to light loams—at least it is so considered by many; and it is reasonable to suppose that if the atmospheric effects upon the particles of a clay soil serve, to some extent, to dissolve the mineral particles, they may easily do the same service for a sandy soil, and help to set loose some of the potash contained in the granitic or feldspathic particles of such a soil. The mechanical effects of the fall working are certainly more useful upon clay than a light loam; but there are other purposes to serve than merely to disintegrate the soil, and mellow and loosen it. There are weeds to destroy, and the forwarding of the spring work by the preparation of the ground for early sowing. These services are as useful for a light soil as a heavy one, and as it is reasonable to look for some advantage from the working in the way of gain in fertility on light as well as heavy soils, it is advisable that owners of either kind should avail themselves of whatever benefits the practice affords. Fall fallowing consists in plowing and working the soil with the cultivator or the harrow. This may be done at such intervals as may be convenient, or which will help to start some weeds into growth, when these may be destroyed by the harrow or cultivator. Heavy soils should be left in rough ridges at the last plowing, with as deep furrows between them as possible, in order to expose the largest surface to the effects of frost and thaw. Light soils may be left in a less rough condition, but the last plowing should be so done as to throw the furrows on edge, and not flat, leaving the field somewhat ridged. A very little work in the spring will put the ground into excellent order for the early crops, and for spring wheat, especially, this better condition of the soil will be of the greatest benefit. When thus treated in the fall, the soil is remarkably mellow, and is dry enough to work much earlier than the compact stubble land which remains as it was left after the harvest. As to the time for doing this work, the sooner it is begun, and the oftener it is repeated, the better. It is not too late to finish when the ground is frozen or there is an inch of snow on the ground

UNLOADING CORN.

Every little help that will ease the troublesome labor of transferring the corn crop from the field to the crib is

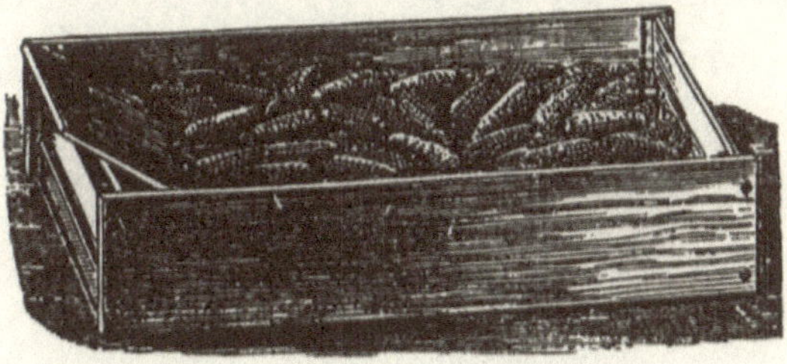

Fig. 66.—BOARD FOR UNLOADING.

gratefully accepted. We have used both of the contrivances here shown (figures 66 and 67), to help in getting the ears out of the wagon-box. At the start it is difficult to shovel up the corn, and until the bottom of the wagon-box is reached, the shovel or scoop cannot be made to enter the load. But if a piece of wide board is placed in a sloping position, resting upon the tail-board of the wagon (figure 66), the shovel can be used with ease

Fig. 67.—UNLOADING ARRANGEMENT.

at the commencement of the unloading. Another plan is to make the box two feet longer than usual, and place the tail-board two feet from the end, figure 67. When the tail-board is lifted, the ears slide down into this recess, from which they can be scooped with ease.

STONE BOATS.

For moving plows, harrows, etc., to and from th fields,

Fig. 68.—PLANK STONE BOAT.

and for many other purposes, a stone boat is far better than a sled or wagon, and is many times cheaper than either. Two plans of construction are illustrated. The boat shown in figure 68 is of plank, six feet in length, one foot at one end being sawed at the angle shown. Three planks, each one foot in width, will make it of about the right proportion. A railing two by three inches is pinned upon three sides, while a plank is firmly pinned at the front end, through which the draw-bolt passes. That shown in figure 69 has some advan-

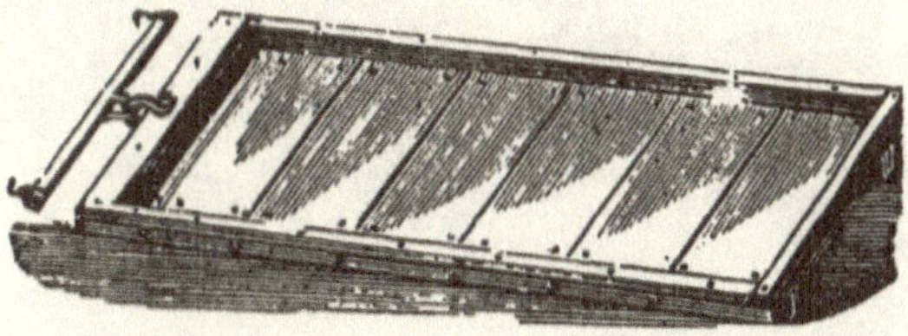

Fig. 69.—STONE BOAT WITH RUNNERS.

tage over the former, a cheaper quality of wood and of shorter length can be used, and when one set of runners is worn out, others can be readily attached without destroying the frame. Oak or maple plank should be used for the best boats, and when runners are used, the toughest wood at hand should be selected. Don't think because it is only a stone boat it is not worthy of being taken care of.

A DUMP-CART.

The dump-cart, figure 70, is a handy contrivance, a good deal used in some parts of this State, and is simply an ordinary ox-cart, the tongue shortened and fastened by a king bolt to the forward axle of a wagon, as shown in the engraving. It can be turned very short, as the wheels have a clear swing up to the cart-tongue, and is very convenient for hauling anything that is to be dumped: such as stones, earth, wood, manure, etc.

The seat of an old mowing machine is fastened to the

Fig. 70.—IMPROVED DUMP-CART.

cart-tongue, on which the driver sits. Horses or oxen may be used.

TO PREVENT WASHING OF HILL-SIDES.

Much damage is done by the washing of hill-sides into deep gullies by heavy rains. Where sloping ground is cultivated this is unavoidable, unless something is done to prevent it. In some cases deep plowing and loosening the subsoil will go far to prevent washing, as it enables the water to sink into the ground, and pass away without damage, by slow filtration. But where the subsoil is not very porous, and when the rain falls copiously and suddenly, the water saturates the surface soil in a few minutes, and the surplus then flows down the slope, cutting the softened earth into many channels, which by and by run together. Then the large body of water possesses a force which the soil cannot resist, and carries the earth down with it, often doing serious and irreparable damage in an hour or less. Of the many plans which have been suggested and tried to prevent this washing, the most successful is the terracing of the slope. This is done by plowing, with a swivel plow, around the hill, or back and forth on the slope, commencing at the bottom and throwing the earth downwards in such a manner that a flat terrace is formed, which has a small slope backwards from the front of the hill. When this terrace has been formed, the plowing is commenced ten or twelve feet above, and another terrace is made in the same manner. This is continued to the top of the slope. If thought desirable, the inner furrows on each terrace may be made to form a water channel, and this may be connected with the channel on the next slope lower down, in some safe manner, either by a shute of boards or of stone, to prevent washing of the soil at these points where the fall will be considerable. This, however, is a side issue, which does not necessarily belong to the main work. The arrangement of the hill-side is shown in figure 71, in which the

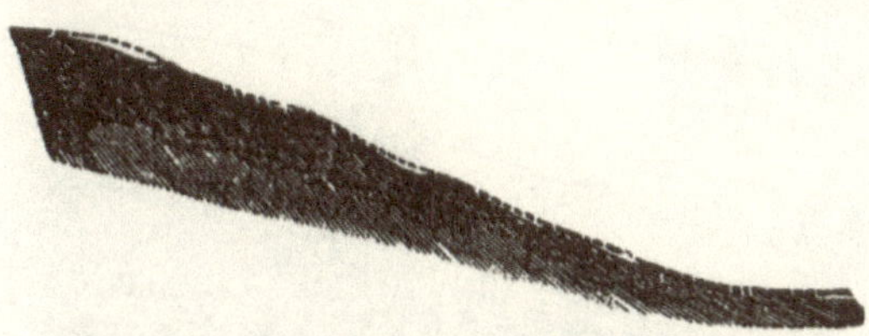

Fig. 71.—PROFILE OF A TERRACED HILL.

original outline of the hill, and the arrangement of the terraces, which are cut out of it, are given. When a heavy rain falls upon the terraced hill, the effect will be to throw the water backwar ls from the outer slope, into the channels at the rear of the terraces; and there, as well as upon the broad surface of the terraces. there is abundant means of escape by sinking into the soil. If not, and the amount of water is too great to be thus disposed of, it may be carried down the slope, by arranging the furrows as drains in the way previously indicated. Hill-sides of this character should be kept in grass, when the slope is too steep for comfortable plowing, after it has been thus arranged; or it may be planted with fruit trees, vines, or timber, upon the slopes, leaving the terraces to be cultivated, or the slopes may be kept in grass, and the terraces cultivated. But in whatever manner the ground may be disposed of, it would be preferable to leaving it to be gullied by rains, barren, useless, and objectionable in every way.

A LOG MINK-TRAP.

A mink-trap is made by boring a two-inch or two and

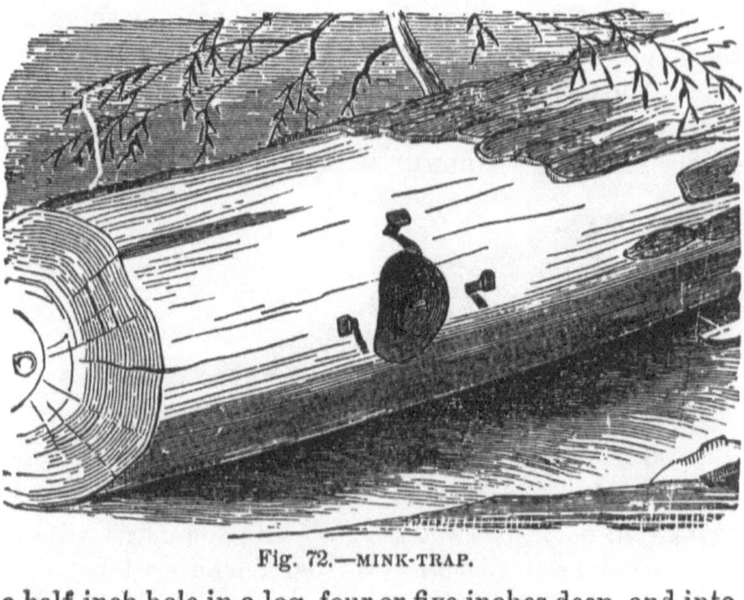

Fig. 72.—MINK-TRAP.

a half inch hole in a log, four or five inches deep, and into the edges of this hole drive three sharpened nails, so that they will project half an inch or so inside, as shown in figure 72. The bait being at the bottom, the mink pushes his head in to get it, but on attempting to withdraw it is caught by the nails. Musk-rat is good bait for them, and a highly praised bait is made by cutting an eel into small bits, which are placed in a bottle and hung in the sun, and after a time become an oily and very odorous mass. A few drops of this are used. The above simple mink-trap may be made by using any block of wood, or a stump of a tree, large or small, and the same plan may be made use of to trap skunks, or, by using a small hole and some straightened fish-hooks, it will serve to catch rats or weasels, enemies of the rural poultry yard, which may be thinned off by the use of this trap.

PLOWING FROM THE INSIDE OF THE FIELD.

There is but one reason why plowing should not be done from the inside of the field, and that is, the imaginary difficulty in "coming out right." There are several points in favor of this method: When a field is plowed, beginning at the outside, there is always a dead furrow running from each corner to the centre; besides this, the team is obliged to run out, and turn upon the plowed land at every corner, making a broad strip which is much injured by the treading, especially if the land is clayey and rather moist. By beginning at the middle, all this is avoided; the horses turn upon unplowed land, and the soil at each plowing is thrown towards the centre of the field, as it should be. There is no difficulty in finding the centre of the field from which to begin the plowing. Suppose we have a rectangular field like the one shown in figure 73; any person who can measure by pacing, is able to find the middle of the ends,

A D and *B C;* the points *K* and *L*. From *K*, pace towards *L*, a distance equal to one-half *A D*, which gives the point *E*. Also the same distance from *L*, towards *K*, giving F, and the work of fixing the central point is done. Run a furrow from *A* and *D* to *E*, and from *B* and *C* to *F;* these define the corners and assist in the turning of the plow. The plowing then begins by back-

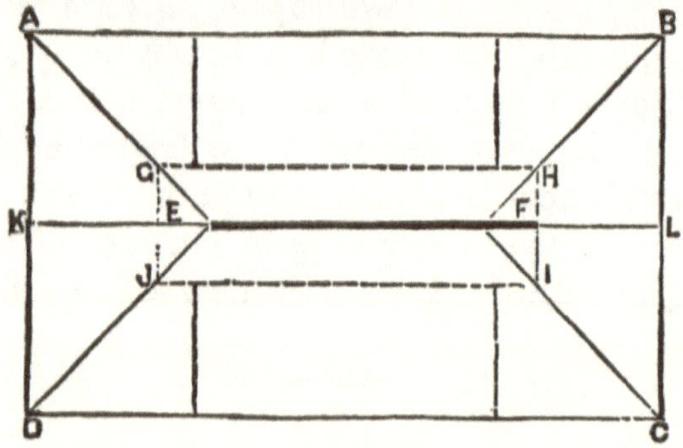

Fig. 73.—PLAN FOR RECTANGULAR FIELD.

furrowing from *E* to *F;* plowing on the ends as soon as possible. After the work has progressed for a time, as far as indicated, for example, by the dotted lines, *G*, *H*, *I*, *J*, pace from the furrow to the outside (see dotted lines), at or near each end of the furrow, as a correction, and, if necessary, gauge the plow until the furrow on all sides is equally distant from the boundary. When the field is of irregular shape, it is not difficult to begin in the centre and plow outward —in fact, this system is of most importance here, because all the short turning in the middle of the field,

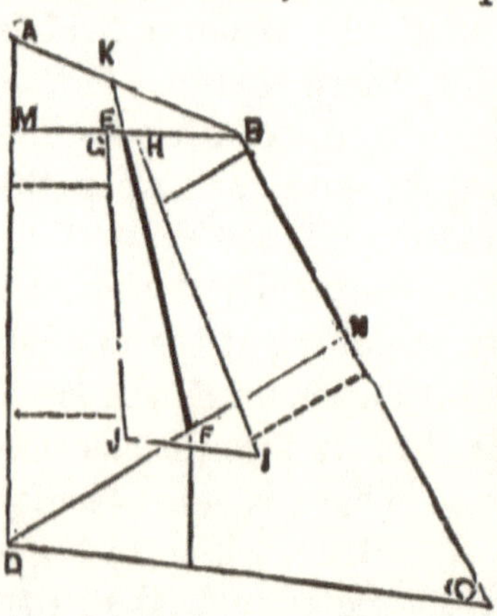

Fig. 74.—PLAN FOR IRREGULAR FIELD.

incident to the irregularity of the field, comes on unplowed ground.

In figure 74 we have a piece of very irregular shape. From a point on *A D*, at right angles to *B*, pace the distance to *B*, and place a stake at the middle point, *E*. In the same way, determine the point *F* on the line *N D*. In a line with *E, F*, measure from *K* a distance equal to *M E* (one-half the perpendicular distance across the end of field), and also in like manner determine the point *F*—which gives the central line, *E F*. The plow should be run from the four corners, as in the first case, to make the corner lines. The plowman will use his judgment, and plow only upon the lower portion at first, until the plowed land takes the shape *G, H, I, J*, when the correction is made. From this time on the furrow runs parallel with the boundary, and the work continues smoothly to the end.

A WIRE-FENCE TIGHTENER.

Having occasion recently to tighten some wires in a trellis, we made use of the following contrivance. Into

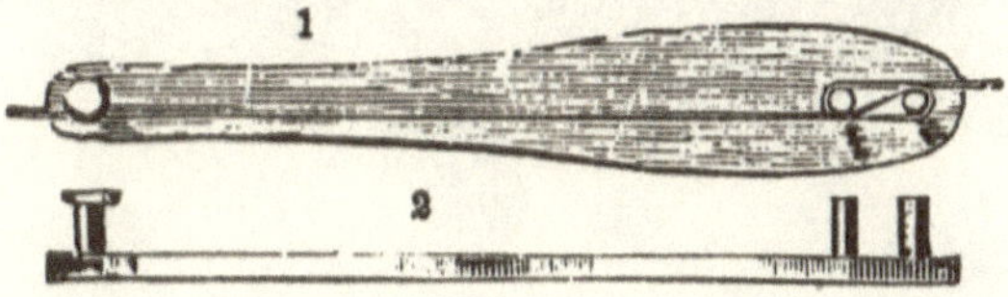

Fig. 75.—WIRE TIGHTENER.

a small piece of wood a few inches long we put two screws about three inches apart, and near to one end one other screw, leaving the heads projecting about half an inch. By placing the wire between the two screws, and turning the piece of wood around, the wire was drawn tight; and by engaging the head of the single screw upon it, the tension was maintained. The operation of the contrivance is shown at 1, and the method of arranging the screws or pins appears as 2. By using a strong piece of wood two feet long, and strong iron bolts, fastened with nuts upon the back side, this device may be used to tighten fence wires.

PLANTING CORN—A MARKER.

What would be thought of a mechanic who should rip his boards from a log with the old-fashioned whip saw and plane them or match them by hand, or who should work out his nails on the anvil one at a time by hand labor? He would hardly earn enough to find himself in bread alone. Yet in an equally old-fashioned, costly, and unprofitable way do thousands of farmers plant and cultivate their corn crops. The ground is plowed, harrowed and marked out both ways, either with the plow, or sometimes by a quicker method, with a corn marker. The seed is dropped by hand and covered by hand with a hoe; the crop is hoed by hand or plowed in the old method, leaving the ground ridged and deeply furrowed, so that in a dry season the corn suffers for want of moisture. All this costs so much that the farmer's labor

Fig. 76.—RUNNER AND TOOTH FOR MARKER.

brings him about fifty cents a day, upon which he lives, grumbling that "farming does not pay." This method would be ruinous in the West where corn is a staple crop, and that it is not so in the East is simply because it is not grown to a large extent. But there is no crop that may be grown so cheaply and easily in the East that produces so much feed as corn. Fifty bushels of corn and four tons of fodder per acre contain more dry nutriment than thirty tons of turnips or mangels, and may be grown with less labor and less cost, if only the best methods are employed. Now, with the excellent implements and machines that are in use for planting and cultivating corn, no farmer can afford to work this crop in the old-fashioned method. There is no longer any need to plant in squares, for the crop may be kept perfectly clean when planted in drills, if the proper implements are used. There are several corn planters by which the seed

Fig. 77.—THE MARKER AT WORK.

may be dropped and covered at the same time in single or double drills, at the rate of eight to twenty acres per day. By using the Thomas harrow a few days after planting, every young weed will be killed, and the crust, which so often gathers upon the surface, will be broken up and the surface mellowed. The harrow may be used without damage until the corn is several inches high. Then anyone of the many excellent horse hoes may be used by which the weeds may be cut out of the rows close to the corn until the crop is so high that farther working is useless. This method of cultivation may cost two dollars per acre, or less, as the ground may have been kept free from weeds in previous years, while on the old-fashioned system it may cost ten dollars per acre, or more, as the weeds may have been allowed to get further ahead.

Nevertheless, there are farmers who will still work on the hand-to-mouth plan, and will still mark out their crops by a marker and drop the seed by hand. For these it will be convenient to have at least a good marker. It will mark uneven as well as level ground; it can be set to any width between rows; any farmer or smart boy can make it, and the inventor, who is a farmer in Canada, does not propose to patent it. The marker is made of two by four scantling, one piece being eight feet long. In this five holes are bored, one for each of the runners, one and one-eighth inch in diameter. The runners are also of two by four timber, and eighteen inches long. Holes one and one-eighth inch in diameter are bored through the runners, in which are placed hard wood pins fourteen inches long. These are driven in from the bottom, the ends being left broad, so that they may not pass through the holes, and projecting an inch and a half. This is shown in figure 76. The small pin which passes through the larger one serves to connect the runner with the principal timber, and by shifting the large pin from one hole to another, the runners may be brought from four feet to one foot, or even six inches apart, and made to mark rows of widths increasing by spaces of six inches up to four feet. When one of the markers meets with an obstruction it is lifted by it, as seen in figure 77, and passes over it. A guide marker is fixed by a hinge to one of the outside runners, and carries a scraper which is held in place by a pin, by moving which the distance of the next row may be regulated. A pair of light shafts may be attached to the marker, and a pair of handles by which it may be guided.

FEED TROUGH AND HALTER

The trough rests on the floor and is four feet long. *A, A,* are inch auger holes; a rope, four feet long, is put through them and tied. Another rope, *D,* has a ring

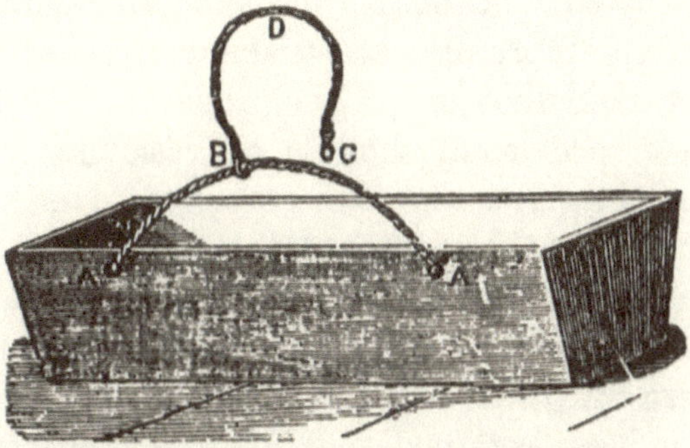

Fig. 78.—FEED TROUGH AND HALTER.

spliced on one end, and a "snap hook" on the other. The longer rope passes through the ring, *B,* and when the rope, *D,* is put over the neck of the cow, the "snap," *C,* hooks into the ring. This allows the animal to stand or lie down with comfort.

THE HORSE-SHOE AND ITS APPLICATION.

Any excess of growth at the toe renders the pasterns more oblique, and, as a consequence, throws undue weight upon the "back sinews," whereas, too great height of heels has a similar effect upon the joints of the extremities, by rendering them too upright. Taking as our guide the foot of the animal that has never been brought to the forge, and which, in consequence, must be considered as a correct model, let the external wall of the hoof be reduced by means of the rasp to a level with the firm unpared sole. If there is no growth of the external wall beyond this level, then there is nothing to be removed.

In the selection of a shoe for the healthy foot, we must bear in mind the object in view, which is to protect the parts from excessive wear. This protection is to be found in a metallic rim of proper size and shape, securely adjusted. Almost every shoe in common use meets this end more or less satisfactorily, and we have already remarked that the proper preparation of the foot that has been previously shod is of vastly more importance than the particular kind of shoe to be adopted. At the same time, there are faults in the shoe most commonly employed, which had their origin in its particular adaptation to the foot after this had undergone more or less severe mutilation at the hands of the farrier, and which have been retained more through custom than through actual necessity, as we have reason to hope. The most prominent of these faults consists in extreme narrowness of rim with a concavity upon the upper or foot surface, in order to prevent the sole from sustaining least weight or pressure, which it is perfectly unfitted to do after being pared down to a point of sensitiveness. In a state of nature we know that every portion of the foot comes to the ground and sustains its share of weight, and in the shod state it should do the same, as far as practicable. Hence, the shoe should be constructed with its upper surface perfectly flat, and with a breadth sufficient to protect a portion of the sole, and to sustain weight. It should be bevelled upon the ground surface, in imitation of the concavity of the sole, and not upon its upper surface, where the space thus formed serves as a lodging place for small stones and other foreign bodies. In shape it should follow the exact outline of the outer wall, being narrowed at the heels, but continued of the same thickness throughout. The lateral projection at the quarters, and the posterior one at the heels are unsightly, of no benefit, and should never be allowed where speed is required.

HOW TO MAKE A FISHING SCOW.

Boat-building should be done during the winter, when in-door work is more agreeable, and leisure is more ample, than in the summer. A boy who can handle tools, may make a very handsome boat or scow, such as

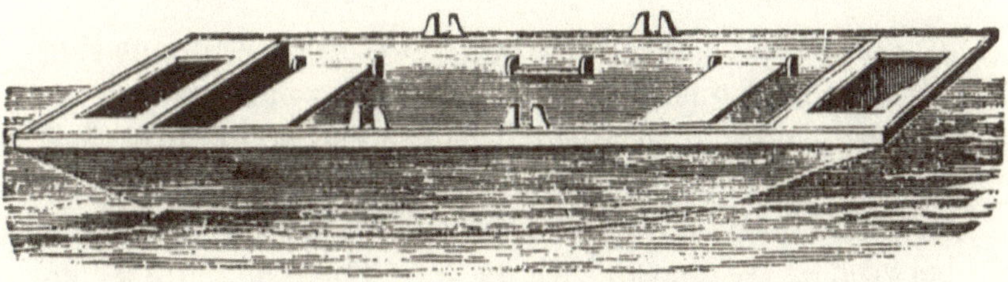

Fig. 79.—VIEW OF FISHING SCOW.

is shown at figure 79, at a cost of five dollars or less, in the following manner. Procure five three-quarter or half-inch clear pine boards, twelve feet in length and eight inches wide; four boards ten feet long, one inch thick, and one foot wide, and three strips ten feet long, one and a quarter-inch thick, and three inches wide. Plane all these smoothly on both sides, and have them all free from loose knots or shakes. Cut two of the one-inch boards sloping at each end to a straight line for two feet, and then slightly rounding the middle of the board. Cut two pieces of the one and a quarter-inch strips into lengths of two feet ten inches, and nail them to the ends of the side-boards, as shown in figure 80. If strips of soft brown paper are dipped into tar and placed between the joints, they will be made closer and more water-tight. Cut the eight-inch boards into three feet lengths, and nail them across the bottom, as shown in figure 80; where the bevel ends, the two bottom boards must be bevelled slightly upon one of their edges, so as to make a close joint. Then take two of the one and

Fig. 80.—PUTTING ON THE BOTTOM.

a quarter-inch strips, and make cuts in each on one side with the saw, one inch deep, as follows: measuring from one end, mark with a pencil across the strip three feet six inches from the end; then mark again across the strip one inch and a half from the first mark, and score between these marks with an ×. Then measure three inches and make another mark, and then an inch and a half and make still another mark, and score as before between these last two with an ×. Then do precisely the same on the same side of the strip, measuring from the other end. Then on the edges of the board score with gauge or make a line with a pencil exactly one inch from the marked side. Then make the cuts on the pencil lines down to the score on the edge, just one inch deep, but no more. Cut away the wood in the places that were marked with an ×, leaving four slots one inch and a half wide, one inch deep, and with three inches between them upon each strip. Nail these strips with the cut side inwards, to the upper edge of the side-board, on the outside of the boat, as seen in figure 81. The spaces left in the gunwales are for the rowlocks. The strips should be well nailed near the rowlocks, and if a quarter-inch, flat-headed, counter-sunk carriage-bolt were used on each side of them, it would be very much better than so many nails. A thin washer, or burr, should be used beneath the nut of each bolt. The rowlock pins should be made of hard maple or oak, in the shape shown at *a*, figure 81. They are one inch thick, one and a half inch wide at the lower part, which fits into the slot, with a shoulder of half an inch, and the top is bevelled off neatly as shown. The seats, of which

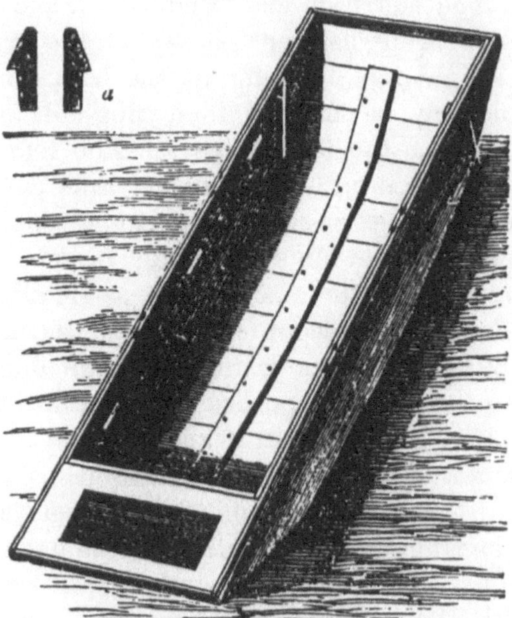

Fig. 81.—INTERIOR OF BOAT.

there are two, are made ten inches wide. The cleats for the seats, one inch thick, one and a half inch wide, and ten inches long, are nailed three inches below the upper edge of the side-board. The middle seat goes exactly in the centre of the boat, with each edge four feet seven inches from the end of the boat. The end seats are placed with the backs two feet from the ends of the boat, leaving eight inches between each seat and the edge of the rowlock nearest to it. There are cleats for three seats, but only two seats are used at once. When one seat is used, the rower sits in the centre, and he can use either of the rowlocks, the boat being double-bowed. When two seats are used, one person only rows at one time, but either can row without changing seats, and one always faces to the direction in which the boat moves. This arrangement of seats is very convenient. Eighteen inches of each end is closed in, and makes a locker for holding fish-lines, hooks, or the "painter," which is a light rope for tying up the boat when not in use. This may be fastened to a ring-bolt or a hole bored in one of the locker covers. The long bottom-board, seen in figure 81, eight inches wide and half an inch thick, is nailed as shown, by wrought nails driven from the outside and clinched on the inside. The seat cleats are nailed in the same manner, as are also the side strips. Every nail is counter-sunk and the hole filled up with putty. The seams are puttied or filled with a strip of cotton sheeting pushed in with the blade of a dinner knife. If the joints are made as well as they may be, this is not needed, but two coats of paint will make all tight. The inside should be painted lead-color, made by mixing lampblack with white paint to a proper shade. The outside may be painted white or a light-green, with the gunwale of a light-blue. A few days will be required to harden the paint before using the boat. None but seasoned boards should be used.

CROWS AND SCARECROWS.

Probably there is no point upon which a gathering of half a dozen farmers will have more positive opinions than as to the relations of the crow to agriculture. It is likely that five of these will regard the bird as totally bad, while the minority of one will claim that he is all good. As usual, the truth lies between the extremes. There is no doubt that the crow loves corn, and knows that at the base of the tender shoot there is a soft, sweet kernel. But the black-coated bird is not altogether a vegetarian. The days in which he can pull young corn are few, but the larger part of the year he is really the friend of the farmer. One of the worst insect pests with which the farmer, fruit-grower, or other cultivator has to contend is, the "White Grub," the larva of the "May Beetle," "June Bug," or "Dor-Bug." It is as well established as any fact can be, that the crow is able to detect this grub while it is at work upon the roots of grass in meadows and lawns, and will find and grub it out. For this service alone the crow should be everywhere not only spared, but encouraged. We are too apt to judge by appearances; when a crow is seen busy in a field, it is assumed that it is doing mischief, and by a constant warfare against, not only crows, but skunks, owls, and others that are hastily assumed to be wholly bad, the injurious insects, mice, etc., that do the farmer real harm have greatly increased. Shortly after corn is planted, the crows appear, and are destructive to young corn. Some assert that the crow pulls up the corn plant merely to get at the grub which would destroy it if the bird did not. How true this may be we do not know, but as the corn is destroyed in either case, it may be as well to let it go without help from the crow. The first impulse of the farmer, when he finds his corn pulled up, is to shoot the crow. This we protest against. Even admitting that the crow does mischief for a short time, it is too useful for the rest of the year to be thus cut down in active life. Let him live for the good he has done and may do. It is vastly better to keep the crows from pulling the young corn, for two or three weeks, and allow them all the rest of the year to destroy bugs and beetles in astonishing numbers. The corn may be protected by means of "scarecrows," of which there are several very effective kinds. Crows are very keen, and are not easily fooled; they quickly understand the ordinary "dummy," or straw man, which soon fails to be of service in the corn-field. It has no life, no motion, and makes no noise, and the crow soon learns this and comes and sits upon its outstretched arm, or pulls the corn vigorously at its feet. A dead crow, hung by a swinging cord to a long slender pole, is recommended as far better than a straw man—as it, in its apparent struggles to get away, appeals impressively to the living crow's sense of caution. But the crow may not be at hand to be thus employed, and if it were, the farmer cannot afford to kill it. Better than a dead crow is a glass bottle with the bottom knocked out, which may be done with an iron rod. The bottle is suspended to an elastic pole by a cord tied around its neck; the end of the cord should extend downward into the bottle, and have a nail fastened to it and within the bottle, to serve as a clapper. If a piece of bright tin be attached to the cord extending below the bottomless end of the bottle, all the better. A slight breeze will cause the tin to whirl, and, in the motion, cast bright reflections rapidly in all directions, while the nail keeps up a rattling against the inside of the bottle. An artificial "bird," to be hung in the same manner, may be made from a piece of cork—one used in a pickle-jar—into which a number of large goose or chicken feathers are fastened so as to roughly imitate a dilapidated bird. A rough head may be carved and put on, to make the deception more complete. As this "bird" catches the wind, it will "fly" here and there in a peculiar manner not at all enticing to the corn-loving crows.

FLOOD FENCE.

The weak point of a fence is where it crosses a stream; a sudden freshet washes away loose rails, and a gap is

Fig. 82.—A FLOOD GATE.

left through which trespassing cattle soon find a passage. Many devices have been used. The one shown in figure 82 is self-acting: when water rises high enough, it opens, and when the flood falls it closes again. It may be made of rails, bars, or fence strips.

CLEARING SLOUGH LAND.

In clearing up land that is covered with tussocks of coarse grass and a tough sod, and digging out ditches to drain such land, much useless labor may be given that could be spared by skilful work. The spade is commonly used for this purpose, but, as in digging dry ground, this slow tool may be replaced to very great advantage by the plow and the horse-shovel. In work ing in swamps these more effective tools may be made available in many cases. To cut off the tussocks with grub-hoes, while they are tough in the summer time, is very hard and slow work; but if a common horse-scraper is used they can be torn up, or cut off, with the greatest ease. The scraper should be furnished with a sharp steel-cutting blade in the front, which may be riveted on, or fastened with bolts, so that it may be taken off and ground sharp. If there are wet and soft places the scraper may be drawn by a chain of sufficient length to

Fig. 83.—THE HORSE-SHOVEL AT WORK.

keep the horse upon dry ground, as shown in figure 83. This plan has been tried by the writer with success, and with a great saving of time and expense; the digging of a pond twenty feet wide along the edge of a swamp, was performed with one man, a boy, a team, and a horse-shovel, as quickly as ten men could have done it with spades. In cutting tough swamp, the plow may be used to break up the surface when the horse-shovel will remove the muck very fast. If the swamp is wet, and water flows in the excavation, the digging may still be done with the horse-scraper by adding to the length of the handles and using planks upon each side for the man to stand upon, and planks upon the inner side of the excavation for the scraper to slide upon with its load of muck. The muck may be thrown in heaps on the side of the pond or ditches, and it will be found convenient to leave it upon one side instead of in a continuous heap, as this will greatly facilitate its final disposal in whatever way that may be.

HOW TO DRESS A BEEF.

There is a way of slaughtering that is not butchering, and it may be done painlessly by taking the right course. The barn floor or a clean grass-plot in a convenient spot

Fig. 84.—THE PROPER PLACE TO STRIKE.

will be a suitable place for the work. To fasten the animal, put a strong rope around the horns, and secure the head in such a way that it cannot be moved to any great distance, and in a position to allow a direct blow to be easily given. The eyes may be blinded by tying a cloth around the head so that there will be no dodging to avoid the stroke. The place for the stunning blow is the centre of the forehead, between the eyes and a little above them. The right place is shown at *a*, figure 84. The best method is to fire a ball from a rifle in the exact spot, and this may be done safely when the animal is blinded, by holding the weapon near to the head, so that a miss cannot be made; otherwise a blow with the back of an axe made when the striker is on the right side of the animal, and the head is fastened down near the ground, will be equally effective. So soon as the animal falls, the throat is divided with a cut from a long, sharp knife; no jack-knife should be used, but a long, deep, sweeping stroke

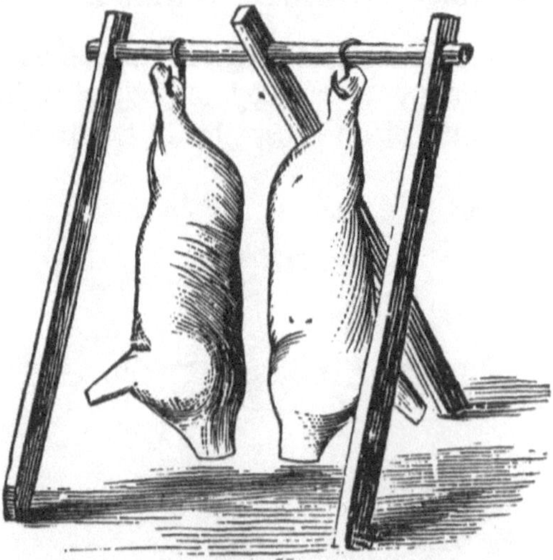

Fig. 85.—RACK FOR A CARCASS OF BEEF.

which reaches to the vertebræ as the head is held back This divides all the blood-vessels, and death is almost instantaneous, but at any rate painless. When the carcass has been freed from blood, it should be turned on its back, and the skin divided from the throat up the brisket, along the belly to the legs, and up the legs to the knees, where the joints should be severed, taking care, however, to cut off the hind feet below the hock joints about two or three inches. The skin is then stripped from the legs and belly, and as near to the back as may be by turning the carcass. The belly is then opened, and the intestines taken out; the brisket is cut through, and the lungs and gullet removed. It is now necessary to raise the carcass. This is done on the rack, the forward legs of which are placed on each side of the carcass, and the gambrels are placed upon the hooks shown in figure 85. The legs of the rack are then raised as far as possible, and as the carcass is lifted, the hinder leg is brought up to hold what is gained until the carcass is clear of the ground; the hide is then wholly removed, the carcass washed and scraped from anything adhering, and then divided down through the backbone, leaving the sides hanging. As a matter of safety from dogs or other dishonest animals, it is well to have the work done in the barn, laying down a quantity of straw to protect the floor, if thought necessary, as the beef should remain at least twelve hours to cool and set.

A FARM CART.

While there are different kinds of farm carts, we have not yet hit upon *the* cart—*i. e.*, one that meets with general approbation. The writer, having much work for a cart, has designed one which is intended to do all the work of the farm more easily than a wagon or any other cart. For the carriage of manure, of fodder-corn, green clover, or other soiling fodder, for hauling roots and such work, a cart is needed with a low body, that can be turned around in its own length to back, or even turn in a manure cellar or on a barn floor. All this can be done with this cart, and when hay, straw, or green fodder is to be loaded, the fore and hind racks may be put on, and greatly increase its capacity. With four-inch wheels, this cart can be drawn, when loaded, over plowed ground or muddy roads, and scarcely sink below the surface. The cart body consists of a frame eight feet long, three and a half feet wide, and fourteen inches deep, thus holding, when heaped, about a cubic yard and a half of manure, or as near as possible one ton. The frame is made of three by four timber for the top, and two by three for the bottom, sides, and cross-bars, and is covered with bass-wood or willow boards on the bottom, the front, and the sides near the wheels. The rear end is closed when desired by a sliding tail-board. The axles are fixed to the frame, as shown in figure 86, and pass through the middle side posts under the upper slide bar and a wide iron strap, which embraces the top of the frame, and passes under the bottom, as shown in the engraving, being screwed by bolts to the timbers. The wheel is the same size as an ordinary wagon wheel, viz., four feet; this brings the bottom of the cart body to within one foot of the ground, and in loading, the lift is only a little more than two feet from the ground. The saving of labor and the effect of work are thus greatly increased, a man being able to load twice as much with the same force, into a cart of this kind, as into a wagon-box four feet high. The rear end of the cart may be provided with a roller, fitted into the rear posts, which serves to ease the unloading of the cart when it is tipped, the rear end then easily moving over the ground as the cart is drawn over the field when unloading manure. But as the cart body is so low there will rarely be any need for tipping the cart. To enlarge its capacity, there

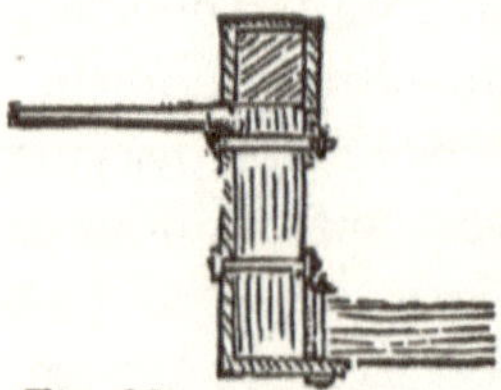

Fig. 86.—AXLE FASTENING.

are movable racks fitted before and behind, as shown in figure 87. The cost of two of these carts is not more than that of a wagon, and may be less, if economy

Fig. 87.—THE CART WITH MOVABLE RACKS.

is exercised in making them. The shafts may be bolted to the sides and so arranged that the cart can be tipped over when the load requires it.

BRACES FOR A GATE POST.

On the side of the post, and near the surface of the ground, spike an inverted bracket, made of a two-inch plank of white oak, or other hard wood. The bracket

Fig. 88.—BRACING A GATE POST.

should be not less than six inches wide, and a foot long. There should be two of these braces, one on the gate side of the post when the gate is shut, and one on the gate side when open. Under the bracket place a flat stone firmly settled in the ground, on which the bottom of the bracket is to rest; a piece of plank, as long as it lasts, will do instead of the stone.

The hang of the gate can then be exactly adjusted by putting a thin stone or piece of wood between the bottom of the bracket and the flat stone or plank. This is a simple and effective method of supporting a post, where there is no other convenient way of bracing, and even in almost all cases, it gives additional firmness. If the lower end of the post is of good size, and is well put in, this method of bracing will hold a very heavy gate.

WHIPPLE-TREES FOR PLOWING CORN SAFELY

We have found it beneficial to cultivate our corn crop until the rows become impassable for a horse, or until it was four feet or more high. But to do this with the wide whipple-tree, the ends of which project beyond the traces, and break down the stalks, is impossible. It may, however, be done by using a whipple-tree specially provided for it. This is made as follows: a piece of oak timber, two inches thick, three wide, and twenty inches long, is rounded at the corners, and deeply grooved at the ends, so that the trace-chains may be entirely imbedded in the grooves. A small hole is bored through each end, into which a small carriage bolt is inserted, being made to pass through a link of the trace-chain, and it is then fastened beneath with a nut.

Fig. 89.—WHIPPLE-TREE.

The trace-chains should be covered with leather where they will rub against the corn, and a flap of leather should be left to cover the front corners of the whipple-tree, as shown in figure 89. A ring or an open link is fastened at the part of the chain which is attached to the clevis, and one at each end by which it is hooked to the traces. With this arrangement one may cultivate his corn without injury, and the same method may be applied to the whipple-trees, for plowing or cultivating amongst trees in the orchard or garden.

WHAT TREES TO PLANT FOR FUEL AND TIMBER.

The attention of our people in the older States is being very properly turned to planting rocky ridges and worn-out pastures with forest trees. This work is done by those who have no expectation of cutting the timber themselves, but with a view to improve their property for future sale, or for their heirs. These old pastures now are worth $10, or less, per acre. Forty or fifty years hence, covered with heavy timber, they would be worth three hundred dollars, or more, per acre. Two elements may safely enter into this calculation of the profit of tree planting: the steady growth of the trees, and the constant increase in the price of fuel and timber. There is great difference in the price of the varieties of wood, but still more in the rapidity of their growth. Hickory grows more rapidly than white oak, and in most markets is worth a quarter more for fuel. Chestnut grows about three times as fast as the white oak, and for many purposes makes quite as good timber. It is in great demand by ship-builders, and cabinet-makers. The chestnut, the tulip tree, and the hickory attain a good size for timber in twenty to twenty-five years, and the spruce and pine need about fifty years. The maples grow quite rapidly, and are highly prized, both for fuel and for cabinet purposes. On light sandy land, the white pine will grow rapidly, and cannot fail to be a good investment for the next generation. As a rule, the more rapid growing trees, if the wood is valuable, will pay better than the oaks.

TO STEADY PORTABLE MILLS.

Figure 90 shows a contrivance for steadying portable mills, which has been used for several years. It is an iron rod of suitable size, about a foot long, fastened by iron brackets to the leg, or post of the mill. Three or four inches of the rod is a screw, and fits one of the brackets through which it runs, and can be turned up or down. The lower end of the rod is pointed, and the upper end squared, that it may be turned with a wrench. The rod is fastened firmly to the side of the post (one on each of the forward posts), and turned down so that the point shall enter the floor sufficiently to hold it firmly.

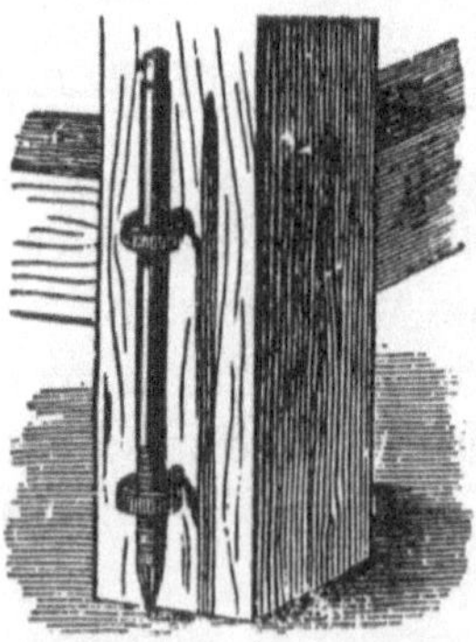

Fig. 90.—LEG OF MILL.

SPLITTING RAILS AND POSTS.

Autumn is the best season for cutting timber, as many farmers have learned by experience. The seasoning process is much more perfect, because there is no layer of growing sap wood. Insects do not work in autumn cut timber, as in that cut in the spring or summer, and the wood does not "powder post." It is best to split the logs into rails or posts at once, and not wait until the timber has become seasoned in the log. The logs will split easier, the rails will season quicker, and be more durable. The splitting of rails is a work that requires good judgment, otherwise much timber will be wasted. Some persons will make rails that are large at one end, and gradually tapering to a sliver at the other, and are worthless for fencing purposes. Set the wedge at the top end of the log, after first "checking" with the axe, by driving with the beetle, so as to divide the log into two equal parts. Now drive in two wedges, as shown in figure 91, both at the same time. Next use a wooden wedge or "glut," either in the end of the log, or on the top a little back from the end. After halving the log, quarter it, and then proceed on the principle that a rail should be about three by three inches. The size of the log will determine the number of rails to be made. For example, in figure 92, six rails are made by first halving the quarter, then splitting off the inner part half-way from the centre, and afterwards halving the outer part. Should the logs be larger, twelve rails are made from each quarter, as shown in figure 93,—or forty-eight rails from the log. In splitting logs into posts, a broad and smooth side is to be sought. Suppose we have the same sized log as the one split into forty-eight rails, or twelve rails per quarter, figure 93—the splitting would be, in each case, from the centre to outside with cross splitting midway. The number of posts would be determined by the size of the posts desired. If the logs are of the size of the quarter, shown in figure 92, there is no cross splitting, unless a small piece for a

Fig. 91.—POSITION OF WEDGE.

stake is taken from the centre. When the logs are only large enough for four posts, and a broad surface is desired, as in bar posts, they may be split by first "slabbing," and afterwards splitting through the centre; all the split surfaces to be parallel. If still smaller, three

Fig. 92.

Fig. 93.

posts can be made, by splitting off two slabs on opposite sides, as in the case above, and not divide the heart, and finally when the log will make only two, it can be halved.

A MIXTURE OF GRASSES.

It is a well-known fact that mixed crops are more productive than those sown singly. Thus one acre sown to oats and barley, or oats and peas, will yield as much, or nearly as much, as two acres sown singly to either crop. So in grass lands, Clover and Timothy, mixed, will produce nearly twice as much as if the ground were seeded to one of these alone. It is also a well-known fact that our grass lands are not so productive as we could wish, and the reason of this may be, and probably is, that we have but one or two kinds of herbage in them. If we examine an old, thick, luxuriant sod, in a pasture or a meadow, it will be found to consist of a variety of grasses and other plants, each of which seems to vie with the other in occupying the soil for itself. This is the result of natural seeding, and gives us a lesson which we may well profit by. There is another reason why grasses should be mixed; this is that the periods of greatest vigor of different varieties occur at different times. We can therefore secure a succession of herbage for a long season by sowing a variety of grass seeds.

To give examples, we might mention that a mixture of Orchard Grass, Red Clover, Timothy, and Kentucky Blue-Grass will produce a pasture which will be in good condition for grazing from April, when the first mentioned grass is in fine condition, up to October, when the last is in its most vigorous state; the Clover and Timothy serving to fill up the interval. With one of these alone there would be but one month of good herbage, and that coarse, if given the whole field to itself. In like manner, a quantity of Rye Grass added to a meadow would help to furnish a quick growing herbage which rapidly and constantly recuperates after cutting or eating down.

The fact is, that we make much less of our advantages in regard to our meadows and pastures than we might. On the average, seven acres of pasture are required to keep one cow through the pasturing season, when by the best management one acre, or at the most two, ought to be sufficient. This is due in great measure to the prevalent fashion of seeding down with but one variety of grass, with clover added sometimes, a fashion which, hereafter, experience teaches us should be more honored in the breach than in the observance.

HITCHING A CRIB-BITER.

Those persons who have a horse that is a crib-biter and windsucker, and which practices his vice when hitched to a post in the street, is recommended to try a hitching-rod, such as shown in figure 94 It consists of a piece of hickory, white oak, or tough ash, about twenty-four or thirty inches long, thickest in the middle, where it may be an inch in diameter. A ferule with a ring is fastened to each end; in one ring a common snap-hook is fixed, and a short leather strap is passed through the other, by which the stick is fastened to the post. The horse thus hitched cannot possibly reach the top of the post, to seize it with its teeth. In the stall such a horse should be hitched with two straps, one at each side of the stall, and of such a length that he cannot reach either side to take hold of the rail or partition of the stall. If a swinging feed-box is used, the crib-biter will be forced to suspend operations, as he cannot draw in the air or "suck wind," unless he has some projecting object that he can lay hold of with the teeth.

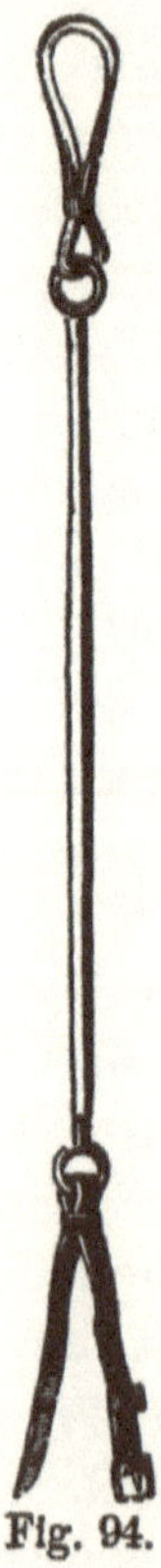
Fig. 94.

HOW TO INCREASE VEGETABLE MATTER IN THE SOIL.

The amount of vegetable matter in the soil may be increased by various methods; one is by large applications of barn-yard manure, say fifty cords to the acre. But this would be very expensive, and is out of the question in common farming. It may be done by putting on peat or muck, when these are near to the fields. But this involves a considerable outlay for labor in digging the peat, and a still larger expense in carting it, whether it first pass through the yards and stables, or be carted to the fields for composting or spreading upon the surface to be plowed in. On some farms this may be the cheaper method of supplying vegetable matter to the soil. But on others the most economical method is the raising of clover, to be fed off upon the land, or to be turned in. If a ton of clover may be worth nine dollars, as a fertilizer, the growing of the plant is a cheap method of improving the land. Two tons for the first crop and a ton for the second is not an uncommon yield for land in good heart. The roots of clover also add largely to the vegetable matter in the soil. The first crop may be pastured, waiting until the crop is in blossom, and then turning in cattle enough to feed it off in three or four weeks. They should be kept constantly upon the field, that the whole crop may be returned to the soil. This will, of course, help the second crop, which may be turned in with the plow soon after it is in blossom. If the equivalent of three tons of dried clover hay, and one ton of roots have been grown to the acre, about thirty-six dollars' worth of manure have been added to the soil, and it has been distributed more evenly than would have been possible by any mechanical process. There has been no expense for carting and spreading peat, or for composting. On the contrary, there has been the equivalent of two tons of clover-hay consumed upon the field, worth, as fodder, twenty-four dollars. This will more than pay the cost of seed, of plowing twice and other labor. This is generally admitted to be the cheapest method of increasing the vegetable matter and the fertility of soils in common farming. And this, it will be seen, requires some little capital.

OPEN LINKS.

An open link, shown in figure 95, is made of three-eighth inch iron rod, and when used to connect a broken chain, is simply closed by a blow from a hammer or a stone There being no rivet, the link is not weakened in any way. Figure 96 shows another link, made of malleable cast-iron, in two parts, which are fastened together by a rivet in the centre. A few of these links may be carried in the pocket, and are ready for instant use in case of an emergency. The last-mentioned links are

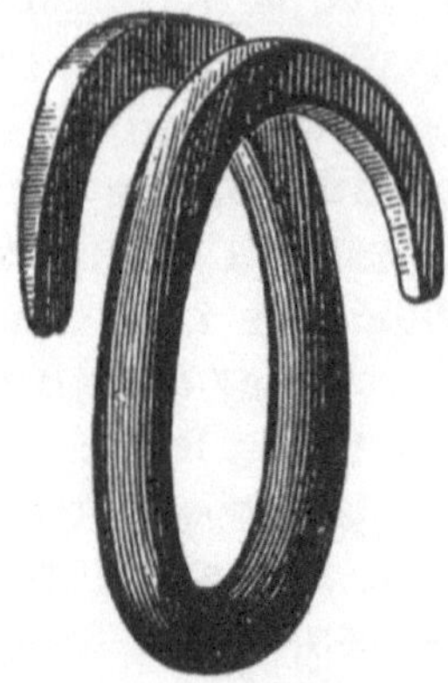

Fig. 95.—COMMON LINK.

Fig. 96.

kept for sale at the hardware stores; the first named may be made in a short time by a blacksmith, or any farmer who has a workshop and a portable forge.

CARE OF THE ROOT CROPS.

Sugar beets and mangels, if early sowed, will need little care. They ought not to stand too thick, however, and it would certainly pay to go through the rows, thinning out all superfluous plants, whether beets or weeds, leaving the plants six to eight inches apart. If the leaves are not so large as to forbid horse-hoeing, this should be done and the crop "laid-by." No root crop should ever be left after horse-hoeing, without a man going through it immediately after, to lift and straighten up any plants which may have been trodden upon, covered with earth, or injured in any way. Ruta-bagas, and any turnips in drills, need the same general culture. One of the great advantages of the introduction of roots into the rotation is that, when properly treated, no weeds ripen seeds. Even red sorrel and snapdragon succumb to two or three years' cropping with mangels or Swedes. This advantage is often lost by careless cultivators, and nothing offers surer evidence of heedless farming. The crop itself may be very fine, but if kept clear of weeds it would be enough better to pay for the trouble, and the weeds would then be where they will make no more trouble forever.

Turnips may be sown as late as the middle of August, but the land should be in good heart, and good tilth. Swedish turnips (rutabagas) sowed as late as the first of August, will usually make a crop delicious for the table, and, though small, bring a good price. Thus they are often used to follow early potatoes by market gardeners, though by them usually regarded as a farm crop.

TRAP FOR SHEEP-KILLING DOGS.

In many places the losses by dogs are so great as to prevent the keeping of sheep altogether ; thus this profitable and agreeable industry is made impracticable over the greater portion of the country ; unless such precautions are taken as will add greatly to its trouble and cost. With small flocks only, this extra cost and trouble are too onerous, and it is only where sheep are kept in large flocks that it will pay to employ shepherds to constantly watch them, or take other necessary precautions. In several of the States—West Virginia and Tennessee more particularly—very stringent laws have recently been enacted for the protection of sheep against dogs, which will go far to encourage the raising of flocks. In other States, where the influence of the owners of dogs is of more weight than that of sheep-owners, these latter are obliged to look out for themselves, and protect their sheep as they may be able. For such the contrivance here described and illustrated, may be useful. It is made as follows: In the meadow or field, where sheep are pastured during the day, a small pen, eight feet square, is made, and fenced strongly with pickets or boards. This pen is divided into two parts (*A*, *B*, figure 97) by a cross-fence. The pen is wholly covered over

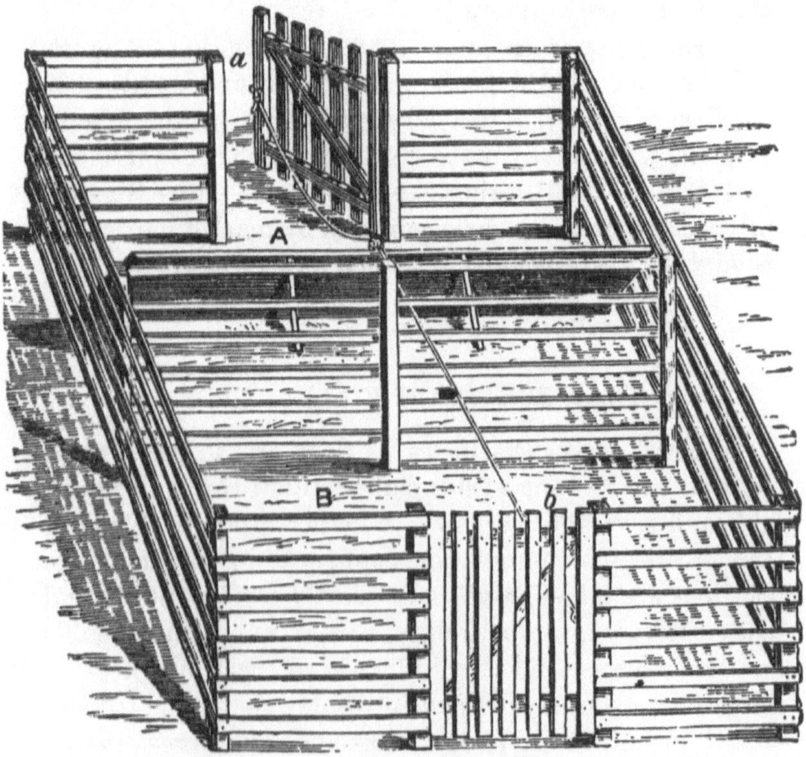

Fig. 97.—TRAP FOR SHEEP-KILLING DOGS.

on the top with strong lath. Two gates (*a*, *b*,) are made so that they will swing open of their own accord, and remain so, unless held closed or fastened. The gate, *a*, is furnished with a latch, by which it is fastened when closed. This gate is intended to admit the dog into the part of the pen, *A*, when he is attracted to it by a sheep confined for the purpose in the other part of the pen (*B*). In the part of the pen, *A*, is a heavy board, reaching across it. One edge of this board rests upon the ground against two pegs, which keep it from slipping backwards. The other edge is kept up by means of two shaky slender supports. A rope is fastened to the upper edge of this board, and to the gates, so that one half of it, when the board is propped up, allows the gate, *a*, to swing open, and the other half holds the gate, *b*, shut, and thus keeps the sheep confined. The trap is now set. A dog, prowling in search of mutton, finds the sheep, and seeks an entry into the pen. He finds the open gate, and rushes in, over the board set upon its edge, and knocks this down. This closes the gate, *a*, which is at once latched and fastened. The gate, *b*, is allowed to swing open, and the sheep is liberated, and, of course, proceeds homeward without delay, while the dog is imprisoned. We need not suggest any method of dealing with the prisoner, as there are many, more or less effective, which will suggest themselves. We think it would be an improvement upon this plan, if the sheep be confined in the pen, where it can be seen by the dogs, and an additional apartment, if not more than one, made, in which other dogs could be trapped. Sheep-hunting dogs usually go in couples, and if only one dog were trapped, the sheep escaping from the pen would be caught by the other before it could reach home. With two or three traps all the dogs could be caught, and in a short time the locality would be rid of them, or, being identified, their owners could be made responsible for their trespasses. It would be necessary to have the pen made very strong, so that the dogs should not tear their way out of the trap, or into the pen in which the sheep is confined. Stout wire-netting would make a safe fence.

So far as regards what are called dog-laws, it would be well if these should provide, amongst other things, that every dog must wear a collar, bearing its owner's name; that the owner of any dog which is caught in pursuit of sheep upon the property of any person other than the owner of the dog, should be held liable for damages for the trespass, and that any dog caught trespassing, and being without a collar bearing its owner's name, should be destroyed by the person capturing it. As any citizen has as much right to keep a dog as another has to keep a sheep, without being taxed for it, and can only be held liable for what damage his dog may do, it does not seem just that any tax should be levied upon dogs. The only just claim that can be made by a sheep-owner is that he shall be protected in the enjoyment of his property, and that the person by or through whom he is injured should recompense him. In the case of irresponsible owners of dogs, from whom no recovery can be made, the dogs should be destroyed by a proper officer. If the right of persons to keep dogs, when they wish to do so, without being taxed, is recognized in this manner, much of the opposition to the enactment of what are called "dog-laws," would be removed, and the protection of sheep made much less difficult, and productive of much greater profit.

HOW TO USE A FILE PROPERLY.

The file is very frequently used in such an imperfect manner as to greatly reduce its value as a mechanical tool. The chief difficulty in using a file is in keeping it in a perfectly horizontal position as it is moved over the work, and in maintaining an equable pressure upon the work meanwhile. Perhaps the most difficult work in filing, and that which is most frequently ill-done, is in sharpening saws. The bearing of the file upon the work is very narrow, and unable to guide its direction, and unless the file is held very carefully the direction varies continually, so that the saw tooth is filed round-

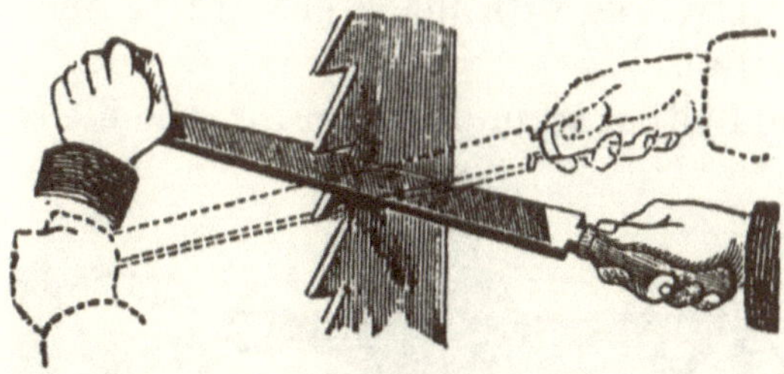

Fig. 98.—IMPROPER USE OF THE FILE.

ing instead of flat, or sloping instead of horizontal, or at exact right angles with the line of the saw, as it should be in a mill-saw or a rip-saw. When the file is held as shown in figure 98 (a very common manner of holding it), it is almost impossible to do good work upon a saw. When the file is pushed on to the tooth, the weight or pressure of the right hand is exerted upon the longer

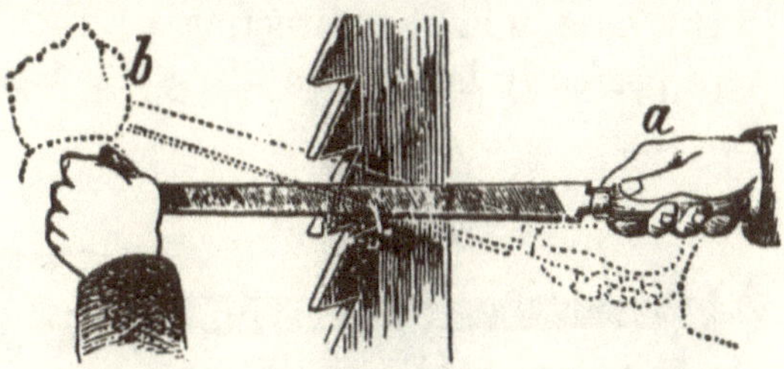

Fig. 99.—ANOTHER WRONG WAY OF FILING.

portion of the tool, making it act as if it were the longer arm of a lever, and thus depresses that portion below the horizontal, as at *a*. When pushed forward, the pressure is then exerted upon the longer portion of the file, which is carried from the horizontal in the contrary direction. The work is thus made round. Or if the pressure of the left hand is guarded against, that of the right hand is seldom altogether controlled, and the work is left sloping, as in figure 99; the position at the commencement being shown at *a*, and that at the finish of the stroke at *b*. This is a very common error with sawyers in mills, as well as with many good carpenters in filing their rip-saws.

To avoid either form of this error, the file should not

Fig. 100.—PROPER METHOD OF FILING.

be held with the ball of the thumb pressing upon the handle of the file, as in figures 98 and 99; but the end of the file should be taken lightly between the thumb and fore-finger, as in figure 100. There is no uneven pressure in this case, and the direction of the file may easily be kept perfectly level. In filing the base of the

Fig. 101.—FILING UNDERNEATH.

tooth, or the under portion of any work which cannot be turned over, the end of the file should be supported upon the ends of the fingers, as in figure 101, or be held by the end of the thumb, in an easy gentle manner. If held lightly, and not grasped too firmly, the arm or wrist will not be tired so soon as when it is held rigidly; and the motion of the file will be more even and regular.

When the arm is wearied by working in one direction, it may be rested by reversing the position of the file, taking the handle in the left hand, grasping the end be-

Fig. 102.—TO REST THE HAND IN FILING.

tween the fingers and thumb of the right hand, and drawing the file towards the body, instead of thrusting it away from it. The file is then held as in figure 102. This is an excellent position in which to hold the file when finishing off a saw tooth, or when touching it up at noon.

A MITRE-BOX.

A mitre-box of an improved form is shown in figure

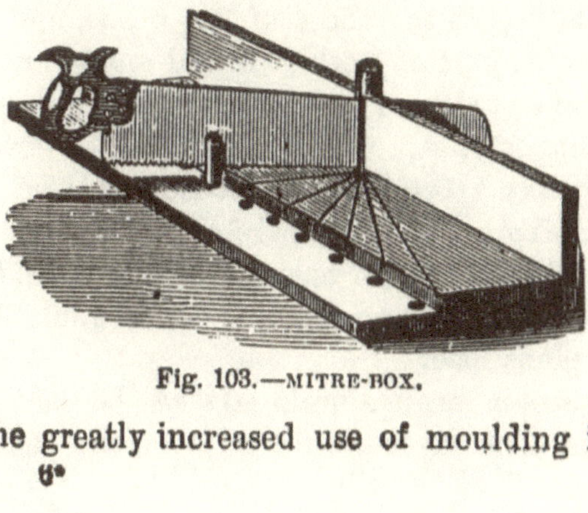

Fig. 103.—MITRE-BOX.

103. The greatly increased use of moulding in house

building renders a mitre-box very necessary in the work-shop. In the one here described, a bevel of any angle may be cut. At the rear of the box is a slotted post, which works in a socket, so that it will turn readily in any direction. From the post, lines are laid out upon the bottom at various angles. At the termination of each line is a round hole, into which a pin may be fitted. The pin is used as a guide for the saw in cutting a mitre-joint, as shown in the illustration.

THE MANURE HARVEST.

In the midst of the harvest of grain, and grass, and tubers, we must not forget the compost heap, in which we garner and store the unsowed crops of a future season. The saying that "anything that grows in one summer will rot before the next," is a safe guide in collecting vegetable matter for the compost heap. When sods, muck, and weeds form a part of the heap, it is not alone the material which we are assiduous in collecting, and put into the heap, that constitutes its whole value. The fermentation induced by the dung and liquid manure, and the action of the lime or ashes added, work upon the earth, adhering to the roots of the weeds, and forming a considerable part of both sods and muck, and develop an admirable quality of plant food. Hence this element of the compost heap, which is generally overlooked as possessing any special value, should never be wanting. It has, moreover, its own offices to perform, in promoting decay, in the formation of humus, and in preserving, locking up, and holding on to valuable ingredients of plant food.

The compost heap should always be laid in even layers, and each layer should go over the entire heap, for thus only can final uniformity be had. We do not mean special-purpose composts, but those made for general farm crops. It would be well if every particle of dung, liquid manure, straw, litter, leaves, weeds, etc., could be worked together into uniform fine compost, and there is really no substantial reason why this should not be done. The gardener would plead for certain special composts. It might, perhaps, be well to make a special hen-manure compost for corn in the hill, and taking the general compost as a basis, to make one for turnips, by the addition of a large percentage of bone-dust. All this may be done—establish once the rule to compost everything of manurial value, and we have in prospect an abundance of farm-made fertilizers at all times and for all crops—victory over weeds, a good place for decomposable trash of all kinds, a sacred burial ground for all minor animals and poultry, whose precincts need never be invaded. There will besides be no stagnating pool in the barn-yard, for all liquids will go to the tank, to be pumped over the compost heaps—no nasty, slumpy barn-yard, for everything will be daily gathered for the growing compost heap, and the harvesting of the manure crop, and its increase day by day, all the year round, will be a source of constant pleasure to master and men.

FASTENING CATTLE WITH BOWS.

Everything connected with this method of fastening cattle in the stable, by means of bows, is so simple in construction, that it is within the reach of every farmer. It requires no outlay, as each one can make all the parts for himself. The bow, figure 104, passes around the animal's neck in the same manner as an ox-bow, and is made of a good piece of hickory, by bending a strip of the right length, and three-quarter inch in diameter, into the bow form. After the bow-piece, *A*, is made of the right size and shape, with one end left with a knob, to prevent the clasp from slipping off, and the other out

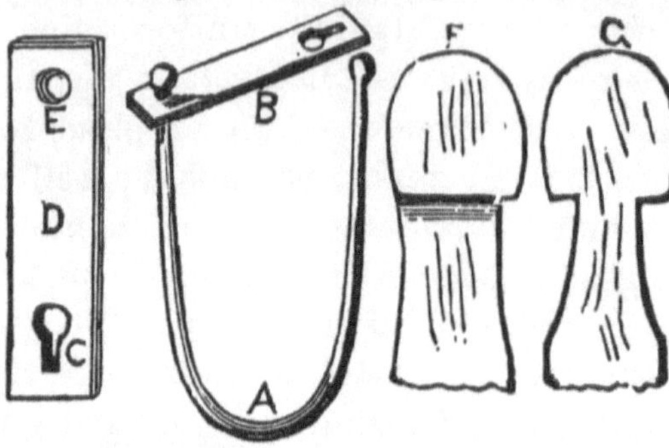

Fig. 104.—BOW AND CLASP.

as shown in front view in figure 104, *G*, and side view at *F*, to fit into the slot, in the clasp, it is carefully bent until its ends are brought together, fastened, and left so for a considerable time, when it will take its form and

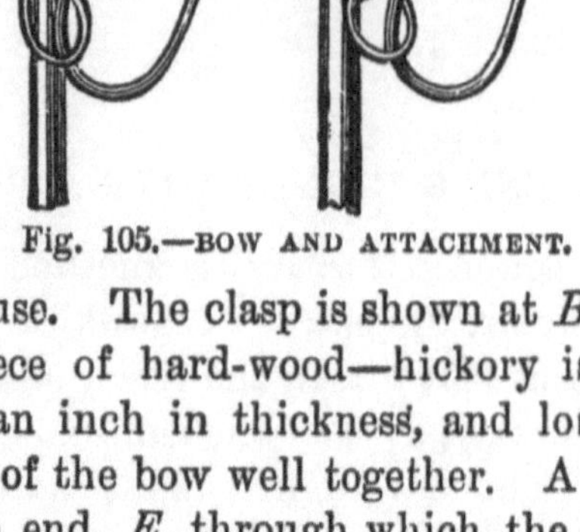

Fig. 105.—BOW AND ATTACHMENT.

be ready for use. The clasp is shown at *B*, *D*, and consists of a piece of hard-wood—hickory is best—three-quarters of an inch in thickness, and long enough to hold the top of the bow well together. A round hole is bored in one end, *E*, through which the bow passes as far as the knob, the other end is cut with a hole for the passage of the other end of the bow, and a slot, *C*, into which its narrow neck springs when the bow is secured about the creature's neck. A smooth, stout hickory pole, two and a half inches in diameter, reaching from the floor to the beam overhead, serves as a stanchion to which to attach the animal, by means of a small bow, and stationary clasp, figure 105, or an iron ring, *A*. If a little more room is desired for young stock, a link or two of chain, *B*, can be inserted between the bow and

Fig. 106.—STABLE SHOWING BOW AND STANCHIONS.

stanchion ring. In fastening the cattle, the bow is raised when it passes around the neck, and the clasp is brought on, and the end of the bow is sprung in place. When the animal is to be let loose, the end of the bow is pressed in, the clasp slips off, the bow falls, and the work is done in less time than it takes to describe it, and everything is out of the way. Figure 106 shows a stable arranged for this method of fastening; aside from the manger, there is but the stanchion poles, one for each animal. There is sufficient freedom of movement o' the head, but not an excess; the animal can stand or lie down with perfect comfort, as the bow moves with ease the whole length of the stanchion. After a week's practice, the animals will take their place with their heads by the side of the stanchion, with a precision that is remarkable. Having used the method, here illustrated, for several years, the writer has found it inexpensive, easy in application, and safe.

THE PRESERVATION OF WOOD.

It is known that the decay of timber first begins through the fermentation of sap within the pores, and that it is continued after this by the absorption of water. The neutralization of the acids in the timber by the use of lime, has been made use of to preserve it from decay with success; but the most effective methods have been to saturate the pores with oils or mineral salts. Creosote and petroleum have been used successfully, but few persons are aware of the enormous absorptive capacity of timber for these liquids. Cypress wood, when dry, will absorb thirty-nine pounds, or five gallons of oil per cubic foot, and California redwood and pine absorb twice their weight when perfectly dry. But it is not necessary for perfect preservation that timber should be fully saturated. One gallon per cubic foot, for the most porous woods, will be fully effective, and a coating of one and three-quarters of a pint per square foot for weather boards, or half as much for shingles, will render them perfectly water-proof. In some careful experiments recently made, dry spruce absorbed, during two days' soaking, nearly two per cent. of its weight of water, and but one-tenth as much when treated with oil; dry pine absorbed sixteen per cent. of its weight, and oiled pine absorbed none that could be ascertained by careful weighing. Pine has proved to be the most easily waterproofed of any timber. Those who wish to preserve shingle roofs, will be able to draw their own inferences as to the usefulness of coating them with crude petroleum.

A NEST FOR EGG-EATING HENS.

In the winter season hens frequently acquire the habit of eating eggs. Sometimes this vice becomes so confirmed that several hens may be seen waiting for another one to leave her nest, or to even drive her off, so that they may pounce upon the egg, the one that drops it being among the first to break it. In this state of affairs there is no remedy, except to find some method of protecting the egg from the depredators. The easiest way of doing this is to contrive a nest in which the egg will drop out of reach. Such a nest is shown in figure 107. It consists of a box with two sloping false half-floors; one of these being depressed below the other sufficiently to make a space through which the egg can roll down to the bottom floor. A door is seen in the side of the nest, through which the eggs can be removed. The sloping half-floors are shown by dotted lines. Upon the back one, close to the back of the nest, a glass or other nest-egg is fastened by a screw or by cement. The false floors may be covered with some coarse carpet or cloth, and the bottom floor with some chaff or moss, upon which the eggs may roll without danger of breaking. If the eggs do not roll

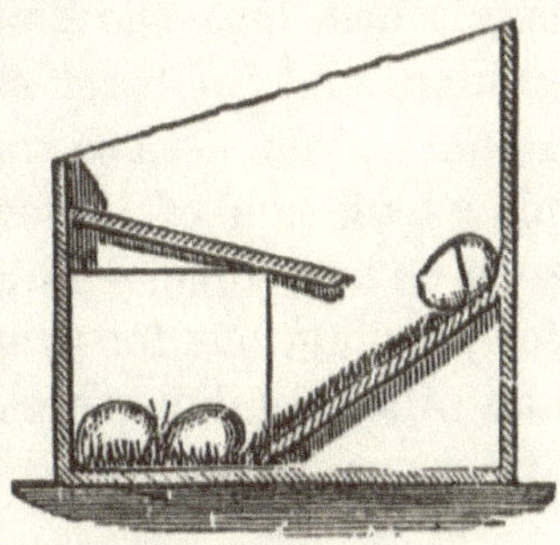

Fig 107.—SAFETY-NEST.

down at once, they will be pushed down by the first attempt of a hen to attack them.

PLOWING GEAR FOR A KICKING MULE.

Below is presented a plan for hitching a mule which has a habit of kicking when harnessed to a plow, but which goes very well in shafts. Kicking is a vice which sometimes belongs to horses as well as mules, and the following expedient has been found effective in

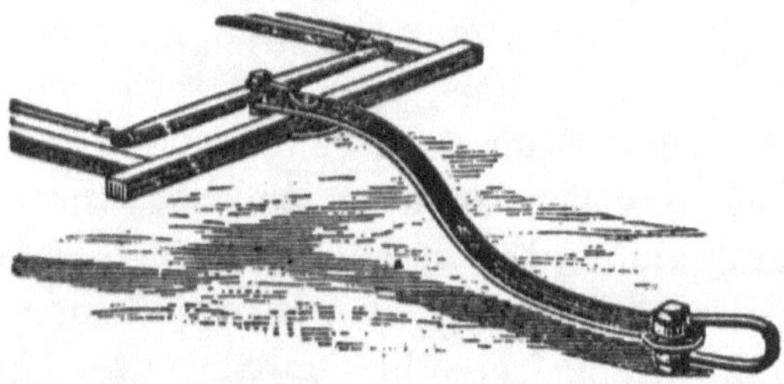

Fig. 108.—PLOWING GEAR FOR KICKING ANIMALS.

curing it. Take a pair of light shafts from a wagon, or make a pair, and fit to the end of it a bent strap of iron, as shown in figure 108. When the mule or horse is hitched into the shafts the end may trail on the ground, and the beast may be exercised with the shafts alone. When used to these, the bent bar is fastened to a plow by means of a clevis, and any difficulty there will soon be overcome. This device has been used, not only for plowing, but for drawing a stone boat, railroad cars, and other similar vehicles.

A LEAF FORK.

A useful plan for making a fork to gather leaves is shown in figure 109. The fork is made of tough ash, with ten teeth, similar to the fingers of a cradle, three feet long, and slightly turned up. The head into which the butts of the teeth are inserted, is thirty inches long. A light cross-bar of tough wood is fastened to the teeth, about eight inches from the head, by means of copper

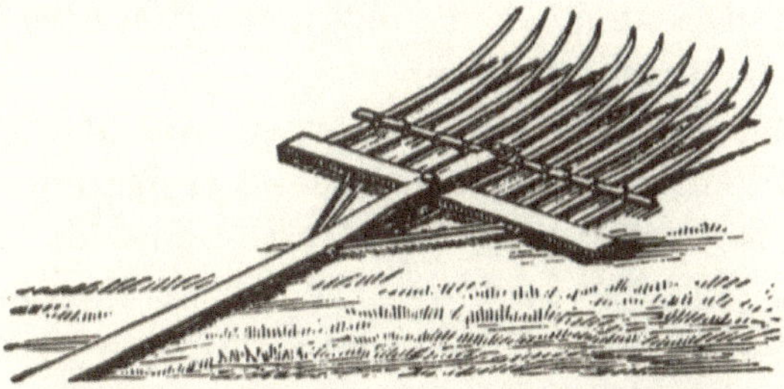

Fig. 109.—FORK FOR GATHERING LEAVES.

wire and a light screw to each finger. A handle is provided and fixed in its proper place, being flattened somewhat to keep it from turning in the hand. The handle should be braced by two strong wires. With such a fork leaves may be loaded very easily and rapidly.

PREPARATION OF THE WHEAT GROUND.

Wheat demands for its perfect development, among other favorable conditions, besides showers and sunshine, depth and richness of soil, thorough tilth, and freedom from excess of moisture. Soil that will yield good clover will bear good wheat. Wheat follows corn very well, but this involves rather late sowing. Where there is a market for new potatoes, which, as they are intended for immediate use, may be freely manured, the potato ground —well plowed and harrowed with a dressing of bone-dust, superphosphate, or, if there is much organic matter in the soil, with a dressing of lime—forms an admirable seed-bed for wheat. One of the best rotations, including winter wheat, is corn on sod, early potatoes, wheat, clover and timothy, the grass to be mowed as long as it is profitable—the manure being applied in the hill for corn, and put on broadcast very liberally for the potatoes. Winter wheat follows none of the usual root crops well, for it ought to be sowed and up before the middle of September, although it often does well sowed nearly a month later.

When wheat follows clover, a crop of clover-hay is often taken off early, and a second crop allowed to grow, which is turned under about the first of August for wheat. In case we have very dry weather in July, the growth of clover will be meagre. If, however, the clover stubble be top-dressed at once, as soon as the early crop is cut, with a muck and manure compost, or any fine compost, "dragged in" with a smoothing harrow, the second crop will be sure to start well, while none of the manure will be lost. Lime, or ashes, if they can be obtained, are to be spread after plowing under the clover and manure, and thoroughly harrowed in. Forty bushels of ashes to the acre is about right, and where hearths of old charcoal pits are accessible—ashes, charcoal-dust, and baked earth, are all excellent—they form a good substitute for ashes and for lime. Sixty to one hundred bushels of evenly dry-slaked lime is a usual application, which, if it could have been mixed with an equal quantity of soil or sods during the slaking, would be all the better.

The soil, and particularly wheat ground, is not well enough tilled in this country. We plow fourteen to sixteen-inch furrows, and use a skim-plow; this leaves the surface so mellow, and covers the sod so perfectly, that we think it hardly needs harrowing at all, and only smooth it over with a harrow, and let it go. The skim plow is a great advantage, but we should take narrow furrows.

The following practice, on heavy land especially, is excellent: Turn under the first crop of clover as deep as possible, just before it is in full blossom; cross-plow the first or second week in August; then put on seventy-five bushels of lime, or more, and harrow it in lightly. Sow early after a soaking rain, and apply at the time of sowing two hundred and fifty pounds or more of super-phosphate to the acre.

HOW TO DRIVE A HORSE-SHOE NAIL.

Most farmers hesitate to attempt to fasten on a loose shoe for fear of injuring the foot by driving the nail in a wrong direction. It is such a saving of time and money to be able to put a shoe upon a horse in a hurried busy time, that every farmer ought to learn how to do it. He may practice upon a piece of soft pine wood in a rough way, when he will find how easy it is, by properly preparing the nails, to make the point come out in exactly the proper place. To prepare the nail it should be laid upon the anvil (which every workshop should have for such work as this), or a smooth iron block, and beaten out straight. The point should then be bevelled, slightly upon one of the flat sides, and the point also bent a very little from the side which is bevelled. It will then be of the shape shown in figure 110. In driving such a nail into a piece of soft wood, or a horse's hoof which is penetrated easily in any direction, if the bevelled side is placed towards the centre of the hoof and away from the crust, the point will be bent outwards, and will come out lower or higher on the crust as the bevel and curve is much or little. A little practice will enable one to cause the point to protrude precisely at the right place. By turning the bevel outwards, in driving the nail, the course will be towards the centre of the

Fig. 110.—NAIL.

foot as shown by the line *b*, in figure 111. The nail is sometimes started in the wrong direction by careless blacksmiths, and the horse is lamed in consequence. If the mistake is discovered, and an attempt made to draw out the nail, a piece of it may be broken off, and at every concussion of the foot the fragment will penetrate further, until it reaches the sensitive parts, and great suffering will follow. Many a horse is supposed to have navicular disease (because that happens to be one of those obscure affections of the foot which has no outward sign), when the trouble is a fragment of nail broken off by a bungling shoer. We have examined the foot of a horse which was killed because of an incurable lameness, and found a piece of nail thus bedded in the centre of the foot, surrounded with an abscess which had eaten into the bone. The torture suffered by this horse must have been intense, and it was supposed to be a case of navicular disease, while the real cause was unsuspected. In driving nails into the hoof, great caution should be exercised. The hand, or the thumb, should be held over the spot where the point of the nail is expected to come out, and if it does not appear when it should do so, the nail must be withdrawn. Use no split or imperfect nail, and have the point very carefully prepared. The course taken by a nail properly pointed and driven is shown by the lines curved outwards at *a*, *a*, in figure 111.

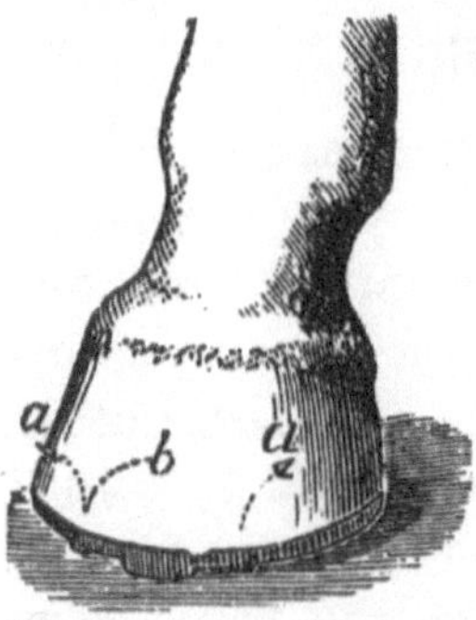

Fig. 111.—DRIVING NAILS.

SCREW-DRIVERS.

To drive a screw with a screw-driver, as it is usually pointed and handled, is a disagreeable task. If the screw goes in with difficulty, the driver slips out of the groove, or it cuts the edges of the groove so that the screw is useless. This is because the point of the tool is not ground properly. It should be ground with an even and long bevel, at least an inch long in small tools, and two inches in large ones. The sides of the bit should be kept straight, and not tapered off nor the corners ground off or rounded. There should be no sharp edge ground upon the end of the tool, and the grinding should be lengthwise, or from handle to point, and not crosswise. The edge should be slightly rounded. The degree of roundness given may be such as would make it equal to an arc of a circle ten to twelve inches in diameter; for small tools this may be lessened considerably. The shape of a well-pointed screw-driver is shown in figure 112. Flat handles should be abolished as a nuisance; after an hour's use of a driver with such a handle, the hand will be stiff and sore. The handle should be round. Screw-drivers are used more frequently than necessary. We have driven hundreds of screws in all sorts of timber, hard white oak even, with the hammer, just as nails are driven, without the use of a screw-driver, and found them to hold perfectly well. This, of course, can be done only with the sharp taper-pointed screws, and if any one uses the old blunt-pointed kind, he is too far behind the times to be much of a mechanic or farmer either.

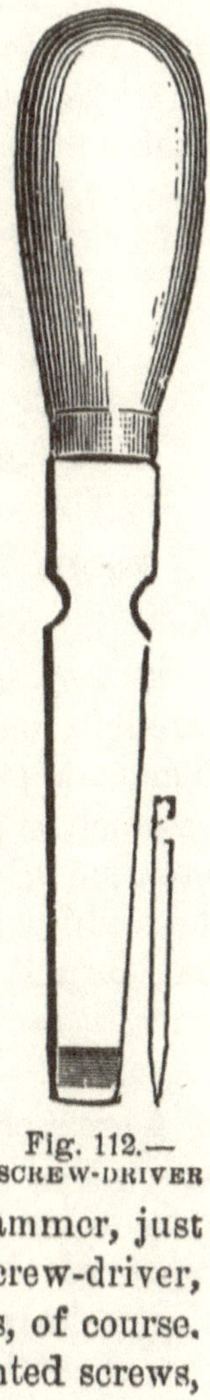

Fig. 112.—SCREW-DRIVER

TO PREVENT COWS SUCKING THEMSELVES.

There are many devices to prevent cows from sucking themselves. A spiked halter is shown in figure 113. A buckle at the upper part, behind the ears, makes it quite easy to detach it. Figure 114 shows

Fig. 113.—SPIKED HALTER.

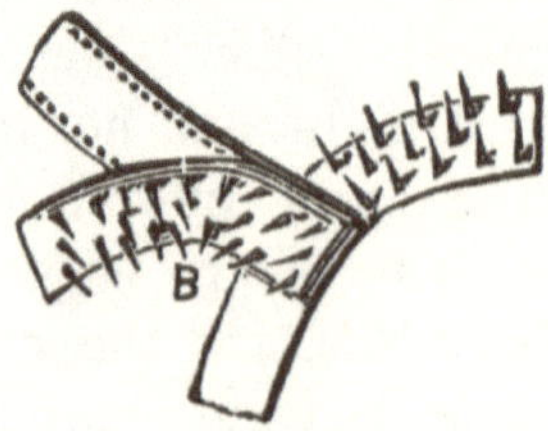

Fig. 114.—MAKING THE HALTER.

how the spikes are secured. The spikes should not be over two inches in length. They are best made of wrought nails, which are sold at the hardware stores. They are placed in an iron vise and the heads flattened as much as possible by pounding with a hammer; they are then driven into a piece of thick leather, and secured by sewing or riveting it upon another piece of leather, as shown at *B* in figure 114.

ABUSE OF BARN CELLARS.

A great change has come over the farm during the last thirty years, in all our thrifty farming districts, in the general use of barn cellars. Formerly such an arrangement of the barn was a novelty, and farmers have slowly learned its great advantages—the greater comfort of cattle, the cheaper cleaning of stables, the more convenient watering of stock, the larger use of peat. muck, and headlands in the compost heap, and the greater value of the manure made under cover. Now the cry is raised of damage to fodder and stock from the barn cellar. Almost any good thing can be perverted and become a nuisance, and it were strange if men who do not read much, and think less, could not abuse the barn cellar, which is the stomach of the farm. The same kind of men not infrequently abuse their own stomachs, and suffer grievously in consequence. "If you make your barn cellar tight, carbonic acid gas and ammonia are thrown off and injure the quality of hay stored in the rooms above, and the health of the cattle in the stables. If you turn your pigs into the cellar to make compost, and keep them from the air and the light, they become diseased, and you put bad meat into your barrel to breed disease in your family." These are not uncommon complaints, circulating in our agricultural journals. Well, suppose we admit these things to be true, what of it? Is there any necessity for having a barn cellar without ventilation? If you leave one end open towards the south, you certainly have ventilation enough—and the gases that are evolved from fermenting manure are not going through two-inch stable plank and the tight siding of the barn when they have the wind to carry them off. If a barn cellar is properly managed, and seasonably furnished with absorbents, the ammonia will be absorbed as fast as it is formed. There will be no odor of ammonia that the nostrils can detect. If the pigs do not do the mixing fast enough, the shovel and the fork, the plow and the harrow, can be added. The making of compost under the barn is nice work for rainy days in winter, and is more likely to pay than any work exposed to the storm. The keeping of pigs under the barn is a question of two sides, and however we may decide it, barn cellars will stand upon their own merits. Any farmer who makes a business of raising pork for the market will find a well-appointed pig-sty, with conveniences for storing and cooking food, a paying investment. If he sees fit to utilize the labor of his pigs by making compost in a well-ventilated barn cellar, their health is not likely to suffer from the wholesome exercise, or that of his family from the use of the flesh. Swine, furnished with a dry sleeping-apartment and plenty of litter for a bed, will keep comfortably clean, and not suffer from overwork in the compost heap. If anything is settled in the experience of the last thirty years, it is the economy of the barn cellar. Our most intelligent farmers, who can command the capital, in-

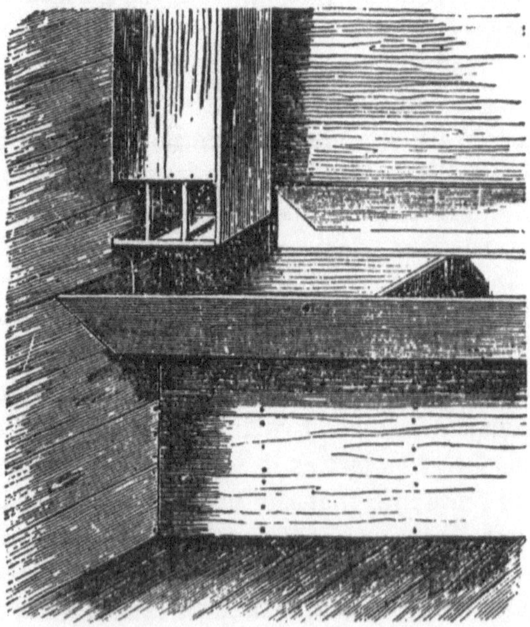

Fig. 115.—HAY RACK AND MANGER.

vest in them. A nice appendage to them is a watering trough fed by a spring or a large cistern in the embankment, to catch all the water, and bring it out by a faucet upon the stable floor above. This works admirably.

HAY-RACK AND MANGER.

A cheap and convenient hay-rack and manger is shown in figure 115. The front of the manger should be of oak or other hard wood plank, two inches thick, and one foot wide, the lower edge of which is placed about two and a half feet from the floor; the bottom should be one foot wide. The side of the hay-rack is one foot wide, the front is eighteen inches wide; the top and bottom being of the same width, so that hay will not lodge. The bottom is made from one and a half inch hard board, and is placed one foot above the top of the manger. Two guards, one inch in diameter, and one foot in length, are placed in an upright position across the opening. At the front of the manger is a swinging door, which is shown partly open. This opens into the feed-passage. The manger may have one end partitioned for feeding grain. All corners should be smoothed and rounded off, and to make it durable, attach a thin, flat bar of iron to the upper edge of the manger by screws or rivets.

A BARN BASKET.

Figure 116 shows a home-made basket or box for use in the barn or in gathering crops. It is made of two pieces of light board, twelve inches square, for the ends, fastened together by laths sixteen, eighteen, or twenty inches long, for bottom and sides. These are securely nailed. The handle consists of a piece nailed to each end, and connected by a light bar. This box is quickly made, and will be found very handy for gathering many crops in the field, as it may be made to hold exactly one bushel, half a bushel, or any other definite quantity, by changing the size. To hold a bushel, which is two thousand, one hundred and fifty cubic inches, the box may be scant twenty inches long, twelve inches wide, and nine deep, or scant eighteen inches long, twelve inches wide, and eleven inches deep. For half a bushel,

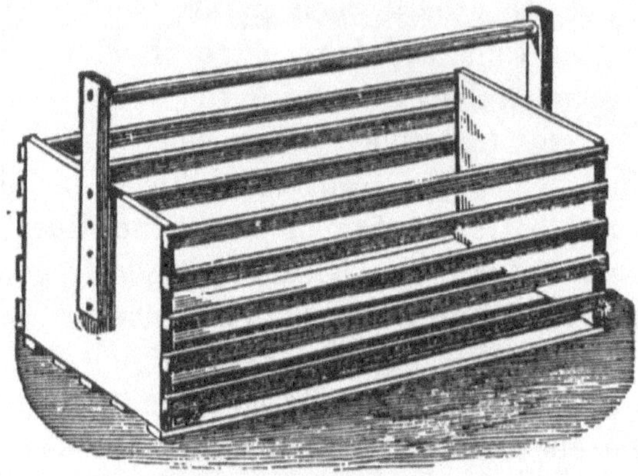

Fig. 116.—CONVENIENT BARN BASKET.

scant eighteen inches long, ten inches wide, and six deep; or fifteen inches long, nine inches wide, and eight inches deep. For a peck, ten inches long, nine wide, and six deep; or eight inches square, and scant eight and a half inches deep.

THE TREATMENT OF KICKING COWS.

It is safe to say that a kicking cow is not naturally disposed to this vice, but has been made vicious by some fault of her owner. There are few men who possess sufficient patience and kindness to so manage a cow, from calfhood until she comes to the pail, that she will be kind and gentle under all circumstances. There are nervous, irritable cows, that are impatient of restraint, which are easily and quickly spoiled when they fall into the hands of an owner of a similar disposition. One who is kind and patient, and who has an affection for his animals, is never troubled with kicking cows, unless he has purchased one already made vicious. Unfortunately, few persons are gifted with these rare virtues, and, therefore, there are always cows that have to be watched carefully at milking time. Cows sometimes suffer from cracked teats, or their udders may be tender from some concealed inflammation, and they are restless when milked; so that, now and then, in the best regulated dairies, there will be cows that will kick. Many devices have been recommended to prevent such cows from exercising this disagreeable habit. Different methods of securing the legs have been tried. The best plan that we have heard of, or have tried, is shown in figure 117. This fetter is fastened to the cow's near leg, by means of the strap in the centre, the curved portions embracing the front of the leg above and below the hock. It will be perceived that, while the cow can move her leg to some extent, and is not hobbled, as when the legs are tied together, yet she cannot lift it to kick, or to put her foot in the pail. We have seen this "fetter" tried upon a cow that had very sore cracked teats, and that kicked furiously when milked, but with the fetter she was unable to kick or hinder milking.

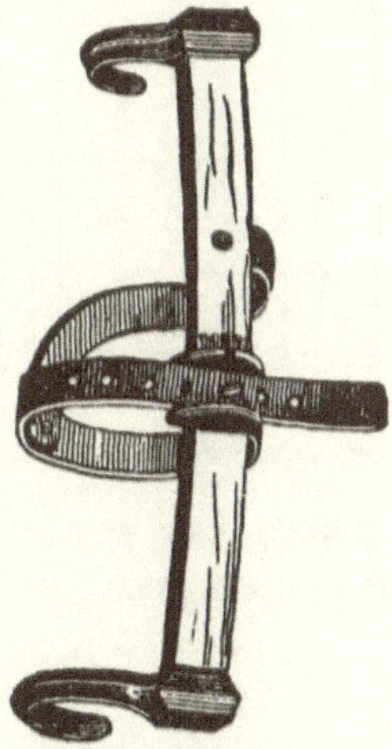

Fig. 117.—COW-FETTER.

HOW TO BUILD A BOAT-HOUSE.

Any kind of a house that is large enough may be used, if provided with the needed fittings named below. Where the level of the water is liable to little change, the house need not be raised much above the surface of the water, but the floor may be made so low that one can easily step out of the boat to the floor. Of course there should be a channel made in the centre of the house, deep enough to float the boat when loaded. The plan of the floor is shown in figure 118, with the boat in the centre. The floor should be protected by a light railing around it (see figure 119), to prevent accidents from slipping when the floor is wet

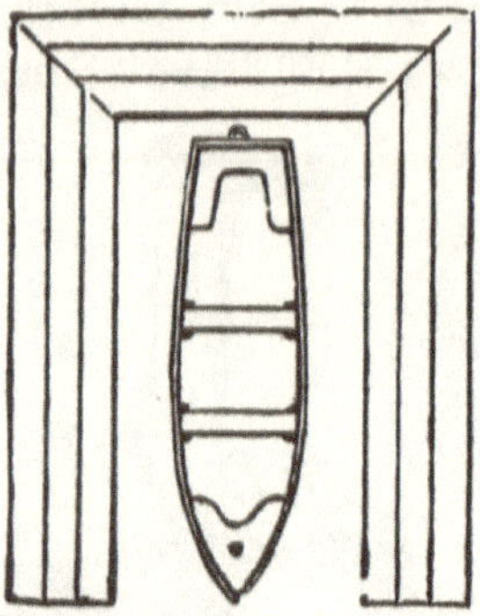

Fig. 118.—PLAN OF HOUSE.

Where the water level changes, the house should be raised on posts, or bents, as may be necessary to keep it

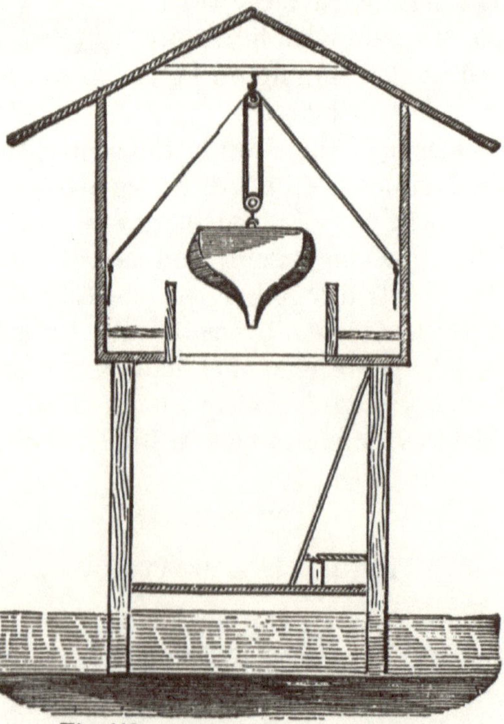

Fig. 119.—SECTION OF BOAT-HOUSE.

above high water. A hanging ladder, that may be drawn up, is provided for use at low water.

WASTE LANDS—MAKE THEM USEFUL.

Waste land abounds everywhere. It is fenced, and has the appearance of farm-land, but the owner, if a farmer, would be better off without it than he is with it. No one locality seems to be better or worse than another in this respect, unless it be that the Southern States have the most waste land, and the Eastern States come next in this respect. There are rocky fields, and fields covered with loose stones; swamps and wet ground, and land covered with wretched brush and small timber, and in the South, especially, barren and gullied hill-sides. It is true, that to clear up these lands, and make them fruitful, will cost in labor, if the labor is valued at the current rates, more than the land would bring if offered for sale. But this is not the right way to look at this matter. In reality, it will cost nothing to clear these lands, because their owners may do it by working when they would otherwise be idle. The way to do it is to set about it. To clear an acre or two at a time, of those fields that can be cleared; and to plant with timber, of some valuable sort, that ground which is too rough for the plow, instead of permitting it to grow up with useless brush. In many cases, the worst trouble that farmers suffer is, that they have more land than they can care for, under their present system of management. Hundreds of farms are worked as grain farms, that are not well suited for any other use than dairy farms, and ground is plowed that should be kept in permanent grass. In some cases, the owners of land have discovered their proper vocation, as in the dairy district of Central

New York, in the fruit and grain farms of the western part of that State, in the pasture farms of the blue-grass region of Kentucky, and in the corn-growing and pork-raising prairies of the West. If the system of culture in these places were changed, the farmers would be poor instead of being rich, and one sees very little waste land in these localities. There are districts where the surface is hilly, and not so well suited for arable purposes as for pasture, but where, instead of grass and cows, side-hill plows and poor corn fields, washed and gullied by rains, are to be seen. Here are waste lands in plenty; and their owners show every sign of poverty and want of thrift. It is not easy to change these circumstances quickly, but it is easy to begin—just as it is easier to start a stone rolling down a hill, than to throw it down bodily; and when it is once started, it goes slowly at first, and may need help, but it can soon take care of itself, and speedily reaches the bottom. It is just so with such improvements as are here referred to. They are necessarily begun slowly, but when one or two acres of these waste places are reclaimed, the product of these adds to the farmer's resources. He is richer than before by the increased value of these acres, and he is better able to reclaim more. When these in their turn are improved, the means for further improvements are greatly enlarged; the ambition of the man to excel in his vocation is excited, and he speedily becomes a neater, better farmer, and necessarily his circumstances are improved. Thus the rough waste lands, which give a disagreeable appearance to the landscape, and are a stigma upon its character and that of our farmers, in the eyes of our own citizens and of foreigners, might in a short time be improved and a source of profit.

A RAT-GUARD.

To keep rats away from anything that is hung up, the following simple method may be used. Procure the bottoms of some old fruit-cans, by melting the solder which

Fig. 120.—GUARD AGAINST RATS.

holds them upon a hot stove. Bore holes in the centre of these disks, and string a few of them upon the cord, wire, or rope upon which the articles are hung. When a rat or mouse attempts to pass upon the rope by climbing over the tin disks, they turn and throw the animal upon the floor. This plan, shown in figure 120, will be found very effective.

A CRUPPER-PAD FOR HORSES.

Many horsemen desire a method by which to prevent a horse from carrying its tail upon one side, and from clasping the reins beneath the tail. We cannot advise the operation of "nicking," which consists in cutting the skin and muscles upon one side of the tail, and tying it over to the cut side, until the cuts heal, when the skin, being drawn together, pulls the tail permanently over to that side. A different form of the operation causes the tail to be carried up in a style that is supposed to be more graceful, and prevents the horse from clasping the reins when driven. As a preventive of both of these habits, the pad shown in figure 121 is often used by horsemen, instead of the cruel and unnecessary operation of "nicking." This appliance is made of leather, is stuffed with hair or wool, and is about three inches in diameter at the thickest part, gradually tapering toward each end, where it is fastened to the crupper straps. It should be drawn up close to the roots of the tail, and by exerting a pressure beneath it, the tail is carried in a raised position, and is not thrown over to one side. If it is, a few sharp tacks may be driven into the inside of the pad.

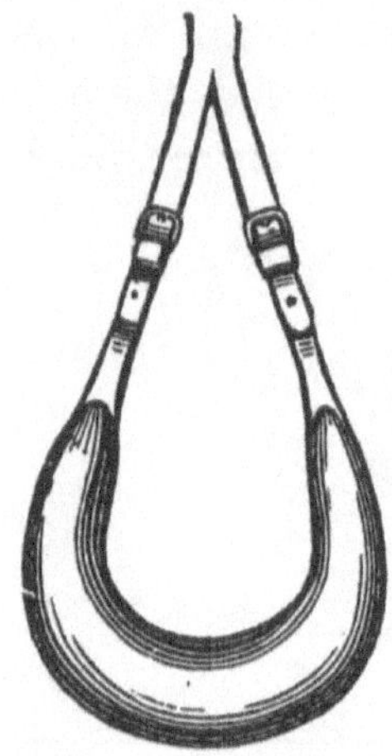

Fig. 121.—CRUPPER-PAD.

A DAM FOR A FISH POND.

In making a fish pond, by placing a dam across a stream, it should be borne in mind that success depends upon the proper construction of the dam, whether it be

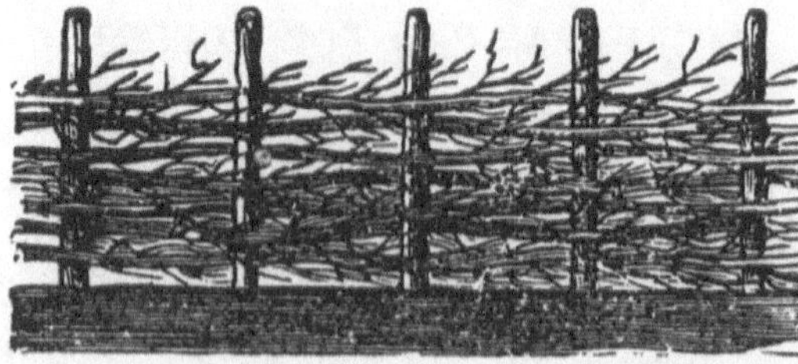

Fig. 122.—STAKES AND BRUSH.

large or small. Any defect here will make the whole useless. The main point in the construction of a dam is to have a complete union between the earth of the bed and that of the dam. This cannot be done by throwing the earth upon an old surface. A new surface must be made, solid and firm, to receive the new earth. In addition, there should be a central core of some strong material, that will serve to strengthen and bind the new construction. In making a dam or embankment to retain or exclude water, the beginning should be to dig a shallow ditch, removing sod or uneven ground, or if the earth is bare, to disturb it thoroughly with the pick, so as to provide binding material to unite with the bottom of the dam. A line of stakes is driven into the ground, and filled with brush woven in, or wattled, as in figure 122. In building the dam, all the sods and vegetable matter should be placed on the outside, where these will root, and bind the surface together; the rest of the earth should be well trodden, or rammed down firmly, and it the soil is puddled by admixture of water in the process of ramming, the work will be better for it. The waterway in the stream should be tightly boarded or planked. Three posts may be driven or set on each bank of the stream, and boards nailed, or planks spiked for a larger structure, so as to retain the earth of the embankments on each side, figure 123. A timber is fitted as a mudsill, to the front and rear posts, and one to the central posts; the latter at such a height as will raise the water to the desired depth. The spaces between these timbers are boarded and planked, and may be filled in with earth, well rammed, and mixed with straw and fine cedar brush, under the covering. If it is desired to raise the water to a greater depth, loose flash-boards may be fitted with cleats, on the centre of the waste-way, or a wire-gauze fence may be placed there, to prevent the escape of the fish. If freshets are apt to occur, a sufficient number of these waste-ways should be provided to carry off the surplus water, and prevent overflowing and wasting of the dam. The dam of a fish pond should always be made high enough for safety against overflow, and to guard against percolation, and washing away by undermining, it should be made three times as wide as it is high, with slopes of one and a half foot horizontal on

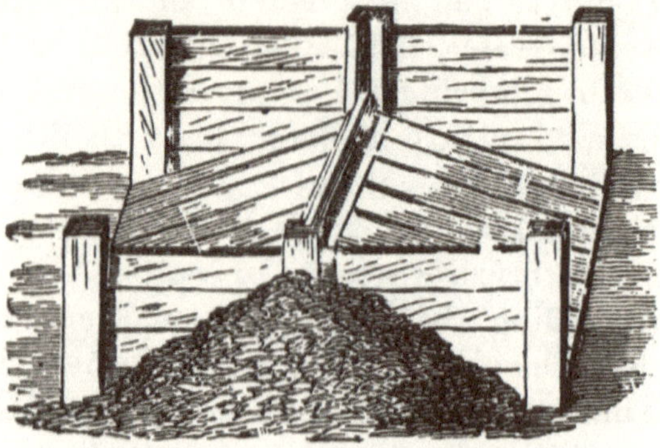

Fig. 123.—WASTE-GATE FOR POND.

each side, to one foot in perpendicular height. If any plants are set upon a dam or embankment, they should be of a small, bushy growth, such as osier willow, elders, etc., but nothing larger, lest the swaying caused by high winds should loosen and destroy the bank.

A WAGON JACK.

In figures 124 and 125 is shown a most convenient home-made wagon jack, in constant use for ten years, and has proved most satisfactory. The drawings were made with such care, the measurement being placed upon them, that the engravings tell nearly the whole story. Figure 124 shows the jack when in position to hold the axle, at *a*. When not in use, the lever falls down out of the way, and the affair can be hung up in a handy place. Figure 125 shows the "catch-board," and the dimensions proper for a jack, for an ordinary wagon, buggy, etc. It is so shaped and fastened by a din between the upright parts of the jack, that it is pushed in position, *d*, by the foot at *c*, when the axle is raised; and falls back of its own accord when the lever is raised a trifle to let the wheel down. All the parts are made

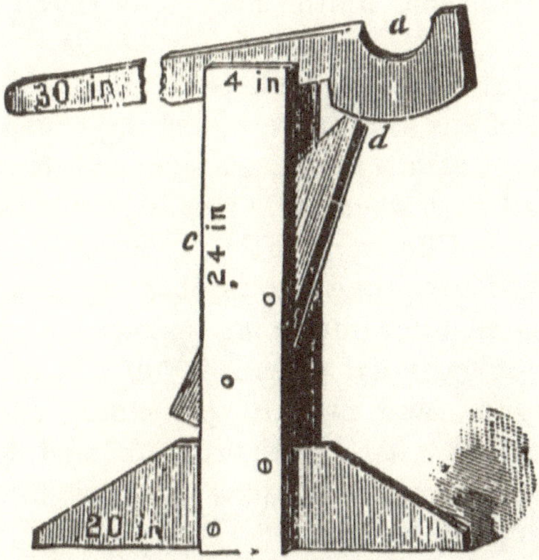

Fig. 124.—MICHIGAN WAGON JACK.

Fig. 125.—CATCH-BOARD.

of inch stuff, the foot board, catch, and lever should be of hard wood; the upright boards between which they are placed can be of pine or other soft wood. Persons who see this simple and convenient wagon jack frequently say, "Why don't you get it patented?" but the inventor thinks that such simple things, which any one can make, ought to be contributed for the common good, and in the same spirit we commend it to any who may be in need of a good wagon jack.

WILL YOU FEED HAY OR WOOD?

A great deal has been said and written about the proper time of cutting hay. The best time, all things considered, is to cut the grass just after it has come into full bloom, though many think the preferable time is just when it is coming into full blossom. As it is impossible to always mow every field just at the right moment, the general safe rule is, we think, to be all ready to begin at full bloom, and finish before it is entirely past.

There is this important fact to be kept in mind, viz., that as soon as grass of any kind has attained its growth, and is full of juices, it begins to change more and more into woody fibre, and that when fully ripe a large part of the stems or stalks differ very little in composition from dry wood. And every one knows that dry wood is neither easily digested nor nutritious. It stands to reason that a stalk of grass cut when it is full of juice containing sugar, gum, and protein compounds, and cured thus, must be more nutritious than if left standing until a part of these constituents have changed into woody fibre. Feeding hay not cut until it is thoroughly ripe, is giving the animals that which is in part only so much wood. The practical lesson is, make a good ready well in advance, now, and have the barns, mows, stacking arrangements, mowers, scythes, horse and other rakes, forks, wagon racks, in short, all things, in perfect order—and the work planned, so as not to let any hayfield get into the fully ripe condition. Head work beforehand will save hard work and worry, and secure better hay.

A BRACE FOR A KICKING HORSE.

Those so unfortunate as to own a kicking horse know something of the patience that it requires to get along with it—and will welcome anything which will prevent the kicking and finally effect a cure. The writer knew a horse, which was so bad a kicker that after various trials, and after passing through many hands, and getting worse all the time, to be perfectly cured in the course of three months by the use of the device here given. This is a simple brace, which acts upon the fact that if the head be kept up, the horse cannot kick. A kicking horse is like a balance, when one end goes up, the other must go down. The brace is shown in figure 126, and consists of a one-half inch iron rod, which may be straight, or, for the looks, bent into a graceful curve. It is forked at both ends; the two divisions of the upper end are fastened to the two rings of the bit, while the lower ends fit upon the lower portion of the collar and hames. The upper ends can best be fastened to the bit by winding with wire, which should be done smoothly, so as not to wear upon the mouth. The lower end is secured by means of a strap fastened to the upper loop, and passing around the collar is buckled through the hole in the lower part of the end of the brace. The brace need not be taken from the bit in unharnessing. Any blacksmith can make such a brace, taking care to have it of the proper length to fit the particular horse. Keep its head at about the height as when "checked up," and the horse will soon be cured.

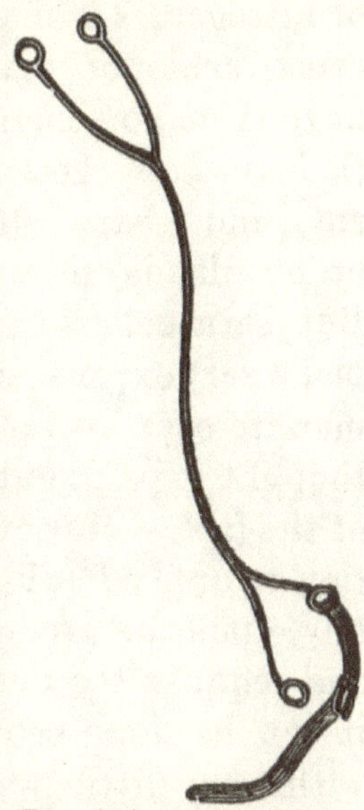

Fig. 126.—THE BRACE.

HOW TO SAVE LIQUID MANURE.

In ordinary farm practice, by far the larger part of the liquid manure of the stock kept is lost. No effort is made to save it. There is no barn cellar, no gutter behind the stabled animals, no absorbents. Analysis shows that the liquid manure is quite as valuable as the solid, or even more so. In 1,000 pounds of fresh horse dung there are 4.4 pounds of nitrogen, 3.5 of potash, and 3.5 of phosphoric acid. In horse urine there are 15.5 pounds of nitrogen, and 15.0 of potash. In 1,000 pounds of fresh cattle dung there are 2.9 pounds of nitrogen, 1.0 of potash, 1.7 of phosphoric acid. In the urine, 5.8 pounds of nitrogen, 4.9 of potash. These are the most valuable constituents of manure, and no farmer can afford to have them so generally run to waste. There is very little loss where there is a gutter well supplied with absorbents, and a barn cellar well coated with dried peat, muck, or headlands, to absorb the liquids as fast as they fall. But barn cellars are still in the minority. Mr. Mechi had a very expensive apparatus for distributing the liquid manure over his farm, by means of tanks and pipes, and thought it paid, but failed to convince his contemporaries of the fact. However that may be, it is out of the question to apply liquid manure in this manner, economically, upon the average farm. It takes too much capital, and requires too much labor. By the use of absorbents, it can be done economically on a small or large scale, with very little waste. Some use a water-tight box, made of thick plank, covering the floor of the stall. This is a very sure way to save everything, and the only objection to it is the expense of the box, and the increased labor of keeping the stalls clean. We used for several years dried salt-marsh sod, cut in blocks eight or ten inches square, taken from the surface of the marsh in ditching. This had an enormous capacity for absorbing liquids, and a layer of these sods would keep a horse or cow comfortably dry for a fortnight. Refuse hay or straw was used on top for purposes of cleanliness. The saturated sod was thrown into the compost heap with other manure, where it made an excellent fertilizer. Later we used sawdust, purchased for the purpose at two cents a bushel, as bedding for a cow kept upon a cemented floor. A bed a foot thick would last nearly a month, when it was thrown out into the compost heap. The sawdust requires a longer time for decomposition, but saves the liquid manure. Our present experiment, covering several months, is with forest leaves, principally hickory, maple, white ash, and elm. A bushel of dried leaves, kept under a shed for the purpose, is added to the bedding of each animal, and the saturated leaves are removed with the solid manure as fast as they accumulate. The leaves become very fine by the constant treading of the animals, and by the heat of their bodies, and the manure pile grows rapidly. It is but a little additional labor to the ordinary task of keeping animals clean in their stalls, to use some good absorbent, and enough of it, to save all the liquid manure. What the absorbent shall be is a question of minor importance. Convenience will generally determine this matter. No labor upon the farm pays better than to save the urine of all farm stock by means of absorbents. These are in great variety, and, in some form, are within the reach of every man that keeps cattle or runs a farm. Stop this leak, and lift your mortgage.

AN OPEN SHED FOR FEEDING.

A feeding-trough in a yard, which can be covered to keep out snow or rain, is a desirable thing, and many devices have been contrived for the purpose, most of which are too costly. We give herewith a method of constructing a covered feeding-trough, which may be made very cheaply of the rough materials to be had on every farm. A sufficient number of stout posts are set firmly in the ground, extending about ten feet above the surface. They should be about six feet apart and in a straight line, and a plate fastened to their tops. A pair

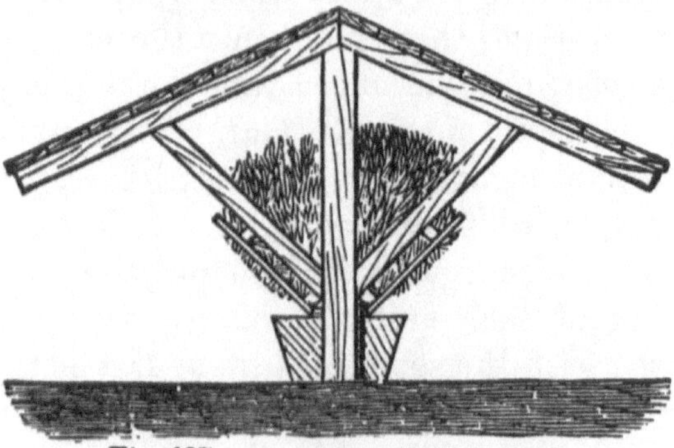

Fig. 127.—AN OPEN FEEDING-SHED.

of rafters supported by braces, as shown in figure 127, is fitted to each post. A light roof of laths is laid, and covered with bark, straw, corn-stalks, or coarse hay. Strips are fastened from one brace to another, and laths or split poles nailed to them, about six inches apart, to make a feed-rack. A feed-trough for grain or roots is built upon each side. For sheep, the shed and rack may be made only eight feet high at the peak, and the eaves four feet from the ground; giving better shelter.

A SHADE FOR HORSES' EYES.

The most frequent cause of weak eyes in horses is a badly-arranged stable. Foul gases irritate and inflame the tender membranes of the eye and head, and horses brought from dark stables into bright sunlight, or onto glittering snow, are dazzled and blinded. The existing weakness or irritation is intensified, and the poor animal suffers unsuspected torments. The remedy is to purify the stable and give it sufficient light, shaded by blinds, from before and behind the horse, or from both sides, avoiding a light from only the front, rear, or one side light. A shade for weak or inflamed eyes may be constructed by fastening wires to the bridle and covering it with oiled cloth in the manner represented in figure 128. Thus a soft, subdued light reaches the eyes, while the horse can still see the ground immediately before him. It will be a timely job to prepare such a shade for use before the snow of winter comes.

Fig. 128.—TO PROTECT THE EYES.

TEST ALL SEEDS—IMPORTANT.

No one can, by merely looking at them, positively tell whether any particular lots of field, garden, or flower seeds have or have not sufficient vitality of germ to start into vigorous growth. Yet it is a severe loss, often a disastrous one, to go through with all the labor and expense of preparation and planting or sowing, and find too late that the crop is lost because the seeds are defective. All this risk can be saved by a few minutes' time all told, in making a preliminary test, and it should be done before the seed is wanted, and in time to get other seed if necessary. Seeds may not have matured the germ; it may have been destroyed by heat or moisture; minute insects may have, unobserved, punctured or eaten out the vital part of a considerable percentage.

Select from the whole mass of the seed, one hundred, or fifty, or even ten seeds, that will be a fair sample of all. For larger seeds, as wheat, corn, oats, peas, etc., take a thin, tough sod, and scatter the counted seeds upon the earth side. Put upon the seeds another similar sod, earth side down. Set this double sod by the warm side of the house or other building, or of a tight fence, moistening it occasionally as needed. If very cold, cover, or remove to the kitchen or cellar at night. The upper sod can be lifted for observation when desirable. The swelling and starting of the seeds will in a few days, according to the kind, tell what percentage of them will grow—a box of earth will answer instead of sods, both for large and small seeds. Small seeds of vegetables or

Fig. 129.—HOME-MADE ROLLER.

flowers, and even larger ones, may be put into moist cotton, to be kept slightly moist and placed in the sun or in a light warm room. For small quantities of valuable flower seeds and the like, half a dozen will suffice for a trial test. With any seed, for field or garden, however good, it is always very desirable and useful to know exactly how many or few are defective, and thus be able to decide how much seed to use on an acre, or other plot.

A FIELD ROLLER.

A very good field roller may be easily made in winter, when timber is being cut. Use a butt-log of an oak tree, in the form shown in figure 129. The log need not be a very large one, because the frame, in which it is mounted, enables it to be loaded to any reasonable extent, and the driver may ride upon it, and thus add to the weight. A roller will be found very valuable in the spring when repeated frosts have raised the ground and thrown out the stones.

A PORTABLE SLOP BARREL.

A barrel mounted upon wheels, as shown in figure 130, will be found useful for many purposes about the farm, garden, or household. The barrel is supported upon a pair of wheels, the axles of which are fastened to

Fig. 130.—PORTABLE BARREL FOR SLOPS.

a frame connected with the barrel by means of straps bolted to the sides. The frame may be made of iron bent in the form shown in figure 131, or of crooked timber having a sufficient bend to permit the barrel to be tipped for emptying. A pair of handles are provided, as shown in the engraving. When not in use, the barrel rests upon the ground, and may be raised by bearing down upon the handles. The barrel may be made to rest in notched bearings upon the frame, so that by raising the handles, the wheels may be drawn away from the barrel, and the latter left in a convenient place until it needs removal. This contrivance will be useful for feed-

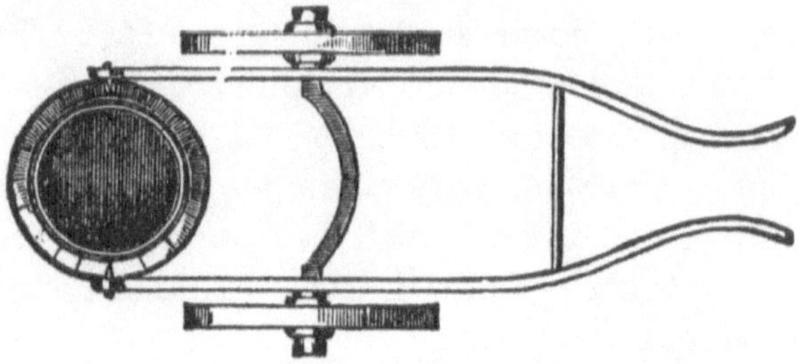

Fig. 131.—PLAN OF FRAME OF BARREL.

ing slops to pigs, or for removing the waste of the house to the barn-yard.

WHERE AND HOW TO APPLY FERTILIZERS.

It is often difficult to decide—for barn-yard or stable manures, or for any artificial fertilizer—whether to use it in the hill or broadcast it; and whether to apply it on the surface, or bury it deeply. Here is a hint or two. If not strong enough to injure the first tender roots, a little manure near at hand gives the plant a good send-off, like nourishing food to the young calf or other animal; the after-growth is much better if the young animal or plant is not dwarfed by imperfect and insufficient diet. Therefore, drilling innocuous hand fertilizers in with the seed is useful, as is putting some well-rotted manure or leached ashes into hills of corn, potatoes, indeed with all planted seeds. But there are good reasons for distributing most of the manures or fertilizers all through the soil, and as deeply as the plant roots can possibly penetrate. The growth and vigor of all plants or crops depend chiefly upon a good supply of strong roots that stretch out far, and thus gather food over the widest extent of soil. If a flourishing stalk of corn, grain or grass, be carefully washed, so as to leave all its roots or rootlets attached, there will be found a wonderful mass of hundreds and even thousands of roots to any plant, and they extend off a long distance, frequently several feet—the farther the better, to collect more food and moisture. Put some manure or fertilizer in place two feet away from a corn or potato hill, or from almost any plant, and a large mass of roots will go out in that direction. So, if we mix manures or fertilizers well through the whole soil, they attract these food-seeking roots to a greater distance; and they thus come in contact with more of the food already in the soil, and find more moisture in dry weather. A deeply-stirred soil, with manure at the bottom, develops water-pumping roots below the reach of any ordinary drouth, and the crops keep right on growing—all the more rapidly on account of the helpful sun's rays that would scorch a plant not reaching a deep reservoir of moisture.

A MILL FOR CRUSHING BONES.

To save the expense of a purchased bone-mill, one may be made as described below, which will crush them into a condition much more valuable for manure than the whole bones, if not quite as good as if finely ground. Make a circular mould of boards, six feet wide and two feet deep. Hoops of broad band-iron are fitted to the inside of the mould, and secured to it about one inch apart. The mould is then filled with a concrete of Portland cement, sand, and broken stone. Place in the concrete when filling binding pieces of flat bar-iron, to prevent the mass from cracking when in use. In the centre place squares of band-iron, as a lining for a shaft by which the crusher is turned. When the concrete is set and hardened, the frame may be taken apart; and, as in setting the concrete will expand somewhat, the iron bands around the mass will be found to have become a tight solid facing to the wheel. The wheel is then set up on edge, and a square shaft of yellow pine, six inches thick, is wedged into the central space. This shaft is fitted to an upright post by a loose band of iron and a swivel joint, so that the wheel may be made to revolve around it. Any other suitable connection may be used for this purpose. A hollow trough of broken stone and well rammed concrete is then laid in the track of the

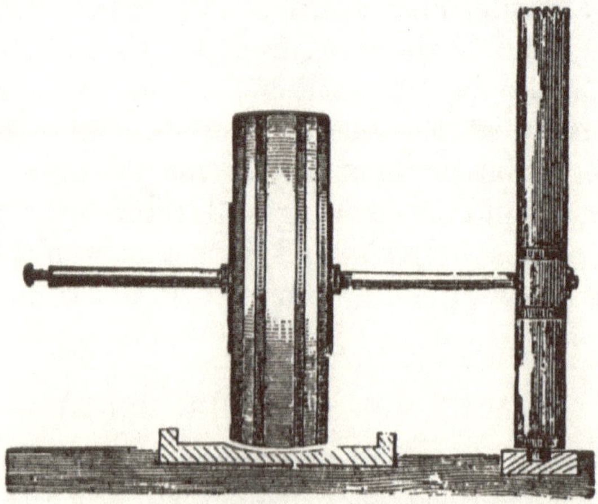

Fig. 132.—HOME-MADE BONE-MILL.

wheel as it revolves, and the crusher is complete and ready for a pair of horses to be attached to it, figure 132. A crusher of this kind may be put up at a country mill, or as a joint affair by a few farmers uniting their efforts, and thus utilizing a valuable fertilizing material, which is now wasted for want of means to render it available.

LIME AND LIMESTONE.

In the first place, limestone, marble, calc-spar, chalk (of rare occurrence in this country), marl, and oyster, and other shells, are all essentially the same in composition, however they may differ in texture, form, and other particulars. They are all different forms of the carbonate of lime; that is, they consist of the alkaline earth, lime, in combination with carbonic acid, and in the case of shells, with animal matter. As a general thing, we only know carbonic acid as a gas. It has a very weak hold of the lime, for if we drop a fragment of limestone into strong vinegar, the acetic acid of the vinegar will unite with the lime (forming acetate of lime), while the carbonic acid, being set free, will be seen to pass off in small bubbles. In this case we free the lime from its carbonic acid, by presenting to it a stronger acid, that of vinegar. But if instead of using another acid to displace the carbonic acid, we place limestone in any of its forms, in a strong fire, the carbonic acid will be driven off by the heat, and there will be left, simply lime. This is called quick lime, or caustic lime, and by chemists oxide of the metal calcium, or calcium oxide. Lime, then, is limestone without its carbonic acid. All the forms of limestone are very little soluble in water; lime itself is more soluble, though but slightly so, requiring at ordinary temperatures about seven hundred times its own weight of water, yet it gives a marked alkaline taste to water in which it is dissolved. Lime in this condition, as quick lime, or when combined with water, "slaked" as it is called, is much employed in agriculture. A small portion of lime is required by plants, but the chief use of lime, when applied to the soil, is to bring the vegetable matters contained in the soil into a condition in which they can be used as plant food. This application of lime as a fertilizer has long been followed by farmers, and in many cases with the most beneficial results. Within a year or so great claims have been made for ground limestone, especially by the makers of mills for grinding it; some of these have asserted that it was superior to burned lime, and superior to nearly all other fertilizers. The question which most interests farmers is, has limestone, however fine it may be, any value as a fertilizer? To this the answer would be both "yes" and "no." Upon a heavy clay soil the carbonate of lime, or limestone in any form, appears to have a beneficial effect; it makes such soils friable and open, so that water and air may penetrate them. While its action upon the vegetable matter in the soil is far less prompt and energetic than that of quick-lime, yet its presence, affording a base with which any acid that may be present in the soil may unite, is often beneficial. To extol ground limestone as "the great fertilizer of the age," to even claim that it is equal to lime itself, is a mistake. Both have their uses. It should be borne in mind by inquirers about the value of ground limestone, that many soils already contain more lime in this form than can ever be utilized, and need no addition.

A FARM WHEELBARROW.

The wheelbarrow is an indispensable vehicle on the farm and in the garden. Applied to hard uses it needs

Fig. 133.—FARM WHEELBARROW.

to be strong and durable. A barrow of the ordinary kind, used on farms, soon becomes weak in the joints and falls to pieces. The movable sides are inconvenient, and the shape necessarily adopted when movable sides are used greatly weakens the structure. It will be noticed at first sight that the wheelbarrow, shown in figure 133, is most strongly supported and braced, that the box, instead of weakening it, greatly strengthens it, and that it is stout and substantial. It is put together at every part by strong bolts, and can be taken apart to pack for transportation, if desired, and a broken part readily replaced.

TO PREVENT THE BALLING OF HORSES.

When the snow upon the roads is cohesive and packs firmly, it collects upon the feet of horses, forming a hard, projecting mass, in a manner known as "balling." This often occurs to such an extent as to impede the motion of the horse, while it causes the animal great discomfort, and is sometimes dangerous to the rider or driver. The trouble may be prevented very easily by the use of gutta-percha. For this purpose the gutta-percha should be crude, *i.e.*, not mixed with anything or manufactured in any manner, but just as imported. Its application depends upon the property which the gum has of softening and becoming plastic by heat, and hardening again when cold. To apply it, place the gutta-percha in hot water until it becomes soft, and having well cleansed the foot, removing whatever has accumulated between the shoe and hoof, take a piece of the softened gum and press it against the shoe and foot in such a manner as to fill the angle between the shoe and the hoof, taking care to force it into the crack between the two. Thus filling the crevices, and the space next the shoe, where the snow most firmly adheres, the ball of snow has nothing to hold it, and it either does not form, or drops out as soon as it is gathered. When the gutta-percha is applied, and well smoothed off with the wet fingers, it may be hardened at once, to prevent the horse from getting it out of place by stamping, by the application of snow or ice, or more slowly by a wet sponge or cloth. When it is desired to remove the gum, the application of hot water by means of a sponge or cloth will so soften it that it may be taken off. As the softening and hardening may be repeated indefinitely, the same material will last for years. For a horse of medium size, a quarter of a pound is sufficient for all the feet.

TO PREVENT CATTLE THROWING FENCES.

To prevent a cow from throwing fences or hooking other cows, make a wooden strip two and a half inches wide and three-quarters of an inch thick, and attach it to the horns by screws; to this is fastened, by a small bolt, a strip of hardwood, three inches wide, half an inch thick, and of a length sufficient to reach downward within an inch of the face, and within two or three inches of the nostrils. In the lower end of this strip are previously driven several sharp nails, which project about one-quarter of an inch. The arrangement is shown in figure 134; the strip, when properly attached, allows the animal to eat and drink with all ease, but when an attempt is made to hook or to throw a fence, the sharpened nails soon cause an abrupt cessation of that kind of mischief.

Fig. 134.—CATTLE CHECK.

FEED BOXES.

In figure 135 a box is shown firmly attached to two posts. It has a hinged cover, *p*, that folds over, and may be fastened down by inserting a wooden pin in the

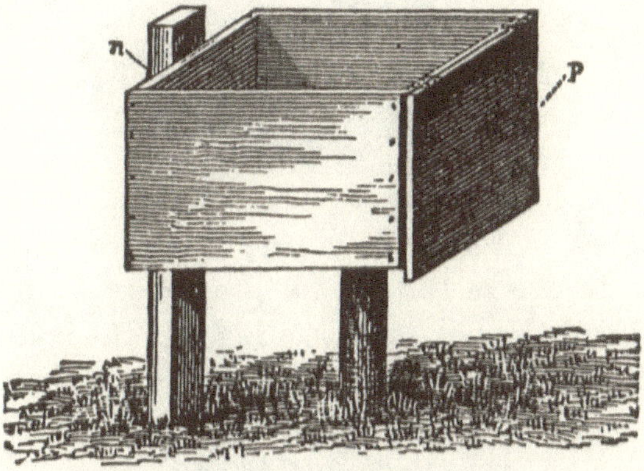

Fig. 135.—COVERED FEED BOX.

top of the post near *n*. The one given in figure 136 may be placed under shelter, along the side of a building or fence. One side of the top is hinged to the fence

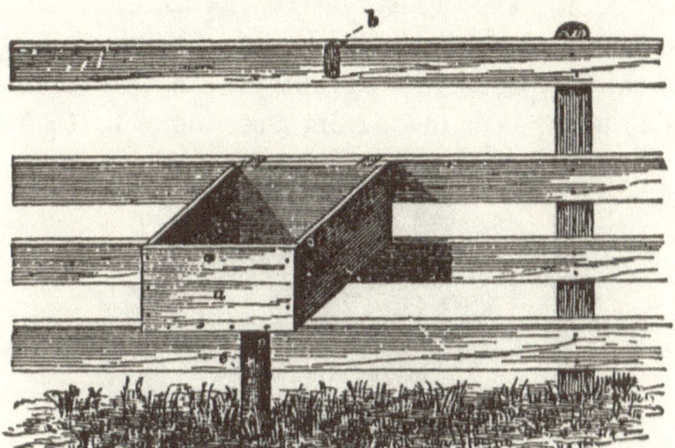

Fig. 136.—HINGED FEED BOX.

or building, the bottom resting upon a stake, *e*. When not in use, the box may be folded up, the end of the strap, *b*, hooking over the pin, *a*, at the side of the box

A good portable box, to be placed upon the ground, is shown in figure 137. It is simply a common box, with a strip of board, *h*, nailed on one side and projecting about

Fig. 137.—PORTABLE FEED BOX.

eight inches. When not in use, it is turned bottom up, as shown in figure 138. The projecting strip prevents three sides of the box from settling into the mud or snow. The strip is also a very good handle by which to carry it.

Fig. 138.—FEED BOX INVERTED.

Those who now use portable boxes will find the attaching of this strip a decided advantage. A very serviceable portable feed box is made from a section of half a hollow

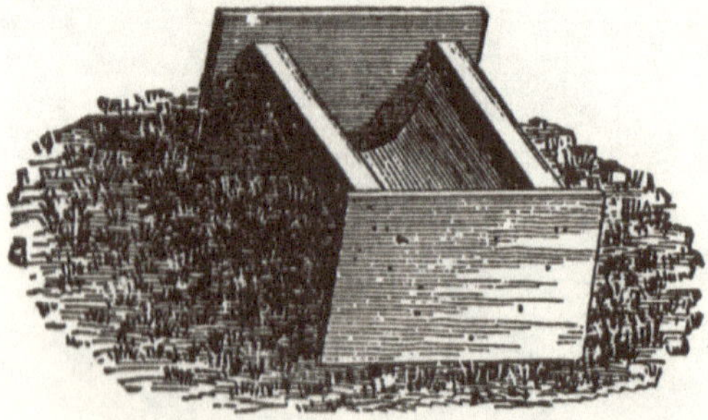

Fig. 139.—BOX FROM HOLLOW LOG.

log, with ends nailed on, as shown in figure 139. By letting the ends project above the sides four or five inches, it may be turned over when not in use, and easily turned back by grasping the sides without the hand coming in contact with earth or snow. All feed boxes and racks should be placed under shelter during summer, or when not in use.

A CATTLE TIE.

Judging from the numerous stanchions and arrangements for fastening cattle in stalls, illustrated from time to time in the public prints, the perfect cattle-fastening has not yet been invented. We do not claim perfection for the arrangement given in figure 140, but it will be difficult to devise a cheaper one, and we doubt if any better or more satisfactory one is in use. The fastening consists of a three-fourth inch rope, which is run through the partitions of the stalls, one long rope being used for the tier of stalls, although short pieces may be employed if desired. This rope is knotted on either side

Fig. 140.—CATTLE TIE.

of each partition, and a good swivel snap for use with a rope, is tied in the rope in front of the centre of each stall. The rope should pass over, very nearly, the front of the manger—from the side of the cattle—and for cattle of ordinary hight, it ought to be about two feet from the floor. When put in, the rope should be drawn up tightly, as it will soon acquire considerable and sufficient slack from the constant strain from the animals. With this arrangement each cow must be provided with a strap or rope about the neck, the rope or strap being supplied with a free-moving iron ring. When the animal is put in the stalls the snap is fastened in the ring, and if the snap is a good one—none but the best swivel snaps should be used—an animal will rarely get free from it. This fastening, it will be noticed, admits of considerable fore and aft motion, and but slight lateral movement. The cost of this arrangement it is difficult to state accurately, it is so small. The rope for each stall will cost less than five cents; the snaps will cost ten cents when bought by the dozen, and the time of putting these fittings in each stall is less than fifteen minutes. The rope will wear two years at least.

A BEEF RAISER.

Two posts are set about fifteen feet high. A deep mortise is cut in the top of each to receive the roller, which is grooved at the points of turning. One end of the roller extends beyond the post, and through this end three two-inch holes are bored. Three light poles are put through these holes, and their ends connected by a light rope. In raising the beef the middle of a stout rope is thrown over the roller; the ends are drawn through the loop, and after the beef is fastened to the loose ends the roller is turned against the loop by means of the "sweep," or lever arms, figure 141. A heavy beef can be easily raised, and may be fastened at any

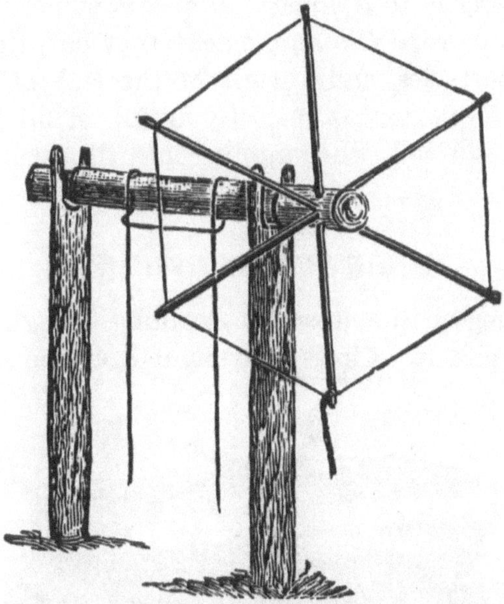

Fig. 141.—A BEEF RAISER.

hight desired, by tying the end of one of the levers to the post with a short rope.

A CEDAR STEM SOIL-STIRRER.

A convenient and quickly-made implement for stirring and mixing manure and fertilizers with the soil, may be

Fig. 142.—A STIRRER MADE OF A CEDAR STEM.

made as follows: A cedar stem is cut about eight feet long, and the branches cut off several inches from the stem, leaving long spurs on all sides for its whole length, as shown in figure 142. A horse is hitched by a chain to the butt end, and the driver guides the implement by a rope fastened to the rear end of the stem. By means of the guide-rope the implement may be lifted over or around obstacles, and turned at the end of the field. Such an implement is specially useful in mixing fertilizers with the soil, when applied in drills for hoed crops.

A HINT FOR PIG KILLING.

Lay a log chain across the scalding trough, and put the pig upon it. Cross the chain over the animal, as

Fig. 143.—SCALDING A PIG.

shown in figure 143. A man at each end of the chain can easily turn the pig in the scald, or work it to and fro as desired.

MENDING BROKEN TOOLS.

Farming tools, such as shovels, rakes, forks, etc., that are much used, will often, through carelessness or accident, become broken, and, with most men, that means to be thrown one side, as utterly useless. By exercising a little ingenuity, they could in a short time be fitted up to do service for several years. The head of hand-rakes often becomes broken at the point where the handle enters, and not unfrequently the handle itself is broken off where it enters the head. In either case the break is easily made good by attaching a small piece of wood to

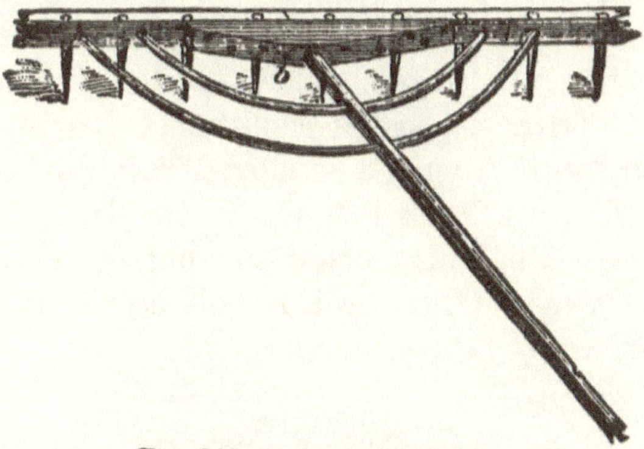

Fig. 144.—A MENDED RAKE.

the head, by small nails or screws, as shown in figure 144. Should the head be broken where one of the bows

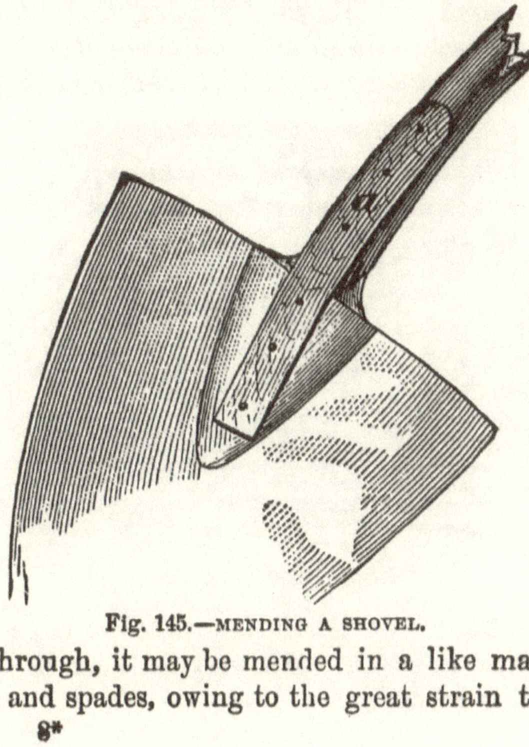

Fig. 145.—MENDING A SHOVEL.

passes through, it may be mended in a like manner, *b*. Shovels and spades, owing to the great strain to which they are often subjected, especially by carelessly prying with them, crow-bar fashion, are frequently broken, and usually at the point where the wood enters the blade. This break, bad as it is, should not consign the broken parts to the rubbish pile, especially if the blade and the handle be otherwise in fair condition. Remove the iron straps or ferule from the handle; firmly rivet a strip of iron, *a*, figure 145, on top of the handle, and a similar one underneath, to the blade and handle, as shown in the engraving. Other broken tools may be made to do good service by proper mending.

A LARGE FEED-RACK.

The width of the rack is seven feet, but it can be any length desired; hight, ten feet; hight of manger, two and a half feet; width, one and one-half foot. Cattle can eat from both sides. The advantage of such a rack,

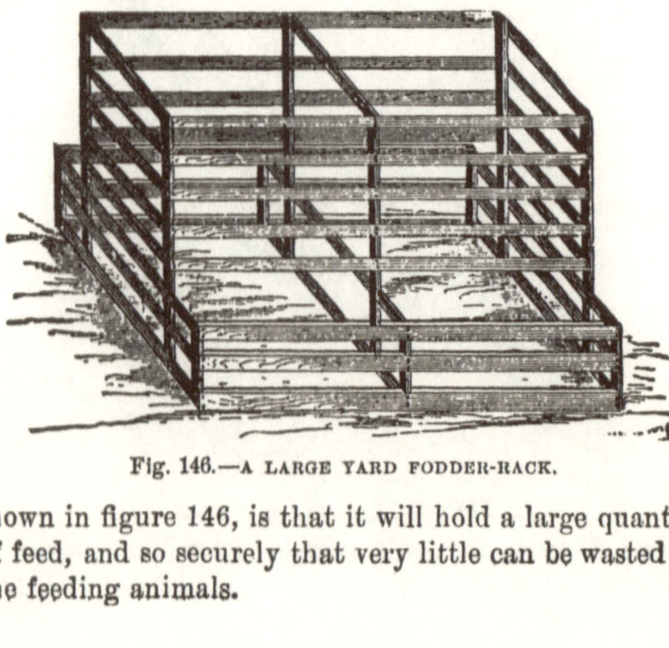

Fig. 146.—A LARGE YARD FODDER-RACK.

shown in figure 146, is that it will hold a large quantity of feed, and so securely that very little can be wasted by the feeding animals.

BARN DOOR FASTENING.

One of the best barns in the country has its large double doors fastened by a bar of iron, about six feet long, which is bolted to one of the doors at its middle point. The ends of the bar are notched, one upon the upper and the other on the under side, to fit over sockets or "hooks" that are bolted to the doors. One hook

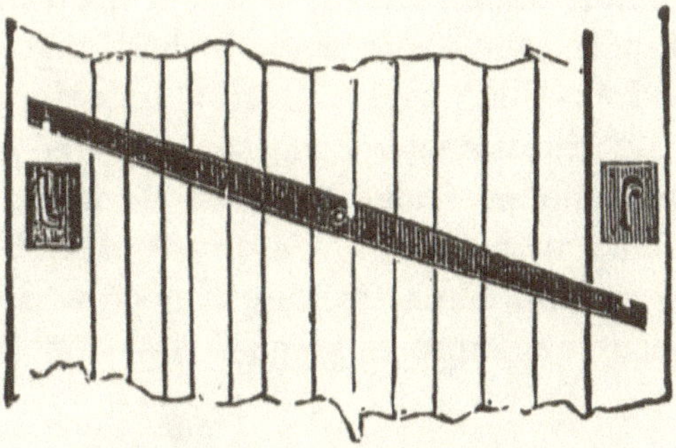

Fig. 147.—IRON BAR DOOR FASTENING.

bends upward, and the other downward, and the bar moves in the arc of a circle when the door is being unfastened or bolted. The construction of this door fastening is shown in figure 147. A wooden bar may replace the iron one, and may be of a size and length sufficient

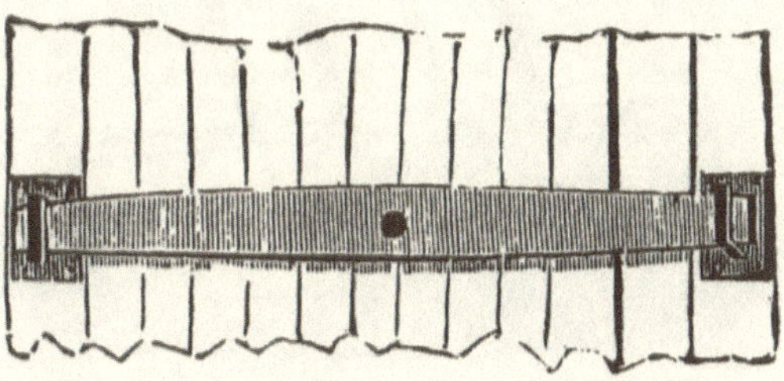

Fig. 148.—WOODEN BAR DOOR FASTENING.

to make the fastening secure. A wooden bar is shown in figure 148. Such a method of fastening could be used for a single door, provided it needs to be opened and closed only from the inside. By putting a pin in the bar near the end that passes by the door-post, so that it will reach through a slot in the door, such a "latch" might be used for any door.

A "FORK" STABLE SCRAPER.

A very handy stable scraper is made of an inch board, five inches wide, and about eight inches longer than the width of a four-tined fork. Bore a hole for each tine a quarter inch in diameter from the edge of the board to about two inches from the opposite edge, the holes passing out upon the side. The lower part of the board is bevelled behind, thus forming a good scraping edge. After the coarse manure is pitched up, the fork is in-

Fig. 149.—A "FORK" BARN SCRAPER.

serted in the holes of the board, and a scraper is at once ready for use, figure 149. To store it, nail a cleat on the floor two inches from the wall, and secure the scraper behind this cleat; place one foot upon the board and withdraw the fork. Notches may be cut in the edge of the board opposite each hole, to assist in placing the tines.

A METHOD OF CURING HAY.

A method of curing hay which has been used for several years with entire satisfaction consists in taking

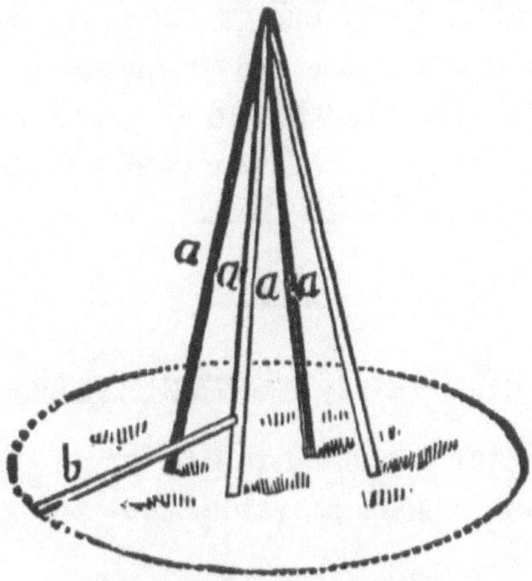

Fig. 150.—THE FRAME.

four slender stakes six feet long, *a, a, a, a* (figure 150),

Fig. 151.—THE SMALL STACK.

fastened together at the upper ends with a loose joint similar to that of an ordinary tripod. One end of the fifth stake, *b*, rests on one of the four legs about a foot from the ground, the other end resting on the ground. The hay is stacked around this frame nearly to the top of the stakes, after which the stake, *b*, is withdrawn, and then the four upright stakes are removed. This is done by two men with hay forks, who raise them directly upwards. As soon as the legs are lifted from the ground the pressure of the hay brings them together, and they can be removed with ease, leaving a small stack of hay, as shown in figure 151, with an air passage running from the bottom upwards through the centre of the small stack, as indicated by the dotted lines.

GRANARY CONVENIENCES.

The better plan for constructing grain bins is to have the upper front boards movable, that the contents may

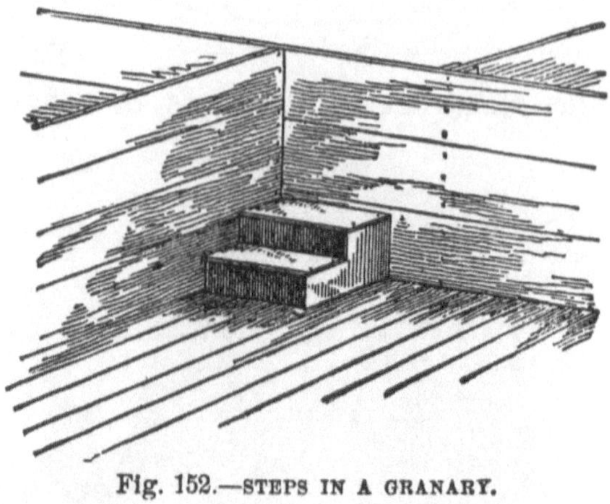

Fig. 152.—STEPS IN A GRANARY.

be more readily reached as they lessen. But as there are tens of thousands of granaries where the front bin boards are firmly nailed, a portable step, like that shown in figure 152, is almost a necessity. It should have two steps of nine inches each, and be one foot wide, and two feet long on top. It is light and is easily moved about the granary.

Every owner of a farm needs a few extra sieves, which, when not in use, are usually thrown in some corner, or

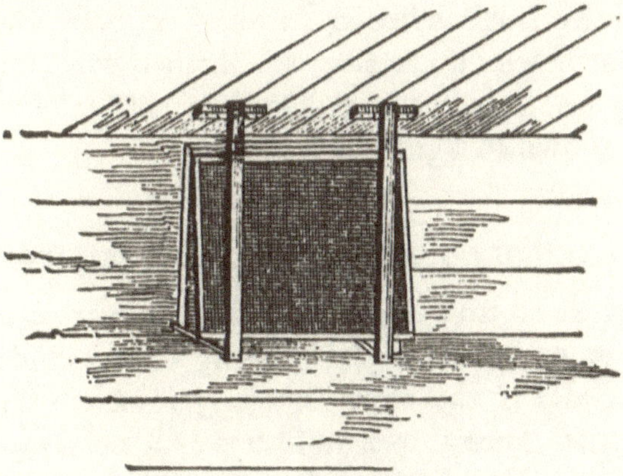

Fig. 153.—A SIEVE RACK.

laid on a box or barrel to be knocked about and often injured by this rough handling, besides being frequently in the way. A little rack, which may be readily made

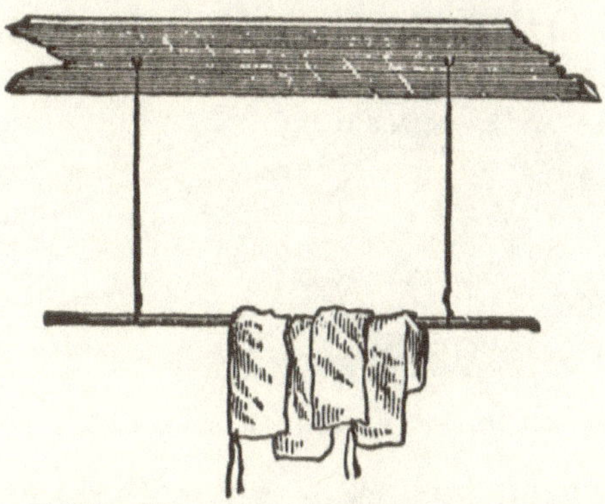

Fig. 154.—A GRAIN BAG HOLDER.

above one of the bins in the granary, as shown in figure 153, is convenient to put sieves out of the way, and keep them from injury.

Grain bags are too expensive and valuable to be scattered about the buildings. A simple mode of securing them is shown, which is at once cheap and safe. In the ceiling over the bins, staples are driven about four feet apart, to which are attached pieces of wire two feet in length. To these wires is fastened a pole five feet in length, over which the bags are thrown when not in use, and they are then out of reach of mice from the bins and wall, as shown in figure 154.

A NON-SLIPPING CHAIN FOR BOULDERS.

One great trouble in hauling boulders or large stones with team and chain is the liability of the chain to slip off, especially if the stone is nearly round. By the use of the contrivance shown in figure 155, nearly all of this trouble is avoided. It consists in passing two log chains around the stone and connecting them a few inches above the ground by a short chain or even a piece of rope or wire. Connect the chains in a similar manner near the top of the stone. The ends of the draught chains are attached to the whipple-trees in any way desired. In

Fig. 155.—METHOD OF FASTENING CHAINS ON A BOULDER.

hauling down an incline, or where the ground is very rough, it will be best to wrap each chain clear around the stone, connecting with whipple-trees by a single chain, thereby preventing a possibility of the chains becoming detached or misplaced in any way.

A PITCHFORK HOLDER.

Having occasion to go into the barn one night, we received a very bad wound from a pitchfork which had fallen from its standing position. This led us to construct a holder, shown in the engravings. The fork-holder is made of an inch board, of a semicircular shape, with five holes large enough to admit a fork handle, bored near the curved side. This board is nailed to a standing post in the barn. A strap or curved bolt is placed some distance below to hold the handles in

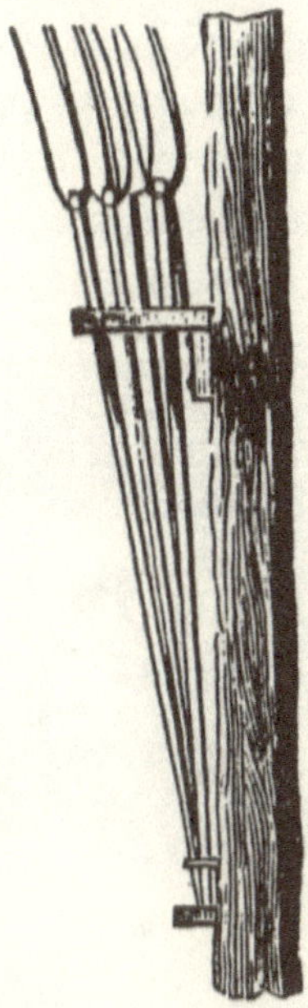

Fig. 156.—FRONT VIEW.

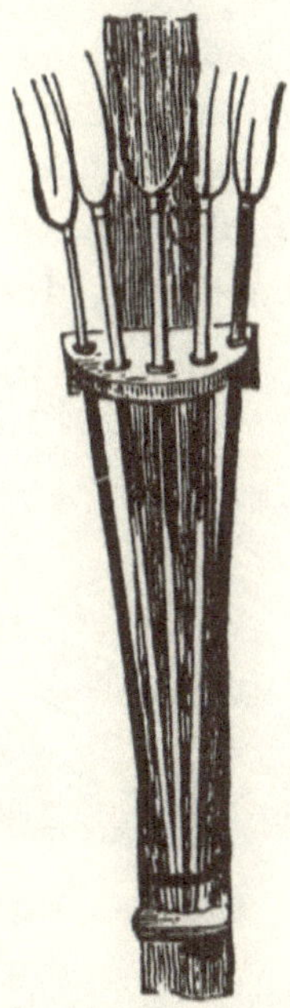

Fig. 157.—SIDE VIEW.

place, as they rest on a bottom board fixed for the purpose. Figure 156 shows the front view of the holder; figure 157 gives the side view.

A CONVENIENT HOG LOADER.

Figure 158 shows the "loader" attached to a wagon, with the rack. The bed-piece consists of two pine boards, six inches wide by nine feet long. These are fastened together by three cross-pieces of the same material, of proper length, so that the "bed" will just fit in between the sides of the wagon-box. A floor is laid on these cross-pieces, on which short strips of lath are nailed, to prevent hogs from slipping. At one end the sides are notched to fit on the bottom of the wagon-box. There are two staples on each side by which the sides are fastened on. The "rack" is made like an ordinary top-box, with the exception that each side is composed of three narrow boards about four inches apart, and nailed to three cleats (the two end cleats to be on the inside, and the middle one on the outside of the rack), and projecting down

Fig. 158.—RACK FOR LOADING HOGS.

the side of the wagon-box. End-boards are made and fastened in like those of an ordinary wagon-box. For unloading the hogs nothing but the bed-piece need be used, which, being light, may be easily thrown on and taken with the wagon.

A HOME-MADE ROLLER.

Take a log six or eight feet long, eighteen or twenty inches in diameter, and put pins in each end for journals, either of wood one and a half inch, or iron one inch. Make a frame of two by four scantlings, or flat rails three or four feet long to suit the size of the roller. Bore holes for journals a little back of centre, and also inch-holes two inches from the back end of scantlings. Fasten these ends together with a chain or rope tight enough to keep the scantlings square with the ends of

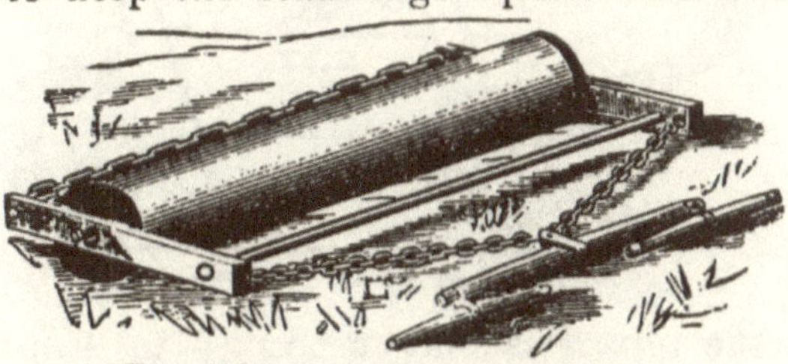

Fig. 159.—A HOME-MADE ROLLER.

the log, figure 159. Fasten the front ends together with a stiff pole or rail, and put a heavy chain across the front, with one end around each front corner. Attach the double-tree at the middle of this chain. The draft chain and the pole will keep the front ends of the frame in position, and the chain behind will prevent the rear ends from spreading. When the roller goes faster than the team, the draft chain will slacken, and the front of the frame will drop and prevent the roller from striking the team. A roller is such a valuable implement that there should be one in use on every farm. Even a rough home-made roller is better than none, whether it is used to break up clods, or to compact the soil after sowing.

A LAND SCRAPER.

In districts where land needs draining, scrapers must be used. A very good one is shown in figure 160. It has one advantage over most scrapers: the team can stay on the bank while the scraper is thrown into the ditch. When the ditch is a large one, fourteen feet or more

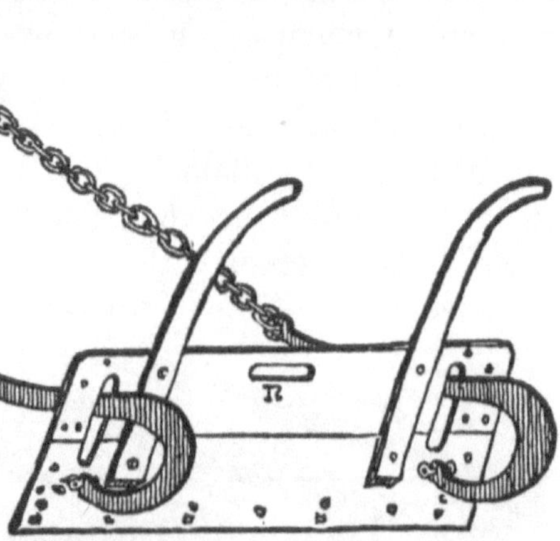

Fig. 160.—A LAND SCRAPER.

wide at the top, it is only necessary to lengthen the chain. The scraper consists of two boards, twelve inches wide and three feet long, fastened firmly together by two strong iron plates, figure 161, *p*, *p*, bolts, and rod-iron nails. The scraper-edge is made of an old cross-cut saw,

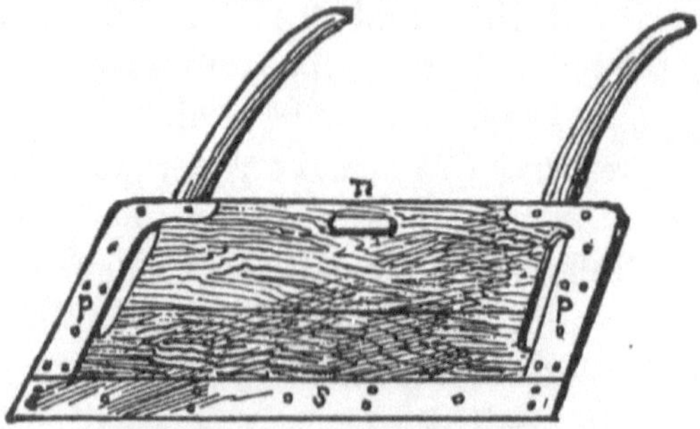

Fig. 161.—FRONT OF SCRAPER.

fastened on with rod-iron nails. Two notches are cut at *p*, *p*, for the hooks to pass through, also one at *n*, for a holder for lifting the scraper when necessary. To make the scraper work perfectly, the rod or hook should have the right bend, as shown at *a*, figure 162,

The hook is fastened to the scraper by two bolts, *b*, *b*,

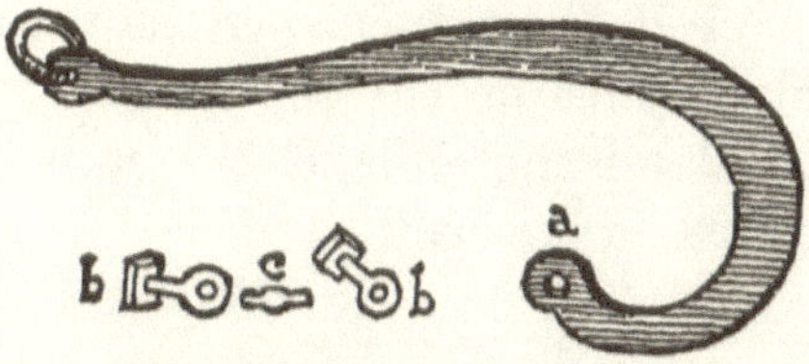

Fig. 162.—THE HOOK-ROD.

figure 162, and small pins, *c*, when the land scraper is complete.

A HOME-MADE BAG-HOLDER.

This bag-holder is one of the most useful articles a man can have in his barn. It consists of a post, *a*, two by four inches, and five feet long, with six one-half inch holes near the upper end, as shown in figure 163. The bar, *b*, passes through a mortise and over the pin nearest

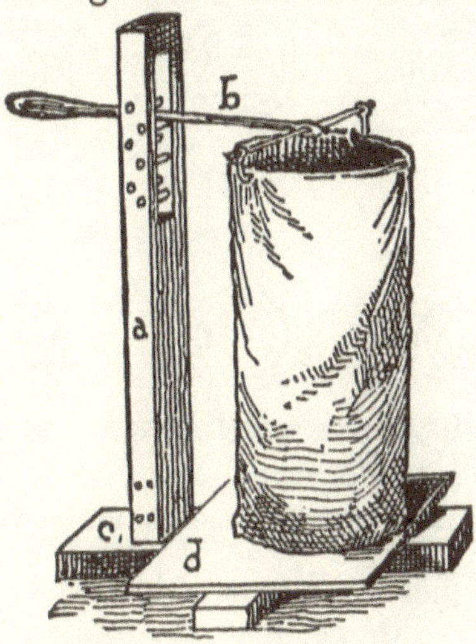

Fig. 163.—A HANDY BAG-HOLDER.

the bag, and under the other pin. This bar can be moved up or down, to suit the length of the bag. The post, *a*, sets in a bed-piece, *c*, two by three inches and two feet long. A board, *d*, eighteen inches square, fastened upon the bed-piece, furnishes the necessary rest for the bag. The mouth of the bag is held open by means of hooks placed on the ends of the cross-bar, with another beneath the main bar.

A SAFETY EGG-CARRIER.

In figure 164, *a* represents the bottom-board of the spring-box, near the edges of which are fastened six wire-coil springs or bed-springs. At *b* is represented a hole made in the board to receive the lower end of the spring, about half an inch of which is bent down for that purpose. Small staples are driven into the board to hold

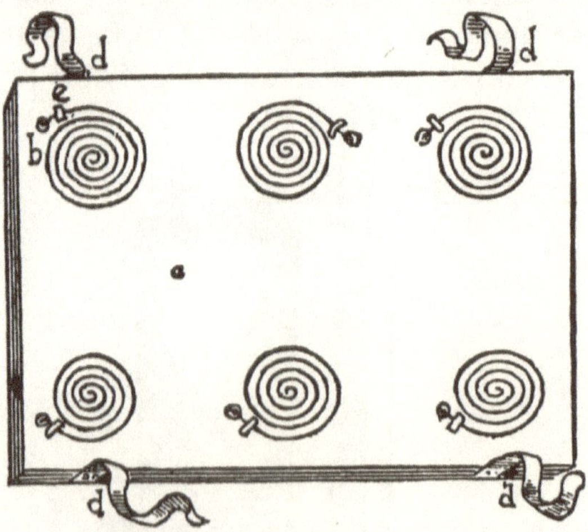

Fig. 164.—BOTTOM-BOARD OF SPRING-BOX.

the springs in place. Scraps of leather or tin might be tacked or screwed down, instead of using staples; *d, d,* are leather straps, an inch or more wide, and long enough to reach from the bottom-board, where each one is fastened by two screws, to the egg-box, after being placed on the springs. Figure 165 represents the side and end boards, which, when placed over the bottom-board holding the springs, forms the spring-box ; screws fasten the side and end-boards to the bottom-board of the spring-box, pieces of tin being nailed around the corners of the box, to give it proper strength, the nails being clinched on the inside.

After securing the springs and straps to the bottom board, the egg-box should be placed on the springs. and the points of the springs placed in holes previously made in the bottom of the egg-box to receive them. Now put a sufficient weight in the egg-box to settle it down firmly on the springs, and fasten the upper ends of the straps to the box, being careful to have the box

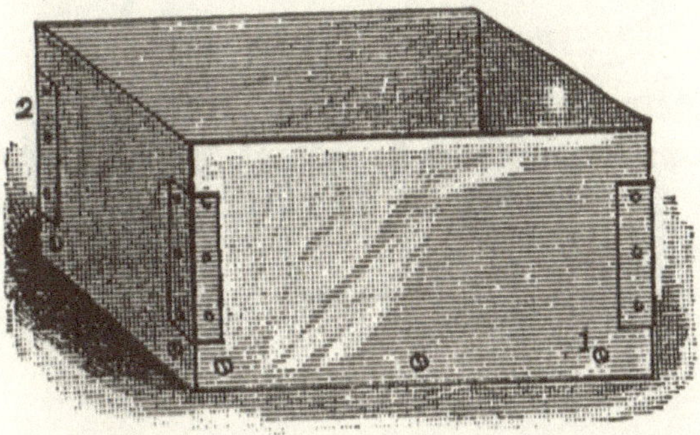

Fig. 165.—FRAME FOR HOLDING EGG-BOX.

set level. Having done this, take the part, figure 165, and put it down over the egg-box to its place, and make it fast to the bottom-board of the spring-box with heavy screws. The object of the bottom, figure 165, is to keep the springs from being strained to one side in going over rough ground. It should be made one-quarter inch or so larger than the egg-box, that the latter may have the benefit of the springs. Our former custom was to put a feeding of hay in the wagon-box, about midway from one end to the other, place the egg-box on the hay, and drive carefully over the rough places. But more or less eggs would be broken, the best we could do, whether they were packed in bran or put in paper "boxes" or

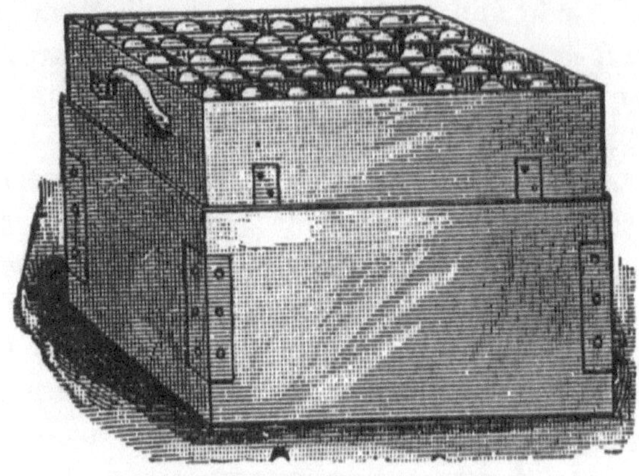

Fig. 166.—EGG-BOX COMPLETE.

cases. After setting the box on springs as described, place it on the bottom boards of the wagon-box, with one end directly over the forward axle of the wagon.

A BUSH-ROLLER.

Figure 167 shows a device which has been made for clearing sage-bush land. It consists of a roller, eight feet long and two and a half feet in diameter, coupled by a short tongue—six feet is long enough—to the forward wheels of a wagon. A standard at each end of the roller-frame supports a cross-piece just clear of the roller. Upon this cross-piece, about four feet apart, and extending to the bolster of the wagon, are bolted two pieces of one and a quarter by six-inch spruce boards. A board is placed across the centre for a seat, thus making a complete and easy-inclining "buckboard." With a span of good horses and this machine, figure 167, one can roll from eight to ten acres of sage-bush in a day; and it is so easily killed, that in two or

Fig. 167.—A HOME-MADE BUSH-ROLLER.

three weeks after such treatment, it will burn off like a prairie on fire.

BROOD-SOW PENS.

Figures 168 and 169 represent a convenient arrangement for brood sows. The pens are not equal to the

Fig. 168.—PLAN OF CHEAP PIG-PEN.

costly piggeries of wealthy breeders, but they answer a good purpose in a new country, where farmers are obliged to get along cheaply. Many who have built expensive houses say these pens answer a better purpose. First, there is a tightly-boarded pen (except in front), sixteen feet by twelve feet. This is divided into four nests, twelve by four feet. A shed roof extends eight feet from the rear. The tops of the nests are covered with boards, and the space between this room and the roof is filled with straw, making it wind-tight, except in front. When young pigs are expected during the cold weather of winter, hang a gunny sack in front of the nest. The doors, figure 169, are the most convenient. The board door is slipped in from the top, between pairs of cross-boards in the pig-pen.

Fig. 169.—DOOR TO PEN.

A RABBIT TRAP.

Rabbits are a great nuisance both in the garden and orchard, and a trap of the following kind put in a black-

Fig. 170.—A GOOD RABBIT TRAP.

berry patch, or some place where they like to hide, will thin them out wonderfully. A common salt barrel, with a notch sawed out at the top, is set in the ground level with the top. There is an entrance box, four feet long, with side pieces seven inches wide—top and bottom four and a half or five inches. The bottom board is cut in two at *b*, and is somewhat narrower than in front, that it may tilt easily on a pivot at *c*. A small washer should be placed on each side of the trap at *c*, that it may not bind in tilting. The distance from *b* to *c* should be somewhat longer than from *c* to *d*, that the board will fall back in place after being tipped. No bait is required, because a rabbit (hare) is always looking for a place of security. The bottom of the box should be even with the top of the ground at the entrance to the top of the barrel. The barrel should be covered closely with a board, as shown in figure 170. Remove the rabbits from the trap as fast as they are caught.

WOODEN STABLE FLOOR.

Elm makes an excellent and durable stable floor; the fibre of the wood is tough and yielding. The planks should be secured in position by wooden pins, as they are constantly liable to warp. Any of the soft oaks make a good floor; the hard, tough varieties are unyielding, and, until they have been in use several months, horses are liable to slip and injure themselves in getting up. Both pine and hemlock make good floors, being soft and yielding, but they are not as durable as many other woods. Planks for a stable floor should be two and a half inches in thickness, and not laid until quite thoroughly seasoned, and then always put down lengthwise of the stall, and upon another floor laid crosswise, as shown at *b*, *b*, *b*, figure 171. The planks of this floor, or cross floor, should be laid one inch apart, that they may the more readily dry off, and offer a better ventilation to the floor above. Unless the upper floor is of material liable to warp, it should not be nailed or pinned, but made as close-fitting as possible. It is not profitable or necessary to have the stall planks more than eleven and a half feet in length, or extend farther back than the stall partition, as shown at *e, e*. This plan leaves a

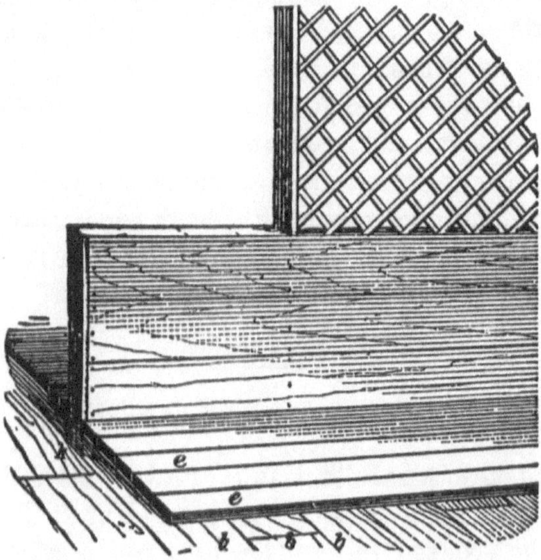

Fig. 171.—MANNER OF LAYING A STABLE FLOOR.

wide smooth walk behind the stalls at *k*, so necessary for ease and rapidity in cleaning the manure from the stable.

Some horse-keepers prefer a slatted floor, similar to that shown in figure 172. Material of the proper length, four inches wide and two inches thick, is set upon edge, as at *h*, with a strip three-quarters of an inch thick and one and a half inch wide placed between the slats, the whole made to fit the stall as closely as possible. By this method it is quite impossible for horses to become so dirty as when lying upon a common plank floor, as the space between the slats form a most admirable channel

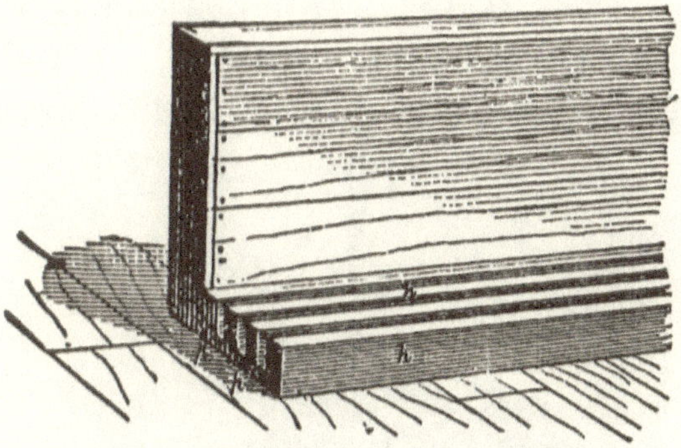

Fig. 172.—A SLATTED STABLE FLOOR.

for carrying off the urine. A few days' constant use somewhat clogs the passages, but they are readily opened by using a home-made cleaner, like that shown in figure 173. Stable floors should have at least one inch descent

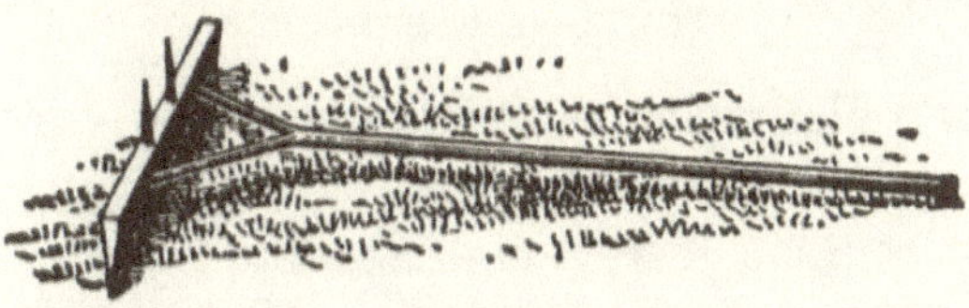

Fig. 173.—A CLEANER FOR A SLATTED FLOOR.

in ten feet, and many make the descent three and even four inches in the same distance, but this is unnecessary. All stabled animals should stand upon floors as nearly level as is consistent with cleanliness.

A RAIL HOLDER OR "GRIP."

Drive two posts, *b*, *b*, figure 174, three feet long, firmly in the ground, four feet apart, between two parallel logs, *a*, *a*. A third post or "jaw," *c*, somewhat shorter, is mortised in a block placed between the logs, and out of line with, or to one side of the posts, *b, b,* so as to hold a rail, *d,* between the three. A lever, *e,* eight feet long, and heavy at the outer end, is mortised into another block, which is placed on the side of *c, b,* both blocks bearing against the posts. The lever and jaw are con-

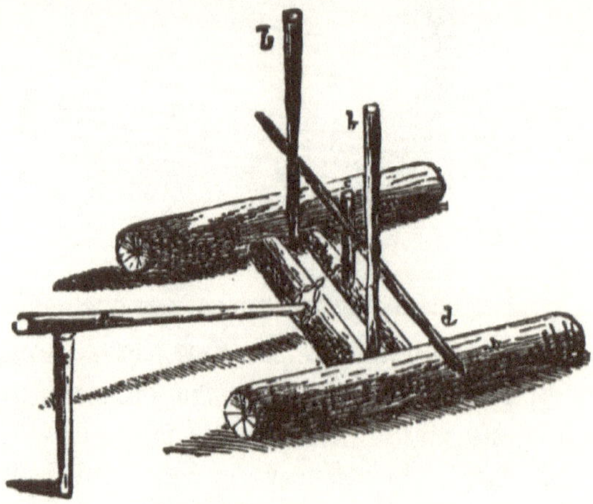

Fig. 174.—A RAIL HOLDER.

nected by a chain passing around the lever, over its block and through a hole in the jaw. An iron pin through a link couples them just enough apart to hold a rail firmly when the lever is on the ground. To remove the rail, raise the lever and rest it upon the small post, *f,* at the farther end, which slackens the chain.

A CHEAP AND DURABLE GRINDSTONE-BOX AND HANGERS.

A good grindstone, well hung, is one of the most valuable aids about the farm or workshop. Those who cannot afford to buy a very neat and handy grindstone frame of the hardware dealers, will find a frame and hangers shown in figure 175, that for convenience, cheapness, and durability is hard to excel. The frame consists of a well-seasoned "trough" of pine or other wood, fourteen inches square (or even one foot square), and from two and a half to three and a half feet in length, to which legs are nailed at *b*, *b*, four inches wide, an inch and a half thick, and bevelled at the top. Supports or hangers, *h*, *h*, are nailed firmly to the side, as indicated; they should be hard wood, and of a size to correspond with dimensions and weight of stone. The shaft may be of iron or wood; fit a piece of sheet lead, or piece of lead pipe, properly flattened out, in the top of each hanger; this will cause the shaft to turn easily, and prevent all squeaking for want of oil. The wooden plug at *r*, is for drawing off the water after each using of the stone, and should in no case be neglected. If one side of the stone is left standing in water, it softens, and

Fig. 175.—A BOX FOR A GRINDSTONE.

the surface will soon wear quite uneven. After the box is completed, give it one heavy coat of boiled oil; then in a few days apply a coat of lead and oil, and with even common care, it will last a lifetime. When the stone becomes worn, it is kept down to the water by simply deepening the groove in the top of the hangers. Always buy a long shaft for a grindstone, for in this age of reapers and mowers, the cutting apparatus of which must be ground, a long shaft for a grindstone is almost a necessity, or truly a great convenience. If the grindstone is to stand out-doors, always cover it with a closely fitting wooden box when it is not in use.

A "LADDER" FOR LOADING CORN.

Take a plank two inches thick, ten inches wide, and eight feet long. Nail upon one side of it cleats, of one-inch by two-inch stuff, at easy stepping distances apart. At the upper end nail upon the underside of the plank a cleat projecting four inches upon either side, to which

Fig. 176.—A "LADDER" FOR LOADING CORN.

attach small ropes or chains, and suspend the ladder from the hind end of the rack, so that one end of the plank will rest upon the ground. This makes a very convenient step-ladder, up which a man can carry a large armful of fodder, and thus load his wagon to its full capacity with greater ease than two men could load it from the ground. I find it of great convenience to me when hauling corn fodder alone. The "Ladder" is shown in figure 176.

PROTECTING OUTLET OF DRAINS.

One of the greatest annoyances in underdraining is the trouble arising from the outlet becoming choked or filled up by the trampling of animals, the action of frost, or even of water in times of freshets. This trouble

Fig. 177.—END OF TILE DRAIN.

is quite successfully overcome by the arrangement as shown in figure 177; it consists of a plank, ten or twelve inches in width, and five or six feet in length, with a notch cut in one side, near the centre. This plank is set upon

Fig. 178.—LOGS AT END OF DRAIN.

edge at the outlet of the drain, with the notch directly over the end of the tile, and is held in position by several stakes on the outside, with earth or stone thrown against the opposite side This plan is best for all light soils, while for heavy clay land the one shown in figure 178 is just as good, and in most cases will prove more durable. It consists of two logs, eight or ten inches in diameter, and from three to ten feet in length, placed parallel with the drain, and about six inches apart; the whole is covered with plank twenty inches long, laid crosswise. Flat stones will answer and are more lasting than planks. The whole is covered with earth, at least eighteen inches in depth; two feet or more would be better, especially if the soil is to be plowed near the outlet.

A LOG BOAT.

A convenient boat for dragging logs is shown in figure 179. The runners, *d, d,* are two by six inches and four and a half feet long; the plank is two by nine inches, and three and a half feet long. A mortise is made at *h* for the chain to pass through. The cross-piece, *c,* is four by seven inches, and three and a half feet long, and worked down to four and a half inches in the middle. Notches are cut into the cross-piece four inches wide and two inches deep, to receive the scantlings, *e, e,* two by

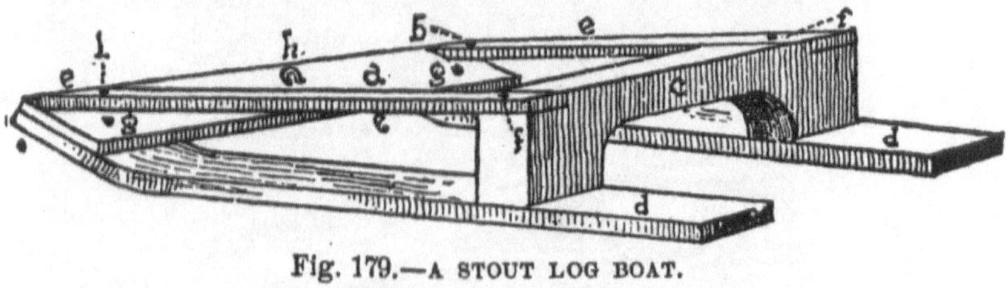

Fig. 179.—A STOUT LOG BOAT.

four inches, and three feet long, which are fastened down by strong bolts, as shown at the dotted lines, *f. f.* The two bolts in front, *b. b,* go through the scantling, plank and runner, while the bolts, *g, g,* pass only through the plank and runner.

It will be more convenient to load the logs by horses,

as shown in the illustration, figure 180. The boat is raised with its upper side against the log. The chain is fastened to the cross-piece at *a*, with the large hook, and the other end is put around the log, under the runner and cross-piece at *b*, and pulled through between the runner and scantling at *c*, when the end of the chain, *d*, is fastened to the whippletree. As the team is started, the

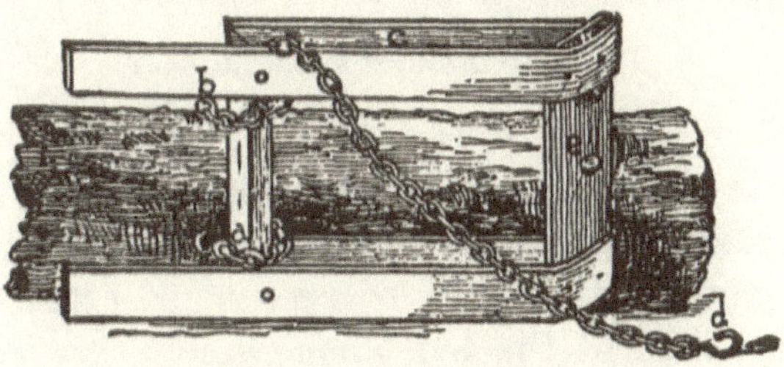

Fig. 180.—LOADING THE LOGS.

boat tips over, with the log on top. Loosen the chain from the two-horse evener, and pull it back through the runner and scantling at *c*, and through the hole.

CHEAP AND DURABLE WAGON SEATS.

It is tiresome to be jolted over rough roads, in a wagon without springs, with a simple board for a seat; but no farmer or cartman need adhere to this practice, when comfortable and portable seats can be so easily and cheaply made.

For a one-man seat, that shown in figure 181 is the simplest and most durable, and should be one foot longer

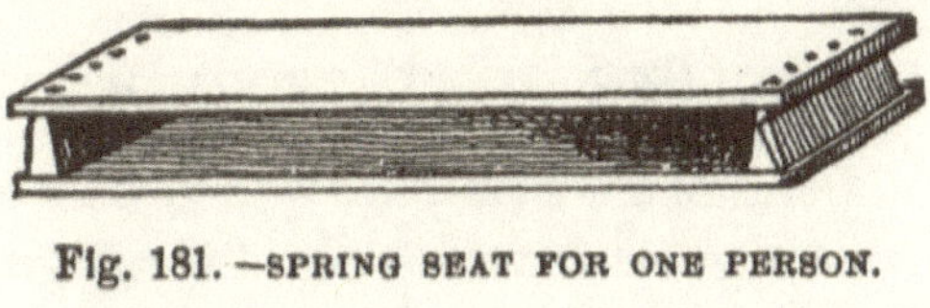

Fig. 181.—SPRING SEAT FOR ONE PERSON.

than the wagon-box is wide; the connecting blocks should be four inches high, and placed near the ends.

The one shown in figure 182 is arranged for two persons, the connecting block being placed in the centre, the ends being kept a uniform distance apart by bolts, with the nut upon the lower side, out of the way. The hole

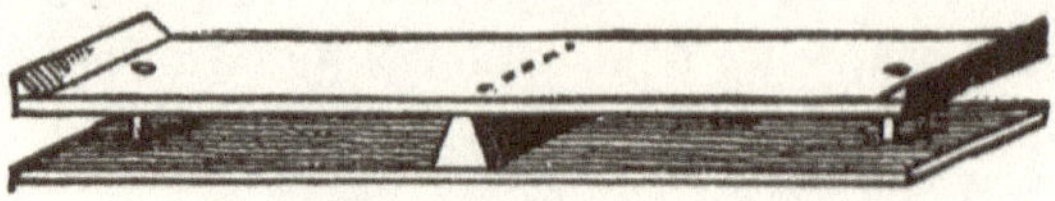

Fig. 182.—A DOUBLE SPRING SEAT.

for the bolt through the lower board should be just large enough to allow the bolt to play freely.

In figure 183 is shown a seat a little more expensive, yet far more elastic. Both boards are eight inches longer than the width of the box upon which they rest. At each end of the top-board is mortised or nailed in a strip of hard wood, one inch thick, two inches wide, and about seven inches in length, which is made to pass freely up and down in a corresponding notch sawed in

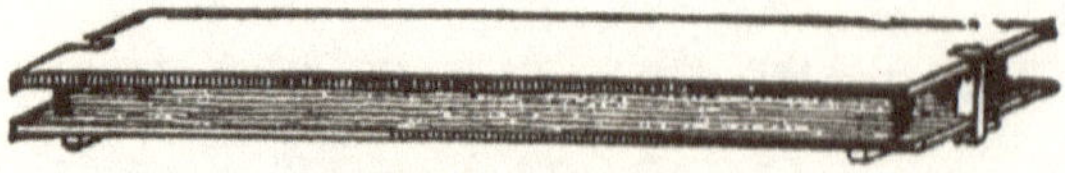

Fig. 183.—A COILED SPRING SEAT.

the end of the lower board. At or near each corner of the seat is placed a coiling spring. A pin, passed through the wooden strip near the bottom, keeps the seat-boards from separating.

A BAG-HOLDER ON PLATFORM SCALES.

Figure 184 shows a contrivance which does away with the need of a second person in filling grain bags, and is both cheap and simple. It is attached to a platform scales for convenience in weighing, and consists of an iron hoop, nearly as large around as a bag. The hoop has four small hooks on it, at equal distances apart, to which the bag is fastened. Attached to the hoop is a piece of iron about six inches long, exclusive of the shank, which slips into a socket fastened to the front of the upright enclosing the rods, that run from the bottom of the scale to the weighing beam. This iron and hoop are fastened securely together. The shank should fit loosely in the socket, to let the hoop tilt down, so that the bag can be readily unhooked. There is an eye-bolt in the hoop where the iron rod joins it, and a rod

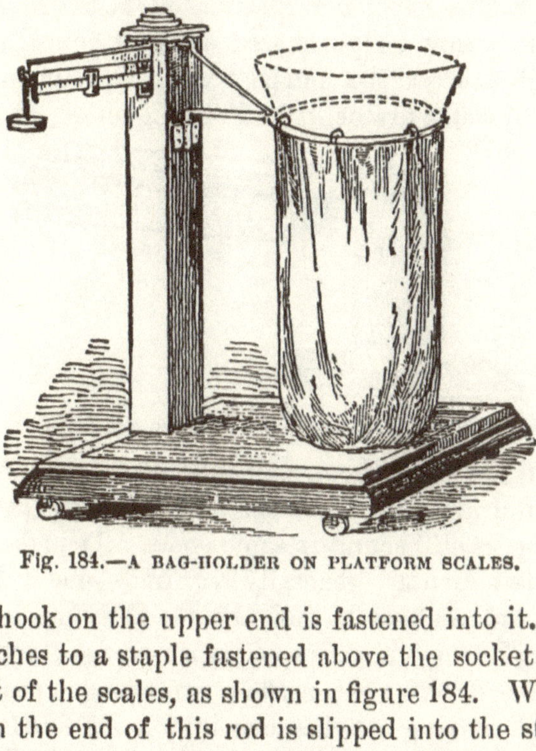

Fig. 184.—A BAG-HOLDER ON PLATFORM SCALES.

with a hook on the upper end is fastened into it. This rod reaches to a staple fastened above the socket on the upright of the scales, as shown in figure 184. When the hook on the end of this rod is slipped into the staple, it lifts the hoop to a level position, and is of sufficient strength to hold a bag of grain. The hoop should be high enough to allow a bag to clear the platform of the scales. When filled, a sharp blow of the hand removes the hook of the sustaining rod, and lets the hoop tilt downward, when the bag rests on the platform. The hoop can be swung to one side, and entirely out of the way. We have a sort of hopper made out of an old dish pan with the bottom cut out. It is very convenient to keep grain from spilling while filling the bags.

MAKING BOARD DRAINS.

On very many farms, wooden drains are used in place of tiles, but mostly in new districts where timber is cheap, and tiles cannot be purchased without much expense. They will answer the purpose well, without much expense. Wooden drains, if laid deep enough, so that the

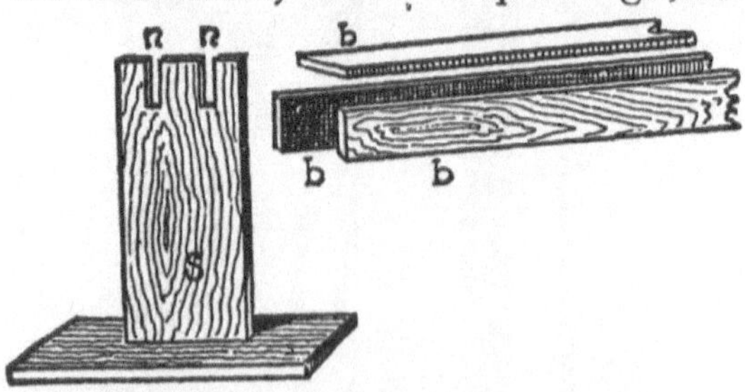

Fig. 185.—FRAME FOR HOLDING BOARDS.

frost will not affect them, will last many years. We know of an old drain that has been built twelve years, where the timber is still sound in some spots. To make wooden drains, two men are generally required—one to hold the boards, and another to nail them. This mode of constructing board drains can be improved upon by making a "standard," which consists of an upright board three feet high, having notches cut into it six inches apart, one inch wide, and several inches deep, to hold the boards firm. The boards *b*, *b*, figure 185, are laid into the notches, *n*, *n*, when the top board can be quickly and easily nailed on. Another method, shown in figure 186, consists of two posts, driven into the ground about three feet from a fence, with a board nailed across from

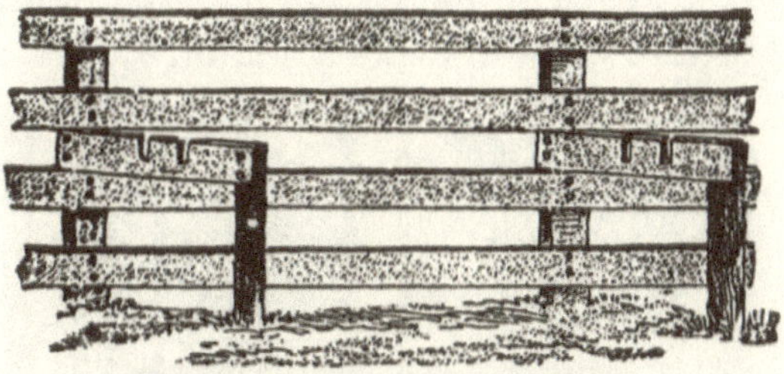

Fig. 186.—FRAME BY A FENCE.

each post to the fence. Notches are then cut into each cross-board several inches deep, when it will be ready for use.

PUT THINGS IN THEIR PLACES.

We have in mind an extensive and well-tilled farm, where a large space in the end of a wagon-shed is called a tool-room. The tools are deposited in the barn, wood-shed, crib, in the field, hung in trees, anywhere but in the right place. The tool-room floor is covered with heaps of rusty iron, old leather, broken harness, fragments of tools, and other accumulations of forty years of farm life. The old iron should be sorted over, and any bolts, nuts, rings, hooks, etc., that are good, may be put in a box by themselves, and the rest should go to the junk dealer. There may be a few straps and buckles of the old harness worth saving. If so, oil the leather and lay it aside; throw the rest out of sight. Put a light scaffold near the roof-plates, and pile many small articles upon it; they will be out of the way and within easy reach. Make a drawer in a bench for holding small tools, and a row of pigeon-holes for nails, screws, etc. Across one end of the room, in front of the plate, fasten a long narrow board by pegs, so that a six-inch space will be between the plates and board. Let the pegs be a foot apart and stand out beyond the board some five or six inches, upon which to hang long-handled tools. About four feet from the floor make a similar rack for shovels,

Fig. 187.—SECTION OF A TOOL ROOM.

picks, chains, whippletrees, etc. Bring all the tools to this room, except those needed every day in the barn. There should be a paint-pot in the tool-house, to use on a rainy day for painting the tools. Figure 187 shows a section of a well-arranged tool-room.

Lay down this law to your man-servant and maid-servant, to your son and daughter, to your borrowing neighbor and your good wife, to all that in your house abide, and to yourself: "That whoever uses a tool shall, when his or her work is done, return the tool to the tool-houseand place it where it was found."

WATER-SPOUT AND STOCK-TROUGH.

The water-trough for the stock should not be immediately under the pump spout, but some ten or twelve feet distant, a spout being employed to convey the water. This spout (figure 188) is made of two good pieces of clean white pine, inch stuff. One piece is four inches and the other is three inches wide, nicely planed and jointed. If securely nailed, it will not leak for a long time, but when it does, let it dry, and then run hot pitch down the joint. The trough should be made of two-inch oak, or pine of the same thickness may do, if kept well painted, inside

Fig. 188.—WATER-TROUGH.

and out. Instead of nailing on the sides to the ends, have the ends fitted into grooves, and use rods, with burrs on them to bring the sides up tightly to their places. When the trough leaks, tighten up the burrs a little with a wrench, and the trouble generally ceases for the time. Even the best trough is by no means very lasting, and its longevity is increased by keeping it thoroughly painted, inside and out, with good paint. Where there are horses that destroy the edges of the trough with their teeth, it is a good plan to rim it all around with thin iron. The spout, where it goes under the pump, can have a strap slipped over the nozzle of the pump.

A DESIRABLE MILKING SHED.

(*See Frontispiece.*)

We recently observed a peculiarly constructed building used as a milking shed during the warmer portions of the year. It is a common frame structure, thirty-five feet in length and eighteen feet wide, with posts eight feet high. The sides and ends are boarded up and down with eight-inch stuff, leaving a space three inches wide between the boards for ventilation, light, etc. A row of common stanchions are placed along each side. A door is made at one end, through which the cows enter. If grain is fed, it is placed in position before the cows are admitted. A small quantity of salt is kept on the floor, immediately in front of the stanchions, thus allowing the cows to obtain a supply twice each day. This manner of salting is an inducement for the cows to enter the building and take their accustomed places; it also tends to keep them quiet while milking. This arrangement, for cleanliness, ventilation, etc., is far superior to the common basement stables, and is a great improvement over the usual plan of milking in the open yard, where broken stools, spilled milk, and irritable tempers are the rule rather than the exception. No matter how stormy it may be without, this shed always secures a dry place, with comparative quiet. A greater supply of milk is obtained with such a shed. The floor of the stable portion may be of earth, covered with coarse gravel.

WEAR PLATE FOR HARNESS TUGS AND COLLARS.

In the manufacture of improved harness trimmings, devices are employed to prevent, as much as possible, the wear and breaking of the tugs where the buckle tongue enters them. This is quite an important point with those purchasing new harness. The simple contrivance, such as is shown in figure 189, consists of a

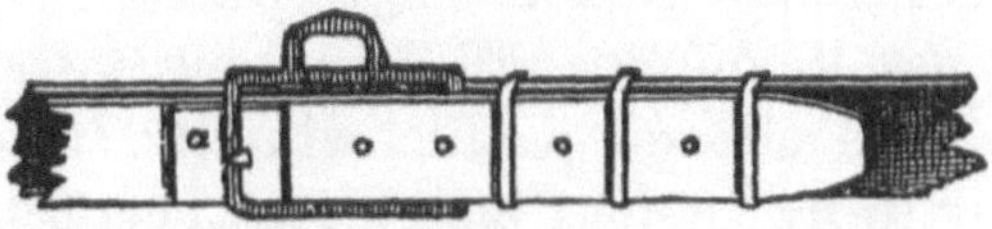

Fig. 189.—WEAR PLATE FOR TUG.

thin iron plate a little narrower than the tug, and about two inches in length, with a hole for the reception of the buckle-tongue when placed between the tug and the buckle. The strain from the buckle upon the tug is equally distributed over the entire surface against which the plate rests. A harness thus equipped will last many years longer than those not so provided. There is another part of the harness that is the cause of much trouble—mainly, the part where the tug comes in contact with the collar. The tug and its fastenings to the hame soon wear through the collar, and compress the latter so much that during heavy pulling the horse's shoulder is often pinched, chafed, and lacerated. This is worse than carelessness on the part of the teamster, as the collar should be kept plump at this point, by re-filling when needed; yet, very much of this trouble may be avoided by tacking to the

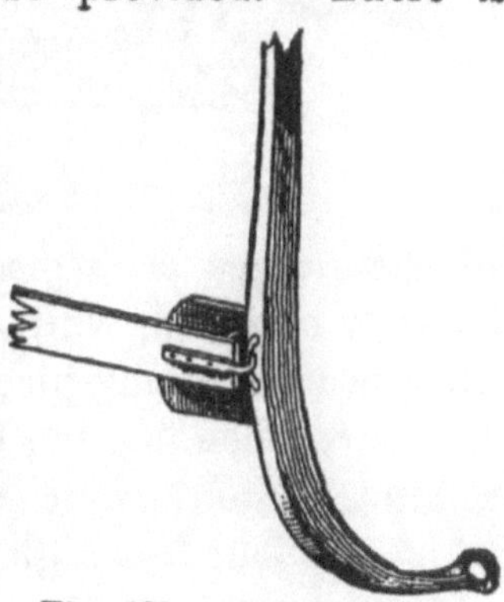
Fig. 190.—WEAR PLATE FOR HAMES.

underside of the hame a piece of leather, as shown in figure 190. It will be found not only to save the collar, but prevent chafing of the shoulder.

POTABLE WATER FENCE.

The water fence, shown in figure 191, is one of the best we have ever used, and those who live near or on tide-water will find such an one very useful. This fence is made usually of pine; the larger pieces, those which lie on the ground and parallel with the "run" of the fence, are three by four-inch pieces, hemlock or pine, and connected by three cross-bars, of three by four-inch pieces, mortised in, three feet apart. Into the middle

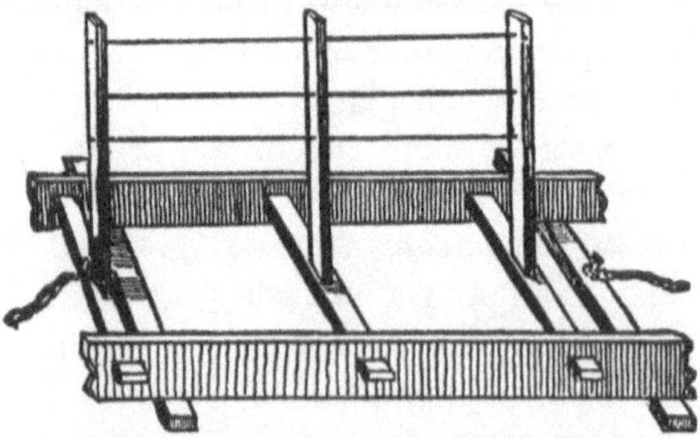

Fig. 191.—SECTION OF A WATER FENCE.

of these three cross-pieces (the upright or posts), are securely mortised, while two common boards are nailed underneath the long pieces to afford a better rest for the structure when floating on the water, or resting on the ground. Stout wires are stretched along the posts, which are four feet high.

DITCH CLEANER AND DEEPENER.

Open ditches require constant attention to prevent their being choked with weeds and accumulations of silt.

Keeping them cleaned out with a hoe is a difficult and laborious task, while drawing a log down them is unsatisfactory and ineffective. To run a plow along the bottom is not only a disagreeable task, but frequently does more harm than good. In view of these facts we devised the simple and effective implement shown in figure 192.

The centre-piece is six by eight-inch oak, eight feet long, and shaped as shown in the cut. The wings, or

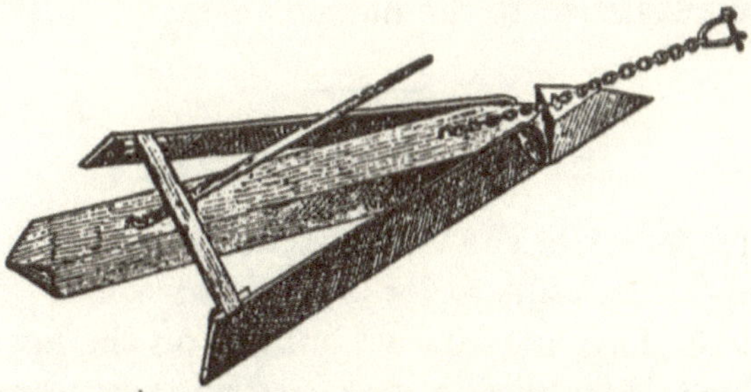

Fig. 192.—A CLEANER FOR DITCHES.

scrapers, are made of oak, or other tough wood; boards ten inches wide. They are attached to the centre-piece at the forward end by an inch bolt that passes through all three pieces. They are connected at the rear end by a strong cross-bar of hard-wood. Twelve or fifteen inches back of this bar the end of the lever is attached to the centre-piece by an eye and staple. A short chain is fastened underneath the centre of the cross-bar, with an eye-bolt passing through it. The chain is attached to the lever with a hook, and may be lengthened or shortened as required.

The implement is drawn by two horses, one on each side of the ditch. A man stands on the centre-piece, and handles the lever. If the ditch is narrow and deep, the rear ends of the wings or scrapers will naturally be forced upward to a considerable hight, and the lever chain should be lengthened accordingly. In wide, shallow ditches, the cross-bar will nearly rest on the centre-piece, and the chain must be short. The scrapers are forced down hard by bearing on the lever. If the bottom of the ditch is hard, two men may ride on the implement. Long weeds catching on the forward end must be removed with a fork. A strap of iron is fastened across the forward ends of the scrapers where the bolt passes through to prevent them from splitting. The horses may be kept the proper distance apart by means of a light pole fastened to the halter rings.

HOW TO BUILD A DAM.

A form of crib, shown in figure 193, is built of logs, about eight feet square for ordinary streams. The bottom should have cross-pieces pinned on the lowest logs. The stones that fill the crib rest on these cross-pieces

Fig. 193.—A CRIB FOR A DAM.

and hold everything secure. The crib can be partly built on shore, then launched, and finished in its place in the dam. All the logs should be firmly pinned together. The velocity of the stream will determine the distance between the cribs. The intervening spaces are occupied with logs, firmly fastened in their places. Stone is filled

Fig. 194.—LOG FRAME FOR A DAM.

in between the logs, and the bottom is made water-tight with brush and clay.

A dam without cribs, built of timbers spliced together, and reaching quite across the stream, is shown in figure 194. The frame is bound together with tiers of cross-timbers about ten feet apart. The sides of this framework of spliced logs are slanting and nearly meet at the top. The interior is filled with stone and clay, and planked over tightly, both front and rear. For a small stream with an ordinary current, this is perhaps the cheapest and most durable dam made. The engravings fully illustrate the construction of the two forms.

DRIVING HOP AND OTHER POLES.

The usual method of driving stakes, etc., is to strike them on the upper end with a sledge or other heavy article; but in the case of hop or other long poles this mode is impracticable. Hop poles are usually set by making a hole with an iron bar and forcing into it the lower end of the pole. Poles and other long stakes often need to be driven deeply in the ground, and this may be done quickly, and without a high step or platform, by using a device shown in figure 195. This consists of a block of tough wood, one foot in length, four or five inches square at the top, made tapering, as shown, with the part next the pole slightly hollowed out. Take a common trace chain, wind closely about the block and pole, and hook it in position. With an axe, sledge, or beetle, strike heavy blows upon the block. Each blow serves only to tighten the grip of the chain upon the pole. In this way, quite large poles or stakes may be quickly driven firmly in the ground. To keep the chain from falling to the ground when unfastened from the pole, it should pass through a hole bored through the block.

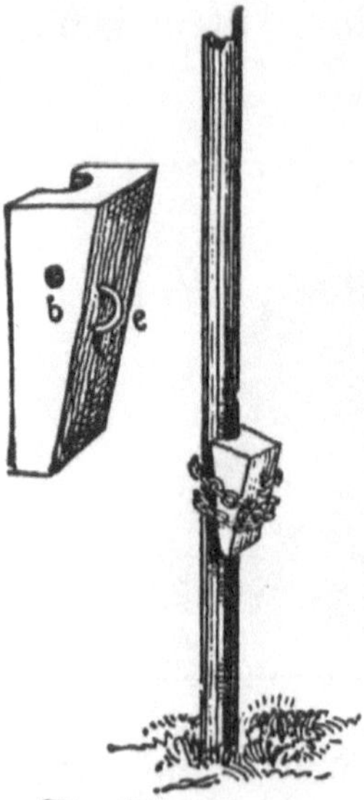

Fig. 195.—DRIVING BLOCK.

A CONVENIENT GRAIN BOX.

The box here represented, figure 196, is at the foot, and just outside of the bin. It serves as a step when emptying grain into the bin. The front side of it is formed by two pieces of boards, hung on hinges at the outside corners, and fastened at the middle with a hook and staple. The contrivance opens into the bin at the back, thus allowing the grain to flow into it. When a quantity of grain is to be taken from the bin, the cover is fastened up, the front pieces swung round, giving a chance to use the scoop-shovel to fill bags or measures.

The box is a foot deep and sixteen inches wide. Its length is the same as the width of the bin. The first four boards, forming the front of the bin, may be made stationary by this arrangement, as, at that convenient hight, bags may be emptied over by using the box as a step. The cost of this is about seventy-five cents. An improvement has the front piece and ends nailed together,

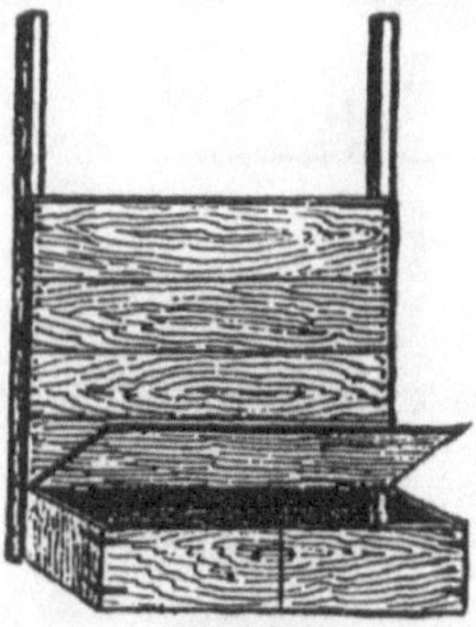

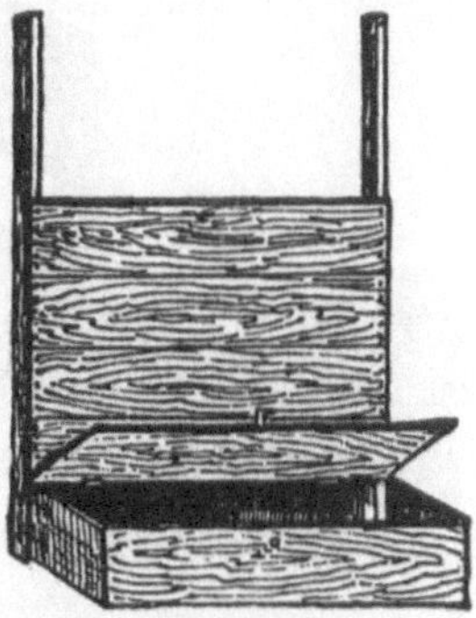

Fig. 196. GRAIN BOXES. Fig. 197.

and the whole fastened to the bin-posts by hooks and staples from the end-pieces, as shown in figure 197. Then the whole could be removed by unhooking the fastenings, and the cover could be let down, to form the lower board on the front of the bin, if desired.

A ROAD-SCRAPER.

A road-scraper is shown in figure 198, which consists of a heavy plank or hewn log, of oak or any other hard timber, six feet long, six inches in thickness, and ten inches wide. A scantling, *b*, two by four inches thick and six feet long, and the brace, *c*, are secured to the log, *a*, by a strong bolt. The edge of the scraper is made of an old drag-saw, and secured by rod-iron nails. The scantling serves as a reach, and is attached to the front part of a heavy wagon, when in use. When the road is very hard, it becomes necessary sometimes for the driver to stand on the scraper, to make it take better hold. The scraper should be shaped about as

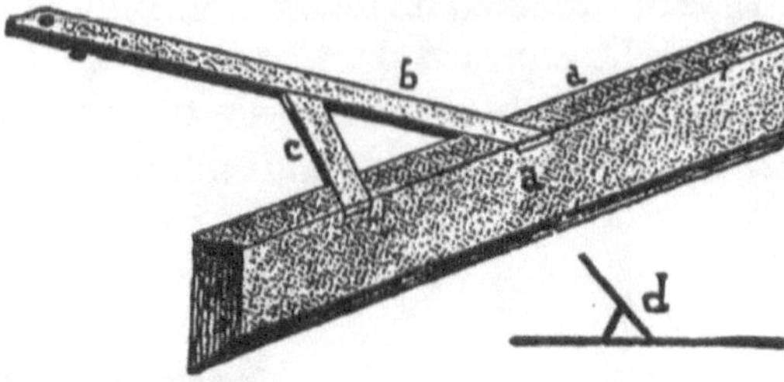

Fig 198.—A ROAD-SCRAPER.

shown at *d*, in the engraving, so as to make it run steady, and cause the loose dirt to slide to one side, and leave it in the middle of the road.

AIDS IN DIGGING ROOT CROPS.

Figure 199 shows a carrot and sugar beet lifter, made in the following manner: Take a piece of hard wood, two and a half by three inches, and six feet long, for the main piece, *a*, into which make a mortise two feet from

Fig. 199.—A ROOT LIFTER.

the wheel end, to receive the lifting foot (figure 200); attach two handles, *b*, *b*, at one end, and a wheel, *c*, at the other. This wheel can be set high or low as desired, by the set screw, *d*, in the clevis, *e*. Figure 201 shows the lifting "foot" separate from the machine. This is made of flat iron or steel, five-eighths inch thick and three inches wide, with a steel point and a small wing at the bottom. It is in the curved form seen in the engraving. The roots are first topped with a sharp hoe or sickle, two rows of tops being thrown into one, which leaves one side of the rows clear for the lifter. The horse walks between the rows and the foot of the implement enters the ground at the side of the roots in a

FIG. 200.

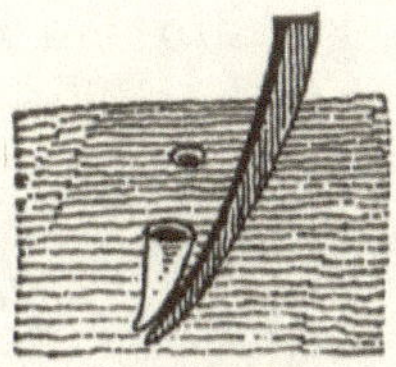

FIG. 201.

slanting direction, as shown in figure 201, lifting the roots so they may be rapidly picked up. The implement is very easily made to run deep or shallow, by simply changing the wheel and lifting, or pressing down upon the handles. A "foot," made in the form of figure 200, may be placed in the centre arm of a common horse hoe with sides closed, and used as above.

THE WOOD-LOT IN WINTER.

A few acres in trees is one of the most valuable of a farmer's possessions; yet no part of the farm is so mistreated, if not utterly neglected. Aside from the fuel the wood-lot affords, it is both a great saving and a great convenience to have a stick of ash, oak, or hickory on hand, to repair a break-down, or to build some kind of rack or other appliance. As a general thing, such timber as one needs is cut off, without any reference to what is left. By a proper selection in cutting, and the encouragement of the young growth, the wood-lot will not only continue to give a supply indefinitely, but even increase in value. A beginning, and often the whole, of the improvement of the wood-lot, is usually to send a man or two to "brush it," or clean away the underbrush. This is a great mistake. The average laborer will cut down everything; fine young trees, five or six years old, go into the heap with young poplars and the soft underbrush. The first point in the management of the wood-lot is, to provide for its continuance, and generally there are young trees in abundance, ready to grow on as soon as given a chance. In the bracing winter mornings one can find no more genial and profitable exercise than in the wood-lot. Hard-wooded and useful young trees should not have to struggle with a mass of useless brush, and a judicious clearing up may well be the first step. In timber, we need a clean, straight, gradually tapering and thoroughly sound trunk. In the dense forest, nature provides this. The trees are so crowded that they grow only at the upper branches. The lower branches, while young, are starved out and soon perish, the wounds soon healing over are out of sight. In our open wood-lots, the trees have often large heads, and the growth that should be forming the trunk is scattered over a great number of useless branches. Only general rules can be given in pruning neglected timber trees; the naked trunk, according to age, should be from one-third to one-half the whole hight of the tree; hence some of the lower branches may need to be cut away. All the branches are to be so shortened in or cut back as to give the head an oval or egg-shaped outline. This may sometimes remove half of the head, but its good effects will be seen in a few years. In removing branches, leave no projecting stub on the timber, and cover all large wounds with coal-tar. Whosoever works in this manner thoughtfully cannot go far astray.

SWINGING-STALL FRONTS.

The value of swinging-stall fronts is appreciated by those who have used them. They prevent the animals from putting their heads out into the alleys, and endangering themselves thereby. The "cribber," or "windsucker," has been made such by want of a contrivance like the one shown in figure 202. Anyone with a moderate knowledge of the use of tools can put it up, as the engraving shows how it is made; *a, a,*

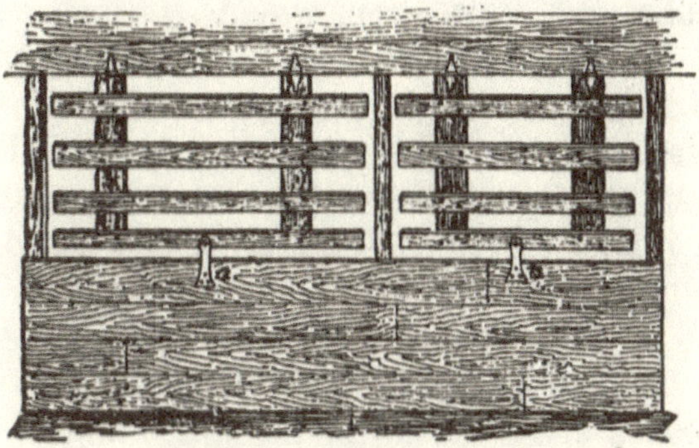

Fig. 202.—FRONT OF STALLS.

being straps to fasten the "fronts" down into place when they are not raised to feed the stock. Inch stuff constitutes the material. The cleats to which the strips are attached should be four inches wide, with the sharp, exposed edges taken off with a plane. The strips should be from two to two and a half inches wide, and attached with screws or wrought nails. The hinges can either be of wrought iron or of heavy leather. If more durable fronts are desired, oak, or yellow pine can be used, though it is much more expensive. Unplaned lumber will answer, but to make a neat, workmanlike job had better use planed lumber.

SAVE ALL CORN FODDER EVERYWHERE.

The profits of farming, as in other business, is the margin between receipts and expenditures. The receipts are largely augmented by saving wastes; these wastes in farming are enormous in the aggregate. The losses in this direction, that might be saved, would make the business very profitable, where it is now barely paying, or not doing that. Take corn stalks, for example. The leaves and a portion of the stems that produce each bushel of corn have a certain amount of nutriment that would support and increase the weight and growth of animals. Yet of our great corn crop, seventeen hundred to two thousand million bushels annually, only a very small part of the fodder is turned to much account. At the very lowest estimate, the stalks yielding one bushel of corn are on the average worth ten cents for feed, even including the great corn regions—a total of two hundred million dollars. At the South, generally, little value is attached to corn stalks as fodder. At the West, many farmers let their cattle roam in the fields, pick off some leaves, eat a little of the stalk, and trample the rest down; they pack the earth so much in trampling on it, that the damage thus done to many fields surpasses the value of the food obtained.

Nearly the whole of a corn stalk, except a very little of the thin, hard outside coating, affords nutritious fodder, if it is cut at the proper time, is well cured and judiciously fed. It needs to be cut when not so green as to mould in the shock, but not so ripe as to lose all its succulence and become woody. Experience and observation will generally indicate to every one the proper time of cutting it.

In shocking corn, the stalks should be kept straight and parallel. The shocks should be large enough to not have too many stalks exposed to the weather, yet small enough to dry and cure through. For somewhat heavy corn, twelve hills square (one hundred and forty-four hills), is abundant for one shock. A good mode of shocking is this: When the shocks are set nearly perpendicular, draw the tops together very firmly with a rope, and tie temporarily—two men working together. Bind with straw or with stalks. For the latter choose tough, nearly ripe, long, slender stalks. "Bend-break" the top with the thumb and finger every two or three inches. Thrust the butt end into the shock and towards the centre nearly two feet, and carefully bend-break it at the surface to a right angle. Insert a similar top-broken stalk two feet distant; bring the top of the first one firmly around the shock, bend it around the second stalk close to the shock, and then bend the second stalk around and over a third one; and so on, using as many stalks as required by size of shock and length of binders. Bring the end of the last one over the bend in the first, and tuck it under the binder into a loop, into which insert a stalk stub, pushing it into the shock to hold the loop. All this is more quickly done than described.

IMPROVED BRUSH RAKE.

One of the most disagreeable tasks connected with a hedge fence is gathering and burning the annual or semi-annual trimmings. It is generally done with pitchforks, and often causes pain. To have a long shoot, covered with thorns an inch long, spring out from a roll of brush and hit one square across the countenance, is exasperating in the extreme. To avoid this danger, many expedients are resorted to. Among the best of these is a long, strong rail, with a horse hitched to each end by means of ropes or chains eight or ten feet long. A boy is placed on each horse, and two men with heavy sticks, eight or ten feet long, follow. The horses walk on each side of the row of brush, and the men place one end of their sticks just in front of the rail, and hold them at an angle of about forty-five degrees, to prevent the brush from sliding over it. When a load is gathered, the horses are turned about, and the rail withdrawn from the brush.

The device shown in figure 203 is an improvement on this method. A good, heavy pole, eight to twelve feet long, has four or five two-inch hard-wood teeth set in it, as seen in the cut. These teeth may be twelve to

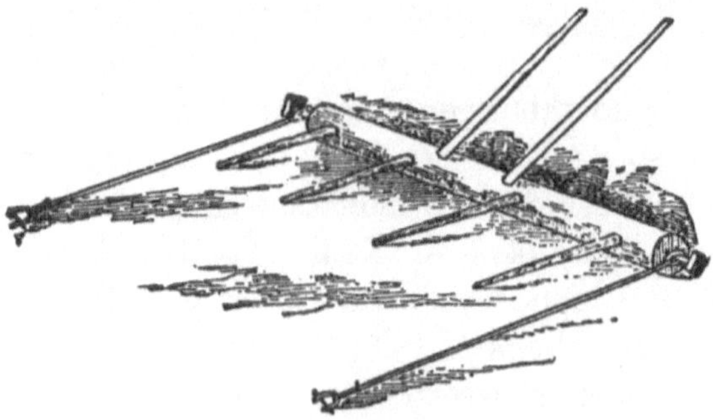

Fig. 203.—A BRUSH RAKE.

twenty inches long, and slide on the ground in front of the pole similar to those of a revolving hay rake. The handles are six to eight feet long, of ash or other tough wood, and fit loosely into the holes in the pole. Two horses are employed, one at each end of the rake. One man holds the handles, and raises or lowers the teeth as necessary. When a load is gathered, the handles are withdrawn, the ends of the teeth strike the ground, throw the pole up, and it passes over the heap. After a little practice, a man can handle this rake so as to gather up either large or small brush perfectly clean, and do it rapidly.

DIGGING MUCK AND PEAT.

A dry fall often furnishes the best time in the whole circle of the year for procuring the needed supply of muck or peat for absorbents in the sty and stable. The use of this article is on the increase among those farmers who have faithfully tried it, and are seeking to make the most of home resources of fertilizers. Some who have used muck only in the raw state have probably abandoned it, but this does not impeach its value. All that is claimed for it has been proved substantially correct, by the practice of thousands of our most intelligent cultivators, in all parts of the land. There is considerable difference in its value, depending somewhat upon the vegetable growth of which it is mainly composed, but almost any of it, if exposed to the atmosphere a year before use, will pay abundantly for digging. This dried article, kept under cover, should be constantly in the stables, in the sties and sinks, and in the compost heap. So long as there is the smell of ammonia from the stable or manure heap, you need more of this absorbent. Hundreds of dollars are wasted on many a farm, every year, for want of some absorbent to catch this volatile and most valuable constituent of manure. In some sections it is abundant within a short distance of the barn. The most difficult part of supplying this absorbent is the digging. In a dry fall the water has evaporated from the swamps, so that the peat bed can be excavated to a depth of four or five feet at a single digging. Oftentimes ditching, for the sake of surface draining, will give the needed supply of absorbents. It will prove a safe investment to hire extra labor for the enlargement of the muck bank. It helps right where our farming is weakest—in the manufacture of fertilizers. It is a good article not only for compost with stable manure, but to mix with other fertilizers, as butcher's offal, night soil, kainite, ashes, bone dust, fish, rock weed, kelp, and other marine products. Dig the muck when most convenient and have it ready.

A CLEANER FOR HORSES' HOOFS.

The engraving herewith given shows a simple and convenient implement for removing stones and other substances from between the frog and the ends of a horse's shoe. Its value for this and other purposes will be quickly appreciated by every driver and horse owner. When not in use, the hook is turned within the loop of

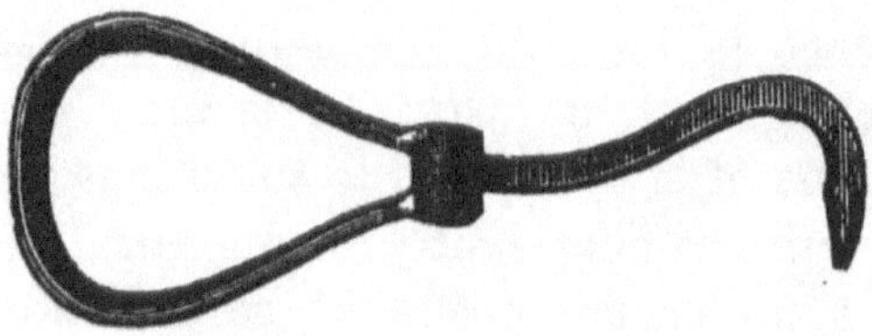

Fig. 204.—A HOOF-CLEANER.

the nandle, and the whole is easily carried in the pocket. The engraving shows the implement open, two and one-half times reduced in size. If horsemen keep this cleaner within easy reach, it will often serve a good turn, and be of greater value than a pocket corkscrew.

COLD WEATHER SHELTER FOR STOCK PROFITABLE

Not one farmer in a hundred understands the importance of shelter for stock. This has much to do with success or failure of tens of thousands of farmers. Animals fairly sheltered consume from ten to forty per cent. less food, increase more in weight, come out in spring far healthier ; and working and milk-producing animals are much better able to render effective service. The loss of one or more working horses or oxen, or of cows, or other farm stock, is often a staggering blow to those scarcely able to make the ends of the year meet, and the large majority of such losses of animals are traceable to diseases due, directly or indirectly, to improper protection in autumn, winter, or spring. Of the food eaten, all the animals use up a large percentage in producing the natural heat of the body at all seasons, and heat enough to keep up ninety-eight degrees all through the body is absolutely essential. Only what food remains after this heat is provided in the system can go to increase growth and strength, and to the manufacture of milk in cows and of eggs in fowls. When heat escapes rapidly from the surface, as in cold weather, more heat must be produced within, and more food be thus consumed. In nature this is partly guarded against by thicker hair or fur in winter.

Any thinking man will see that an animal either requires less food, or has more left for other uses, if it is protected artificially against winds that carry off heat rapidly, and against storms that promote the loss of heat by evaporation of moisture from the surface of the body. A dozen cows, for example, will consume from two to six tons more of hay if left exposed from October to April, than if warmly sheltered, and in the latter case they will be in much better health and vigor, and give much more milk. Other cattle, horses, sheep and swine will be equally benefited by careful protection.

GOOD STONE TROUGHS OR TANKS.

Figure 205 shows an unpatented stone water tank, or trough, neat, effective, and readily constructed by almost any one. These troughs may be of any length, width and depth desired, according to their position, use, and the size of stones available. Here are the figures of the one shown: The two side-pieces are flagging stones, six feet long and twenty-seven inches wide. The bottom-piece is four feet ten inches long, two feet wide; and the two end-pieces, two feet long, twenty inches wide, or high. These stones were all a little under two inches thick. Five rods, of three-eighths inch round iron, have a flat head on one end, and screw and nut on the other; or there may

Fig. 205.—A STONE TROUGH.

be simply a screw and nut on each end; they must not extend out to be in the way. Five holes are bored or drilled through each side-piece, which is easily done with brace and bit in ordinary stone. The middle hole is four to five inches above the bottom edge, so that the rod through it will fit under and partially support the bottom stone. The end rods are about four inches from the ends of the side-pieces, and stand clear of the end stones in this case so that the dipper handles hang upon them; but they may run against the end stones. When setting up, the stones being placed nearly in position, newly-mixed hydraulic cement is placed in all the joints, and the rods screwed up firmly. The mortar squeezed out in tightening the rods is smoothed off neatly, so that when hardened the whole is almost compact solid stone-work—if good water-lime be used. Almost any flat stones will answer, if the edges of the bottom and end-pieces be dressed and a somewhat smooth groove be cut in the side-pieces for them to fit into or against. The mortar will fill up any irregularities. A little grooving will give a better support to the bottom-piece and the ends than the simple cement and small rods. It will be noted that the side-pieces extend down, like sleigh runners, leaving an open space below. A hole can be drilled in a lower edge to let out the water in hard freezing weather, and be stopped with a wooden plug. Such tanks will keep water purer than wood, and last a century or longer, if not allowed to be broken by freezing. Any leakage can be quickly stopped by draining off the water and applying a little cement mortar where needed. When flagging or other flat stones are plentiful, the work and cost would be little, if any, more than for wooden tanks. They can be set in the ground if desired. The iron rods need painting, or covering with asphalt, to prevent rusting.

ARTIFICIAL FEEDING OF LAMBS.

It frequently happens that artificial feeding of lambs is necessary, and to do it successfully good judgment is required. The point is to promote a healthy and rapid growth, and not allow the lambs to scour. The milk of some cows, especially Jerseys, is too rich, and should be diluted with a little warm water. Farrow cows' milk, alone, is not a good feed, since it frequently causes constipation. It may be given by adding a little cane molasses. Milk, when fed, should be at about its natural temperature, and not scalded. Lambs, and especially "pet" lambs, are often "killed with kindness." Feed only about a gill to a half pint at first. After the lamb has become accustomed to the milk, it may be fed to the extent of its appetite. When old enough, feed a little flax seed and oats, or oil-meal if early fattening is desired.

There are various methods of feeding young lambs artificially. A satisfactory way is to use a one-quart kerosene oil can with the spout fixed so as to attach a nipple; the milk flows more freely from this than from a bottle, on account of the vent. Let ewes and lambs have clean, well-ventilated apartments. When the weather is mild and warm turn them out into the yard. If it is not convenient to let the ewes out, arrange partitions and pens, so that the lambs may enjoy the outside air and sunlight.

A CONVENIENT BAILED BOX.

The common box with a bail, or handle, is a useful farm appliance; it answers the purpose of a basket, is much more durable, and a great deal cheaper. Instead of a flat bail, we would suggest, for heavy work, a green hickory or other tough stick, to be chamfered off where it is nailed to the sides of the box, the portion for the

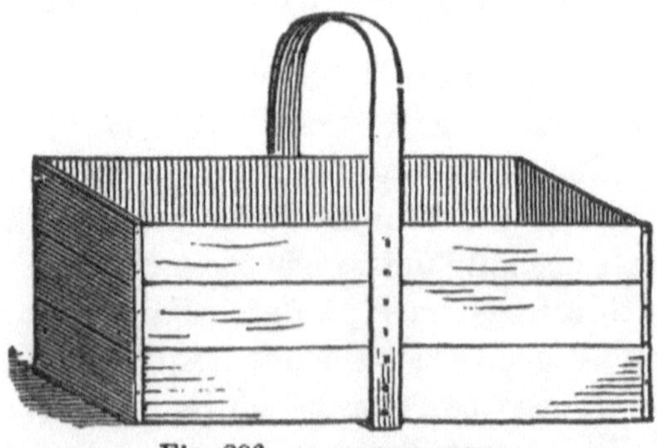

Fig. 206.—A BAILED BOX.

hand being, of course, left round. It will be found useful to have these boxes of a definite size, to hold a half-bushel or a bushel. A legal bushel is two thousand one hundred and fifty (and a fraction) cubic inches. A box may be made of this capacity of any desired shape. Ends a foot square, and side-pieces and the bottom eighteen and a half-inches long, will make a bushel box. If desired narrower, make the ends eight inches high and fourteen inches wide, with the sides and bottom two feet long. Such a box, shown in figure 206, holds a very little more than an even bushel. It is inexpensive.

SAWDUST FOR BEDDING.

We have tried for two years dry sawdust in the cows' stable, and on the whole like it better than any bedding we have ever tried. It makes a more comfortable bed, completely absorbs the urine, and the cow is kept clean with less labor than when any other is used. The objection to salt-marsh sods, dried, or to headlands, and dry muck, is that they soil the cow, and make it necessary to wash the bag before milking. Straw, of all sorts, soon becomes foul, and, without more care than the ordinary hired man is likely to bestow, soils the cow's bag also. Dry sawdust is clean, and makes a soft, spongy bed, and is an excellent absorbent. The bag is kept clean with the aid of a coarse brush without washing A charge of fifteen bushels in a common box-stall, or cow stable, will last a month, if the manure, dropped upon the surface, is removed daily. The porous nature of the material admits of perfect drainage, and of rapid evaporation, of the liquid part of the manure. The sawdust is not so perfect an absorbent of ammonia as muck, but it is a much better one than straw, that needs to be dried daily, in the sun and wind, to keep it in comfortable condition for the animals. In the vicinity of saw and shingle mills, and of ship-yards, the sawdust accumulates rapidly, and is a troublesome waste that millowners are glad to be rid of. It can be had for the carting. But even where it is sold at one or two cents a bushel, a common price, it makes a very cheap and substantial bedding. The saturated sawdust makes an excellent manure, and is so fine that it can be used to advantage in drills. It is valuable to loosen compact clay soils, and will help to retain moisture on thin, sandy and gravelly soils. There is a choice in the varieties of sawdust for manure, but not much for bedding. The hard woods make a much better fertilizer than the resinous timber. To keep a milch cow in clean, comfortable condition, we have not found its equal.

A CHEAP ENSILAGE CART.

The adoption by many farmers of the silo method of preserving fodder, has made it necessary to change the manner of feeding live stock. When the ensilage is removed twenty feet or more from the silo to the feeding rack, it is best to have some means of conveying it in

Fig. 207.—AN ENSILAGE CART.

quantities of from one to two hundred pounds at a time. This can be done cheaply and quickly by a small hand-cart, one of which any farmer having the tools can make in half a day. A good form of ensilage cart is shown in figure 207, and is simply a box eighteen inches wide, three feet long, and two and a half feet in hight. A wooden axle, of some tough fibre, is nailed to the bottom, ten inches from the end, and wheels from one to two feet in diameter are placed upon the axle. Suitable wheels can be made from planks, with cleats nailed on to keep them from splitting. Handles and legs are attached as shown in the engraving. The axle being near the centre, throws nearly the whole weight of the load upon it while being moved. It will be found easier to handle than a barrow, and not so liable to upset when unequally loaded. It is a cheap arrangement, and may be used for various other purposes as well as for moving ensilage.

MILKING AND MILKING TIME.

Any one who has had to do with dairy farming knows that there are a great many poor milkers, against a few who understand and practice the proper method of removing the milk from a cow. It is a well-known fact that some persons can obtain more milk from a cow with greater ease and in quicker time than others. In the first place, there must be an air and spirit of gentleness about the milker, which the cow is quick to comprehend and appreciate. It is not to be expected that a cow, and especially a nervous one, will have that easy, quiet condition so necessary to insure an unrestrained flow of milk, when she is approached in a rough way, and has a person at her teats that she justly dislikes. There must be a kindness of treatment which begets a confidence before the cow will do her best at the pail. She should know that the milker comes not as a thief to rob her, but simply to relieve her of her burden, and do it in the quickest, quietest, and kindest way possible. The next point in proper milking is cleanliness: and it is of the greatest importance if first-class milk and butter are the ends to be gained in keeping cows. No substance is so easily tainted and spoiled as milk; it is particularly sensitive to bad odors or dirt of any kind, and unless the proper neatness is observed in the milking, the products of the dairy will be faulty and second-class. Those persons who can and will practice cleanliness at the cow, are the only ones who should do the milking. It matters not how much care is taken to be neat in all the operations of the dairy, if the milk is made filthy at the start; no strainer will take out the bad flavor. Three all-essential points are to be strictly observed in milking: kindness, quickness, and neatness. Aside from these three is the matter of the time of milking. It should be done at the same hour each and every day, Sundays not excepted. It is both cruel and unprofitable to keep the cows with their udders distended and aching an hour over their time. We will add another *ness* to the essentials already given, namely: promptness.

A REVOLVING SHEEP HURDLE.

An easily moved feeding hurdle is shown in figure 208. It consists of a stout pole or scantling of any convenient length, bored with two series of holes, alternating in nearly opposite directions, and twelve inches apart. Small poles five or six feet long are so placed in the holes that each adjoining pair makes the form of the letter X. These hurdles are arranged in a row across the field, and the sheep feed through the spaces between the slanting poles. The hurdles are moved forward by revolving them, as shown in the engraving. By using two rows of these hurdles, sheep may be kept on a narrow strip of land, and given a fresh pasture daily by advancing the lines of hurdles. This method of feeding off a forage crop is one of the most effective and inexpensive for en-

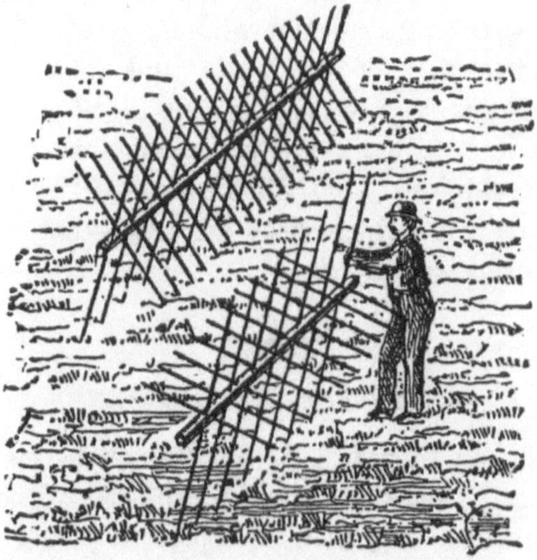

Fig. 208.—A REVOLVING HURDLE FENCE.

riching worn-out land, especially if a daily ration of grain or oil-cake is given to the sheep.

LIGHTS IN THE BARN.

It is estimated that nine-tenths of all fires are caused by carelessness. Winter is the season when the lantern is frequently used in the barn, and we give a word of caution. Never light a lamp or lantern of any kind in the barn. Smokers may include their pipes and cigars in the above. The lantern should be lighted in the house or some out-building where no combustibles are stored. A lantern which does not burn well should never be put in order in the hay-mow. There is a great temptation to strike a match and re-light an extinguished lantern, wherever it may be. It is best to even feel one's way out to a safe place, than to run any risks. If the light is not kept in the hand, it should be hung up. Provide hooks in the various rooms where the lights are used. A wire running the whole length of the horse stable, at the rear of the stalls, and furnished with a sliding hook, is very convenient for night work with the horses. Some farmers are so careless as to keep the lamp oil in the barn, and fill the lantern there while the wick is burning. Such risks are too great, even if the buildings are insured.

A NEST FOR SITTING HENS.

The nest box shown in figure 209 can be made to contain as many nests as desired, and be placed in the poultry house or any other convenient place. When a hen is set in one of the nests, the end of the lever is slid from under the catch on top of the box, and the door falls over the entrance to keep out other hens. They rarely molest the sitting hen after she has held exclusive possession three or four days, and the drop may be raised

Fig. 209.—BOX OF HENS' NEST.

again. The box legs should not be over six inches long. The step in front of the nests, four to six inches wide, is a continuation of the bottom of the box. It is a vast improvement on old barrels, broken boxes, and other makeshift hens' nests so generally employed.

BARN-YARD ECONOMY.

A dark stream, often of golden color, always of golden value, flows to waste from many an American barn-yard. This liquid fertility often enters the side ditch of the farm lane, sometimes of the highway, and empties into a brook, which removes it beyond the reach of plants that would greatly profit by it. Mice may gnaw a hole into the granary and daily abstract a small quantity of grain, or the skunks may reduce the profits of the poultry yards, but these leaks are small in comparison with that from the poorly-constructed and ill-kept barn-yard. The most valuable part of manure is that which is very soluble, and unless it is retained by some absorbent, or kept from the drenching rains, it will be quickly out of reach. Manure is a manufactured product, and the success of all farm operations in the older States depends upon the quantity and quality of this product. Other things being equal, the farmer who comes out in the spring with the largest amount of the best quality of manure will be the one who finds farming pays the best. A barn-yard, whether on a side-hill or on a level, with all the rains free to fall upon the manure heap, should be so arranged as to lose none of the drainage. Side-hill barn-yards are common, because the barns thus located furnish a convenient cellar. A barrier of earth on the lower side of the yard can be quickly thrown up with a team and road-scraper, which will catch and hold the drenchings of the yard above, and the coarse, newly-made manure will absorb the liquid and be benefited by it. It would be better to have the manure made and kept under cover, always well protected from rains and melting snows. Only enough moisture should be present to keep it from fermenting too rapidly. An old farmer who let his manure take care of itself, once kept some of his sheep under cover, and was greatly surprised at the increased value of the manure thus made. In fact, it was so "strong" that when scattered as thickly as the leached dung of the yard, it made a distinct belt of better grain in the field. The testimony was so much in favor of the stall-made manure that this farmer is now keeping all his live stock under cover, and the farm is yielding larger crops and growing richer year by year. If it pays to stop any leak in the granary, it is all the more important to look well to the manure that furnishes the food, that feeds the plants, that grow the grain, that fills the grain bin. At this season the living mills are all grinding the hay and grain, and yielding the by-products of the manure heap. Much may be saved in spring work by letting this heap be as small as out-door yard feeding and the winds and rains can make it, but such saving is like that of the economic sportsman who went out with the idea of using as little powder and lead as possible. In farming, grow the largest possible crops, even though it takes a week or more of steady hard work to get the rich, heavy, well-prepared manure upon the fields. More than this, enrich the land by throwing every stream of fertility back upon the acres which have yielded it. Watch the manure heap as you would a mine of gold.

A CHEAP MANURE SHED.

Many farmers waste much of their stable manure by throwing it out of doors to be acted upon by sun and rain. We recently saw a very cheap, sensible method of almost wholly preventing such loss. A board roof, ten feet square, is supported by posts eight feet long above ground, which are connected inside by a wall of planks (or of poles, as the one examined was). Near the post at each end, stakes *a*, *a* (figure 210), are set, against which one end of the end-planks rest. This allows the

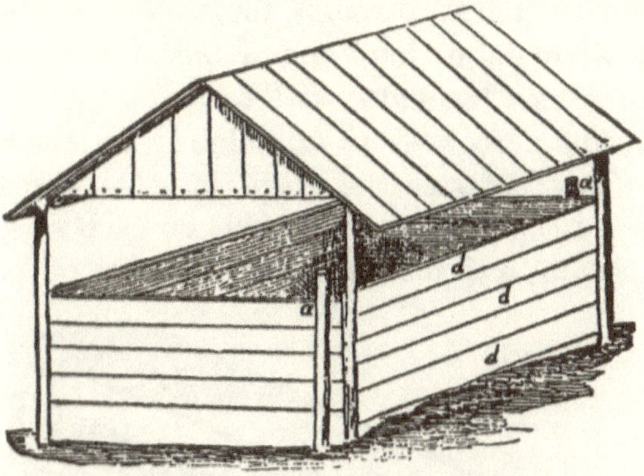

Fig. 210.—A SHED FOR MANURE.

front planks, *d*, *d*, to be removed in filling or loading. It is placed near the stable, preferably, so that the manure from the stable can be thrown directly into one corner, whence it is forked to the opposite corner in a few days, to prevent too violent fermentation. A frequent addition of sods, leaves, and other materials that will decompose, will increase the heap, and improve its value, supplying a manure superior to many of the commercial fertilizers, at less cost.

A SHEEP RACK.

The dimensions of the rack (fig. 211) are: length twelve feet, width two feet nine inches, and hight three feet. The materials are: ten boards twelve feet long, eight of them ten inches wide, one seven inches wide, and one eight inches wide; four boards, two feet nine inches long and twelve inches wide; six posts three by four inches, three feet long; sixty-four slats, sixteen inches long and one inch square; and two strips, twelve feet long and two and a half inches wide. Nail the two narrower boards in the shape of a trough, turn it bottom up, and draw a line through the middle of each side. Set the dividers to four and a half inches, and mark along the lines for holes with a three-quarter-inch bit, and bore the narrow strips to match. Set the slats into the trough, and fasten the strips on their upper ends. Nail two of the boards to the posts on each side, as seen in the sketch, and also the short boards on the ends.

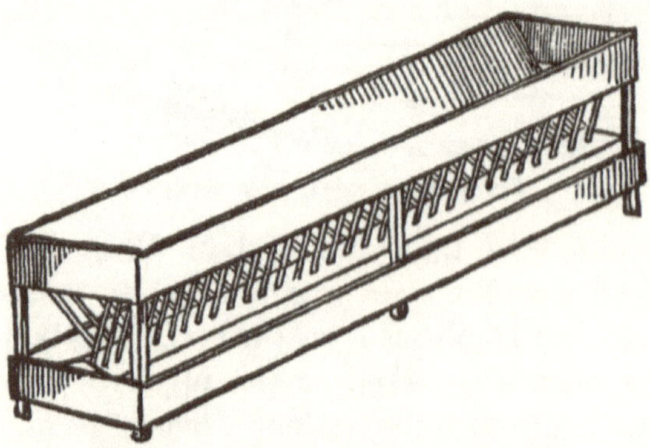

Fig. 211.—FODDER RACK FOR SHEEP.

Lay in a floor one foot from the ground, and set in the trough as shown in the engraving. Fit a board from the slats up to the top of the outside of the frame. The floor need not cover the middle under the trough.

A GOOD PICKET POINTER.

On many farms a picket pointer might never be of use, but anyone wishing to put up a picket fence a hundred or more feet long would save time by making one for the occasion. Pickets may be purchased ready pointed, but true economy consists in doing as much of the work as possible at home. This arrangement does not concern the fancy-topped pickets sometimes seen, but simply the popular square picket with pyramidal point, which makes, after all, one of the neatest fences that can be found for the yard. The waste material from building or fence-making, and an hour's time, will suffice for its making.

Fig. 212.—FRONT VIEW.

A bit of studding material, 30 inches long, has a hardwood strip three inches wide nailed on each side so as to project half of its width forward, thus forming a groove in which the picket is held, as will be seen later. They extend lower down than the central piece and with it form the front leg. The left strip, instead of extending to the top, however, is there replaced by a broader bit of hardwood board five or six inches long and projecting forward three inches, after which the projecting edges on both sides are sawed off at the proper angle for the picket points, say a little lower than 45 degrees.

Fig. 213.—SIDE VIEW.

The two rear legs are strips of lath five feet long, fastened near the top of the front leg and braced so that the forward part is not quite vertical. A block or seat 18 inches long is fastened across them 32 inches from the lower end, and so adjusted as to hold them one foot apart at the ground. The clamp by which the pickets are held in place consists of a half cylindrical block suspended by short lengths of strap iron and connected by a wire on each side to a foot lever, the action of which need be but slight.

Measure from the bevel at the top, down just the length the pickets are to be made, and place a block transversely in the groove at that point, for the stick to rest on. The groove should be at least one-fourth inch wider than the pickets, but a small wedge is inserted at the bottom on the left, so that as they fall into position they are crowded over to the right side.

To do the pointing, first cut all the pickets in a miter box to the right length, and at the proper angle to fit the water ledge over the baseboard, then place one in the groove of the pointer, thrust it down past the clamp, which it will push out, till it reaches the block at the bottom. Apply a little pressure on the foot lever to hold it in place, and then, with a sharp drawing knife, bevel the top, keeping the blade flat on the guides of hard-wood; lift the picket, turn one quarter to the right, thrust down and cut again, and so on until it is finished. With poplar pickets one and one-fourth inches square, I have seen them pointed at a little more than one per minute, which is certainly much better than to lay off each one and cut with a chisel, as I have known a carpenter to do.

STERILIZING OVEN AND BOTTLE TRUCK.

Both oven and truck for milk can be made by any carpenter and tinner. Fig 214 represents the sterilizing oven. It is made on a light frame, of matched lumber; the inside is lined with zinc soldered at the joints. The door should be double, with beveled edges fitting loosely and having felt, rubber or asbestos packing all around the outside. No threshold or extra floor is required. Drainage must be supplied, preferably through the floor.

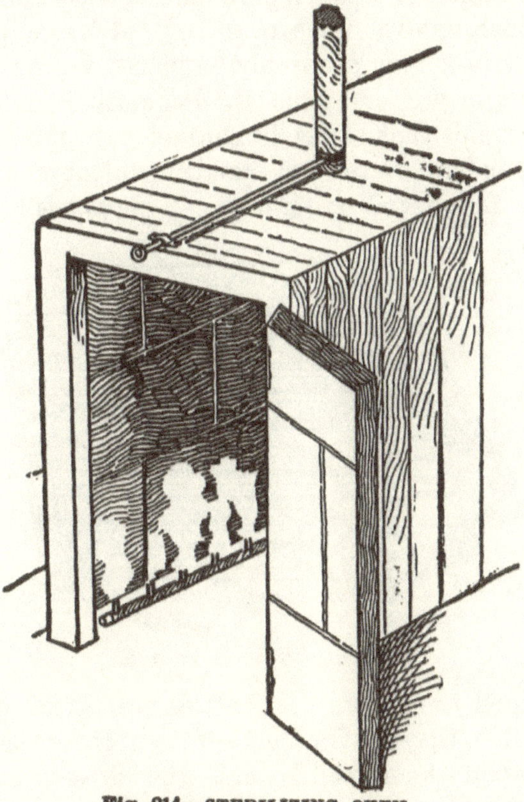

Fig. 214.—STERILIZING OVEN.

Steam is introduced by a row of jets eight to 12 inches apart in a steam pipe laid on or near the floor on the two sides and back and connected with steam supply. A valve just outside regulates the amount to be used. The pipes at the end just inside the door are capped so that no steam escapes except at the short nipples, or simply holes drilled in pipe, which will answer very well. A flue opens out of the top of the oven, made of tin, three or four inches in diameter and long enough to go out at the roof. This flue is closed by a damper just above the oven; except after sterilizing it is opened to hasten the cooling and assist in drying off the bottles which are inside. Such an oven is never to be used for the heating of milk, but in it may profitably be placed not only bottles, but tinware, stirrers, faucets, dishcloths, in fact, anything movable that comes in contact with the milk.

A convenient method of handling a large number of bottles is illustrated by fig. 215. This consists of shelves

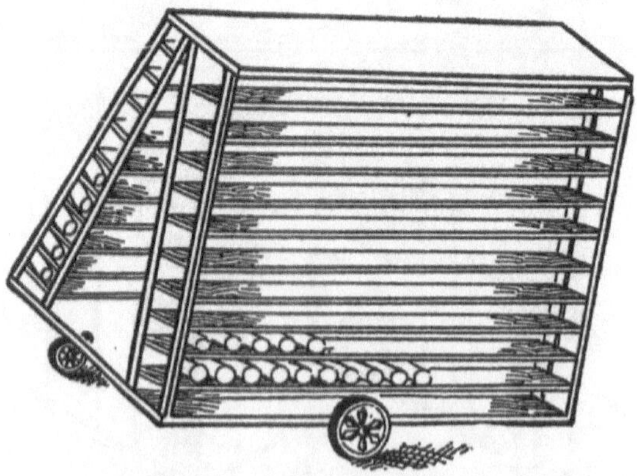

Fig. 215.—BOTTLE TRUCK.

so arranged that when the bottles are placed on them, necks inside, they are inclined sufficiently for the water to drain out of them readily, and the dust does not as readily enter them as it would if they were in an upright position.

The truck is of such a size that when loaded it will readily enter the oven and admit of the door being closed. A good way to mount such a truck is to place it on two wheels in the center, which bear the entire weight. The little wheels, one each at the front and rear, do not quite touch the floor when the truck is level; these latter are also fixed so as to turn around in a socket like a table caster. Thus rigged, the truck may be pushed around wherever wanted to load or unload and saves a vast amount of handling and inevitable breakage.

INEXPENSIVE BUILDING CONSTRUCTION.

Many farmers would like to put up a small building for some purpose or other but are deterred by the expense, the shingling or clapboarding of walls and the shingling of the roof being a large item in the expense account, both for labor and materials. The cut shows a

Fig. 216.—BATTENED BUILDING.

simple and inexpensive plan that will give good satisfaction. The frame of the building is put up and covered, roof and sides, with red resin-sized building paper stretched tightly and lapping so as to shed water if any should ever reach the paper. This costs only $1 per 500 square feet. The boarding is then put on, "up-and-down," and the cracks battened, as shown. Cover the boards and battens with a cheap stain or paint, and they will last for many years. Such a building will not only be inexpensive but it will be very warm, and in later years can, if desired, be clapboarded and shingled by simply removing the old battens.

COVER FOR SAP BUCKETS.

A good cover for sap buckets may be made at a cost of less than one cent by taking a wide shingle (*a*), sawing off four inches of the tip end and fastening to it a small spring wire, as shown in the illustration. The wire can

Fig. 217.—COVER FOR SAP BUCKETS.

be made fast to the shingle by little staples, or by using a narrow cleat like a piece of lath. The wire should be about 30 inches long and will cost less than half a cent. When done, spring the ends of wire apart and it will hug the tree firmly.

A HANDY TROUGH.

For watering or feeding cattle in the barn a handy trough is illustrated, gotten up by a practical farmer. It may be of any desired dimensions, but is usually about four feet long and one and one-half feet wide. If built slanting, stock can eat up clean any feed in it, or the trough can be readily cleaned. It is very handy for watering cattle in winter, as the trough full of water can be rolled down in front of the cattle, and from one to another as soon as they are through drinking. Where running water is handy, it can be let into this tub and quickly rolled in front of the cattle. With wheels made

Fig. 218.—A HANDY TROUGH.

of hard wood this device will last for years, and can also be used for a variety of other purposes about the barn. It is one of those handy contrivances that save labor and add to the pleasure and profit of farming.

SUBSTITUTE FOR FLOOD GATE.

When a flood gate cannot be used, the device shown in the illustration is very desirable; *a* represents the posts or trees to which the device is attached; *b* is a piece of iron

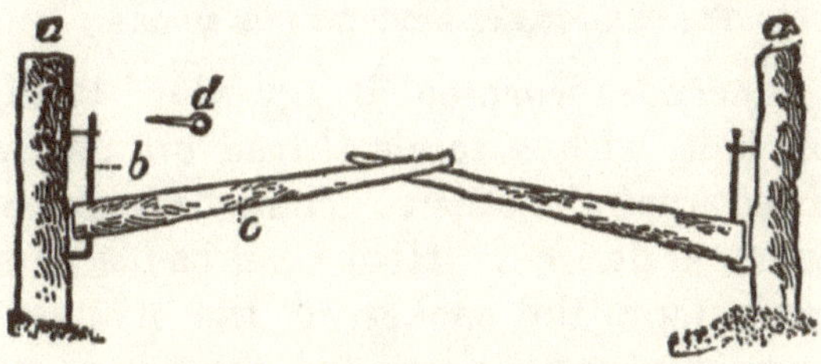

Fig. 219.—FLOOD GATE SUBSTITUTE.

in the shape of a capital L, the lower end of which is driven into the post. Further up is a small iron with an eye which fits over the upper end of this iron. This is driven in or turned in after the poles, *c*, have been placed in position. It is best to make the poles or rails, *c*, of some good timber. Use enough of these to make the fence or gate sufficiently high. These swing around on the rods as the water forces them apart. When the water recedes these can be again placed in position, and there is no loss of fence material. The ends are laid on each other, as in building up a rail fence.

HOOKS FOR SHOP OR STORE HOUSE.

A handy arrangement for hanging up articles, as for instance, tools in the shop, or meats and other eatables in the storeroom, is shown in the accompanying sketch. This plan is particularly to be commended where it is desired to get the articles up out of the reach of mice, rats

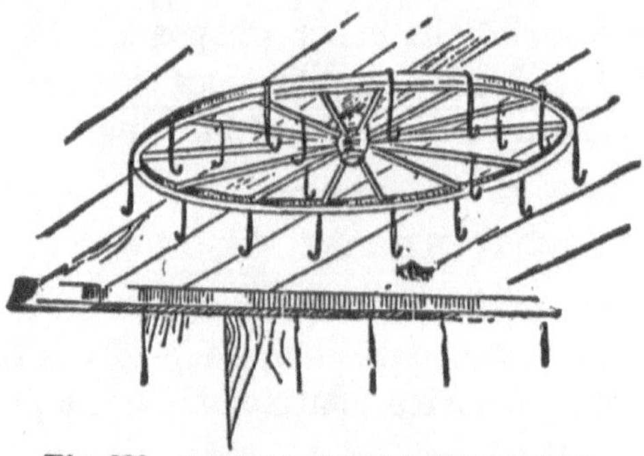

Fig. 220.—CHEAP SUPPORT FOR HOOKS.

or cats. Suspend a worn-out buggy wheel to the ceiling by an iron bolt, with a screw thread on one end and a nut or head upon the other. The wheel can be hung as high or as low as desired. Hooks can be placed all about the rim and upon the spokes, in the manner shown, giving room in a small space for the hanging up of a great many articles. This arrangement is convenient, also, from the fact that one can swing the wheel about and bring all articles within reach without moving.

IMPROVING A PASTURE SPRING.

The average pasture spring is apt to be a mud hole because not protected from the cattle's feet. Where a spring is to furnish the sole supply of water for a pasture year after year, it is worth while to make the most of it. If there is an old iron kettle with a break in the bottom, it can be utilized after the fashion shown in

Fig. 221.—A SPRING WALLED UP.

the cut, provided the source of the spring is a little higher than the point where it issues from the ground. With rough stones and cement, build a water-tight wall about the spring, setting the rocks well down into the ground. Set the kettle with the opening in the bottom, so that the water will rise to its top. A pure supply will thus always be at hand for the stock and a permanent improvement made to the pasture.

A GENERAL FARM BARN.

The ground plan shown in the illustration, fig. 222, provides sufficient stable room for ten cows, three horses, and a box stall, besides a corn crib and a tool house. These are all on the first floor. The building is 40x30, with a feed way running through the middle four feet wide. The building can be made any desired hight, but 20-foot posts are usually most desirable. On the second floor is space for hay, sheaf oats, corn fodder or other coarse food. There should also be on the second floor a bin for oats or ground feed. This is spouted down to the feed way, where it can be easily given out.

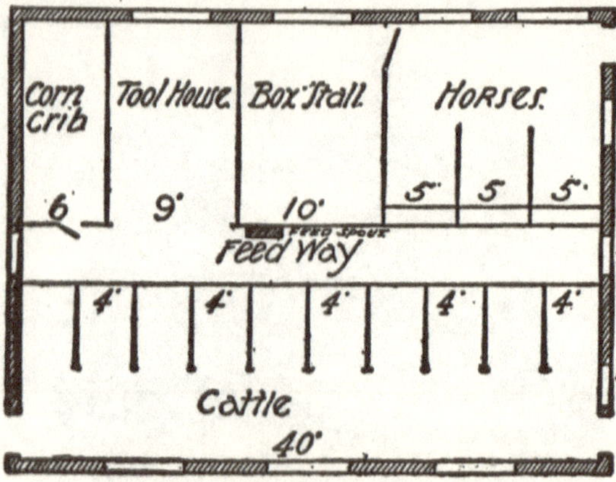

Fig. 222.—GROUND PLAN OF BARN.

The corn crib, of course, can be divided, if it is thought necessary, so that ground feed can be kept in a portion of it. There are plenty of windows in front and back, so that the building is well lighted. This barn can be built cheaply, and is large enough for a small dairy farm.

HANDY CLOD CRUSHER AND LEVELER.

One who has not tried it would be surprised to find how much execution the device shown in the cut will ac-

Fig. 223.—CLOD CRUSHER.

complish. Insert a narrow plank in front of the rear teeth of an A harrow, and the land will be harrowed, the lumps crushed and the surface leveled, at one operation. One can also, by stepping on and off the crosspiece, drag earth from knolls and deposit it in depressions, thus grading the land very nicely.

GIVING SEEDS AN EARLY START IN THE GARDEN.

The ground is often cold when the seed is put into the garden plot. To get the earliest vegetables, have a few boxes without bottoms and with a sliding pane of glass

Fig. 224.—FORCING BOXES.

for a top, as shown in the cut. Let the top slope toward the sun. Shut the slide entirely until the plant breaks ground, then ventilate as one would in a hotbed, as suggested in the right-hand sketch. A few such boxes will make some of the garden products ten days earlier—worth trying for.

A POST ANCHOR.

Where temporary wire fences are used to any considerable extent, the corner or end posts may be anchored, as shown in the illustration. The large rock, *a*, is sunk into the ground as deep as the post is placed and the earth is solidly trampled above it. Place the wire around the stone before it is put into the ground, then pass it around the top of the post. By using a stick, *b*, the wire can be tightened if there is any tendency to become loose. To move the fence, loosen the lower strand from the posts. Begin at one end and make a coil about two feet across. Roll this on the ground, crossing and recrossing the strand of wire with the roll, about every foot of length on the strand. The barbs will hold it and keep the roll together. When the roll is as large as is convenient to handle, cut the wire and begin again. When replacing, fasten one end to the post

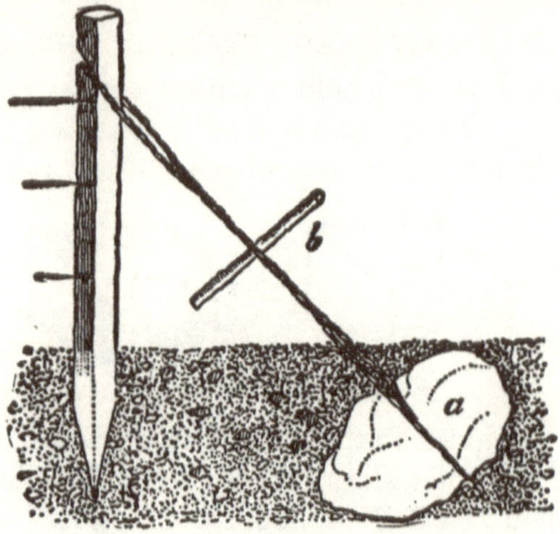

Fig. 225.—ANCHOR FOR END POST.

where the top wire is to stay and roll along the ground close to the posts. Follow with the second one a little further off, and then the third. Experience has proved to me that this is the easiest, quickest and best plan to remove wire fence, as after some practice it can be done quickly.

STONEBOAT FROM TWO BOARDS.

Most of the stoneboats in use are made with runners. I prefer to secure two boards the length desired for the boat, about 15 inches wide and three inches thick. I then measure 12 inches on top of the board and 18 inches on the opposite side, as shown in fig. 1. Saw through on the dotted line, turn the end of the board over and with four bolts fasten it as shown in fig. 2.

Do this with both boards, place them side by side and fasten with strong crosspieces. This makes a good boat,

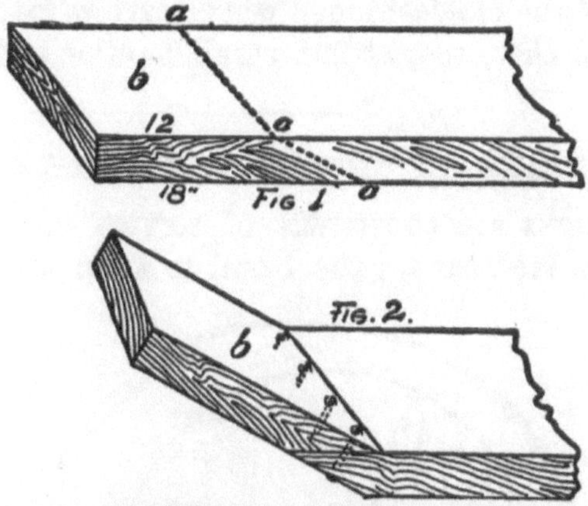

Fig. 226.—EASILY-MADE DRAG.

and in my experience is more desirable than any other kind. They can not only be used for hauling about the place, but are excellent for breaking roads during the winter.

A HANDY GARDEN BARROW.

A great improvement on the ordinary garden wheelbarrow is shown in the cut. The wheels have broad

Fig. 227.—IMPROVED BARROW.

tires, are light and run beneath the body—just in the position to balance the load when the handles are raised.

This barrow can be dumped from the side, as in the case of the ordinary barrow. It is thus possible to make over one of the old-fashioned wheelbarrows into the style shown, and that, too, at but small trouble and expense.

HOMEMADE TRUCKS AND WHEELS.

Low trucks are constantly of service on the farm. Now it is a feed car for the barn, or a two-wheel barrow

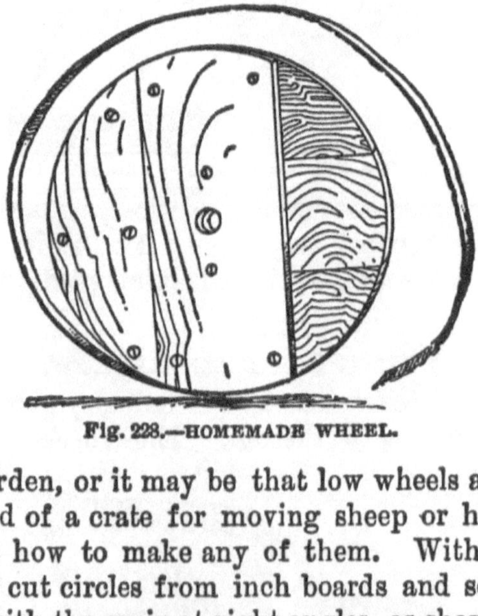

Fig. 228.—HOMEMADE WHEEL.

for the garden, or it may be that low wheels are needed for one end of a crate for moving sheep or hogs. The cut shows how to make any of them. With a "key-hole" saw cut circles from inch boards and screw them together with the grain at right angles, as shown. Two-inch hoop iron binds the edges and keeps them from splitting. Large iron washers help to hold such wheels firmly in place on the axles.

A ROLLER FROM MOWING MACHINE WHEELS.

Cast-off mowing machine wheels may be utilized very readily for making a land roller. Use narrow strips of plank with slightly beveled edges, putting them around the wheels in the manner shown in the cut,

Fig. 229.—SIDE VIEW.

making slots in the planks to fit the cogs on the rims of the wheels. These strips are held firmly in place by "shrinking on" two iron hoops at the ends, as shown. The frame is attached in the usual manner.

MAKING A PICKET FENCE HEN-TIGHT.

On many farms the hens could be given free range if the garden fence were a sufficient barrier to the fowls. The cut shows a picket fence with a picket extending upward for fifteen inches every twelve feet. To these extended ends of the pickets is stretched a twelve-inch

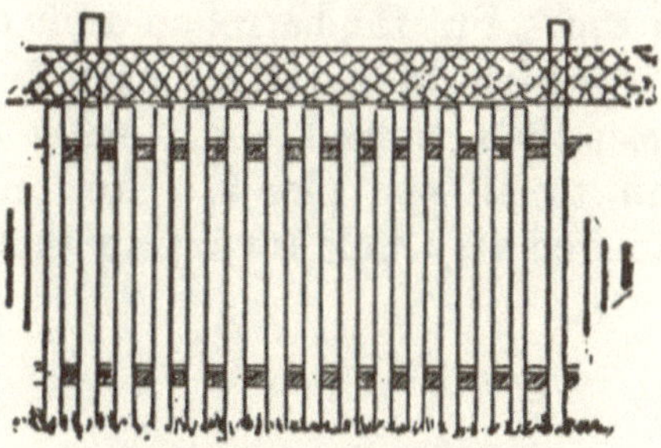

Fig. 230.—PICKET FENCE.

strip of wire netting, as shown in the sketch. In the prominence of the pickets the fowls do not clearly notice the netting until they fly against it. After a few trials they will give up the attempt to fly over. Poultry yard fence can be constructed in this way, using ordinary pickets, and above them any needed width of netting, according as the fowls are Brahmas, Plymouth Rocks or Leghorns.

BARREL STRAWBERRY CULTURE.

Probably many readers have heard of the plan of raising strawberries on the outside of a barrel. If one has only a small city or village lot, or "back yard," the experiment is well worth trying. The accompanying illustration shows one or two wrinkles that may help make the experiment a success. First bore the holes all about the barrel, then put inside a drain pipe made of four strips of board, reaching from the top to the bottom. The joints should not be tight. Now fill in earth about the pipe and set out the strawberry plants in all the holes and over the top. Put the barrel on a bit of plank, on the bottom of which wide casters have been screwed. The barrel can then turned about every few days to bring the sun to all the plants. An ordinary flour barrel will answer very well for trying this interesting experiment.

Fig. 231.—VIEW OF BARREL.

www.ingramcontent.com/pod-product-compliance
Lightning Source LLC
Chambersburg PA
CBHW020056050826
49324CB00034B/366
9781493096305